Championing the Cause
of Leadership

Championing the Cause of Leadership

A Look at the Baseball Dynasties

Ted Meyer

BUSINESS EXPERT PRESS
Leader in applied, concise business books

Championing the Cause of Leadership: A Look at the Baseball Dynasties

Copyright © Business Expert Press, LLC, 2022.

Cover design by Isabelle Zimmerman

Interior design by Exeter Premedia Services Private Ltd., Chennai, India

First published in 2022 by
Business Expert Press, LLC
222 East 46th Street, New York, NY 10017
www.businessexpertpress.com

ISBN-13: 978-1-63742-198-7 (paperback)
ISBN-13: 978-1-63742-199-4 (e-book)

Business Expert Press Human Resource Management and Organizational Behavior Collection

Collection ISSN: 1946-5637 (print)
Collection ISSN: 1946-5645 (electronic)

First edition: 2022

10 9 8 7 6 5 4 3 2 1

*To my late grandfather Francis Richard Everds for teaching me
to love the game of baseball and respect the men in it.*

Description

If your group, team, or organization is not performing at its best, this book is for you. It puts you right into the shoes of the leaders of the great baseball dynasties and demonstrates how they overcame challenges very similar to those we face in business today such as how to reign in highly talented but dysfunctional members of your team, turning around careers that have stalled late in life, how to plan for the future during down cycles in your business, helping your team truly understand the practical benefits of diversity and inclusion, and many more.

Meyer combines his 30 years of representing some of the world's top companies with his deep knowledge of baseball history and looks at leadership from a brand-new perspective—that of the small group of professional baseball teams that became dynasties in one of the most competitive environments of all—the major leagues. This book provides guidance and best practices for encouraging and embracing leadership from all levels in your organization. It addresses the relevance of leaders coming to terms with their own internal struggles and conflicts before they, and as a result their team, can reach their full potential. It teaches how to build a professional and winning culture, the importance of balance, and achieving radical innovation. And it provides example after example of very talented individuals finding their best selves within the context of their teams.

The stories of greatest teams of our greatest game are wildly entertaining, and given the American origin of baseball, they are very applicable to success of any group or team. Whether you are a baseball fan or not, reading *Championing the Cause of Leadership* is a great way to deepen your skillset as a leader and put your team over the top.

Keywords

culture; leadership; crisis management; diversity and inclusion; turn-around; bad behavior; long-term planning; innovation; teamwork; sustained success

Contents

Preface

This book is the culmination of over 30 years of devotion to two passions. The first passion is serving clients. As a management-side labor and employment lawyer, I have worked closely with clients, large and small, on leadership and organizational success. I help them plan. I help them solve problems. I represent them in disputes and work with them on how to avoid them. I have learned a great deal about why some clients succeed in business and why others don't. My second passion is learning the history of baseball. I am fascinated with the game primarily because it mirrors so much of who we are as people and as a society. For a long time, I viewed the former as a job and the latter as a hobby. But at some point, the line between the two blurred, and I began to understand the specific ways the two intersect. In so doing, I have discovered many parallels—and have come to believe that we can learn a great deal about how to find excellence in our organizations, teams, and groups from studying the game of baseball.

The sport of baseball came into being in the early 1800s. It has no single point of origin but rather evolved from a combination of several other games, including cricket, rounders, and town ball. Its rules, metrics, and distances also developed as the game took hold. Part of the reason I believe it became popular was that it is a game that could be played by anyone, anywhere. Men and women of all ages played the game. Teams and leagues were established for everyone who wanted to play. Soldiers on each side of the Civil War played baseball. Both amateurs and professionals played in parks and school grounds. There have been leagues of all kinds, including schools, churches, synagogues, prisons, towns, companies, and industries. Baseball's broad appeal has resulted in the experiences and memories of the game being passed on from generation to generation. The sounds and rhythms of baseball are familiar to and ingrained in all of us.

The language of the game has permeated all segments of society. Succeeding at a client presentation is "hitting a home run." Perceived perfection is "batting a thousand." Being close to an agreement means that you are "in the ballpark." When we work carefully to prepare, we are "covering all the bases." An unusual or unexpected idea is "out of left field." These phrases are commonly used, widely understood, and don't require an explanation. This language is second nature and is, I believe, used not only to communicate a concept but also to allow the speaker to connect at a deeper level with the listener. And it is a reminder of how much more alike we are than different. Baseball connects us in ways that very few other things do.

To best illustrate the concepts in this book, I decided to focus on the most outstanding teams—the dynasties. Doing this created challenges as there are probably some 25 or more great teams who might qualify as dynasties and who have been labeled as such by the historians of the game. As a result, I needed to establish guidelines for which teams would qualify. Webster defines a dynasty as a powerful group or family that maintains its position for a considerable time. In sports, this definition has taken on a requirement of winning multiple championships in a short period, including doing one of the most challenging things to do in competitive sports—repeat as champions after winning one the year before. Winning many games in one season isn't enough. Winning one title isn't enough. Winning a championship every other year isn't enough. So, I settled on the teams who met the following four-pronged test:

1. Winning championships in at least two successive years.
2. Being a dominant team for at least four years.
3. Being the best team of their era.
4. Being generally regarded by historians as a dynasty team.

The difference between those who are and are not on the list is razor-thin, but that is the point. Part of championship success is knowing how to navigate those key pressure moments that do not present themselves often but that the champions (in sports and life) learn to handle, and in some cases, even learn to embrace. How teams successfully dealt with these moments—which can be as short as one day, one inning, or one pitch in the last inning of the last game of a seven-game series following a seven-month season—is particularly important, and just as critical in life.

There were other challenges in identifying the dynasty teams such as comparing teams before and after free agency, changes in the rules over time, and changes in the number of teams eligible for the postseason. Before 1969, only two teams made the postseason—the winners of the National and American Leagues. As of 2020, ten teams made the post-season, and the ultimate champion had to win two or three rounds of playoffs and then win the World Series. When I started this project, I was concerned that I would have to make explanations and assumptions to address these issues. But after studying the dynasty teams, players, coaches, and front-office leaders on those teams, I learned that the greatest teams would always find a way to win and that the cream always rose to the top.

By far, the biggest challenge in identifying the greatest dynasties stemmed from the fact that for nearly half of the 20th century, our so-called American pastime systematically excluded men of color. While this robbed those players of the opportunity to compete in the major leagues, it also deprived fans of all races from seeing the highest level of competition the game could offer. Having separate leagues divided solely by race was bad for everyone. But after studying the Negro League players and teams, I am more convinced than ever that they would have been very competitive in the major leagues and that the elite among them would have ranked among the dynasty teams. As such, I have included teams from the Negro Leagues in this study.

I also realized that the impact of the integration of baseball on American society could not be overstated. After Jackie Robinson opened the door in 1947, other great players followed, including Willie Mays, Henry Aaron, and Roberto Clemente. While progress was slow at first, their efforts and the efforts of other minority players allowed for multiple generations of Americans to see players of different colors working together toward a common goal. For this author, who was born and raised in a lily-white town in the Midwest in the 1960s and 1970s, watching the way Black, Latino, and White players interacted and succeeded on Major League Baseball (MLB) fields helped form me in an unshakable belief that race didn't matter. It was to me diversity and inclusion writ large. Watching minority players in the major leagues taught me not just that diversity *is* important but *why* it is so. To me, Jackie Robinson was one of the most impactful civil rights leaders in American history.

MLB has not only mirrored race relations but other areas of life such as the relationship between labor and management, gambling, owner greed, worker safety, the use of technology, and many other challenges and changes we have faced. The sport has navigated multiple wars, several natural disasters, and two major viral pandemics 100 years apart. Like most people, baseball players fail more than they succeed. Even the best hitters do not reach first base at least 60 percent of the time. Also, projecting how things will turn out is just as tricky in baseball as it is in life. Predicting which team will win a championship in baseball is very difficult. Oddsmakers and sports journalists make annual preseason predictions in all professional team sports, and their success rates in baseball are by far the worst.

So, given that baseball is so rooted in our modern culture, can we learn anything from it that can guide us and our organizations, teams, and groups on our own paths to success? More to the point, what can we learn from the most outstanding teams—the dynasty teams—about finding excellence for our own modern groups and teams? It turns out that we can learn a great deal. One was led by a manager who had tried and failed as a manager of three previous teams. After his third firing at the age of 55, he confronted personal demons that had haunted him his entire life, discovered for the first time how to effectively confront others, and learned to truly connect with his players and coaches. The new bonds he became capable of creating turned out to be key contributing factors in getting through the tough times that are inevitable for all organizations. He also developed a new level of personal confidence that helped him deal with his difficult boss and disarm that boss when necessary. As a result of these forces, the team became capable of playing their best when games, and seasons, were on the line. A personal breakthrough by one key leader or player can profoundly impact the future of an entire franchise.

Another dynasty team had lost at historical levels for 25 years, but in the darkest days of their history, the team was remade entirely based on a thorough long-term plan created by the team's new owner. Earlier in his life, the owner had made a long-term plan for a new business during a two-year hospital stay when he almost died. That business became wildly successful and allowed him to buy a major league franchise. He repeated this strategy with his new team. In doing so, he resisted the temptation to make short-term fixes that would have increased his popularity but not solved problems. Instead, he played the long game, charting a course for years into the future. He thought long and hard about the characteristics of the players he wanted on his new team and poured his resources into acquiring those players. He then completely rebranded the team in substance and appearance, and through a series of innovative changes dramatically improved not just his team, but the entire game of baseball. This represents another common theme—charting a course for future success within the darkest of days is possible and doable.

All of the dynasties featured players who were not stars but who rose to the occasion when most needed by their teams. These "under the radar" players did not care about personal statistics or who received public credit. They were all comfortable in their own skins and were happy to allow the limelight to shine elsewhere. When the chips were down, they delivered. One such player is today almost entirely unknown by even the most avid baseball fan. But that player is second all-time in major league history in batting average in World Series games. He attended medical school *while* playing professional baseball and retired from baseball at the age of 29 to begin his medical residency. He served as a battalion surgeon on the front lines in Korea. He became a cardiologist who practiced for over 25 years. After retiring from his medical practice, he became the president of the American League for 10 years. Throughout his career, he modeled many great lessons for leadership, such as overcoming fear and danger, demonstrating humility, and consistently modeling the highest level of integrity.

The dynasty teams also teach us that leadership can come from any place at any time in an organization, not just from those at the top of the hierarchy. Leadership often came from a player rather than a manager or front-office executive. There are even examples of that leadership coming from rookies or very young players. The point is that these great teams embraced that reality and did not discourage it. They did not overly formalize the leadership hierarchy but instead promoted a culture that accepted leadership from any place within the organization.

Many books on culture and leadership rightly recognize personal character as an essential element of success and promote removing flawed characters from organizations. The dynasty teams understood that it is not that easy. To be successful, teams require talent, and talent is not always accompanied by perfect conduct. The dynasty teams illustrate at least two examples of how to manage bad behavior within organizations. One example teaches the right way, and the other teaches the wrong way. For the team that handled this problem the right way, the dynasty continued and thrived. For the team that handled it the wrong way, the mishandling of the situation contributed to the end of that team's dynasty in that era. This stark contrast teaches much on how to handle and address bad behavior by essential people within organizations.

The dynasties also teach us the importance of leaders being aligned. Many organizations suffer because leaders up and down the chain of command are not on the same page. When this occurs, team members get mixed messages. They wonder if anyone is minding the store. And ultimately, they question whether anyone is watching out for their careers. This is how top people are lost, and it can be a significant contributing factor toward organizational failure. This issue is perfectly framed by one great baseball dynasty that handled this marvelously as they were formed and rose to greatness—but 40 years later, under new ownership, failed miserably.

The dynasty teams also demonstrate over and over that tremendously successful individuals are best defined by finding their success in the success of the team. The greatest players in baseball history are primarily regarded as such because of significant personal statistics. I suggest in this book that it is not the right way to define greatness but that the true test is determined by the impact the individual player had on the team's success. When the analysis is done from this perspective, the greatest player of all time is not one whom historians have generally regarded as such.

Most of the dynasty teams also had to overcome losing—in some cases, many years of losing—before breaking through. And it is not so much that they overcame losing, but that they learned from it. They recognized mistakes they were making over and over, figured out the small marginal changes they could make to turn things around, and then used that knowledge to transform the team. And they kept hope alive rather than falling into the trap of starting to believe that they would never get there.

My journey in uncovering these truths led me to fascinating sources. I learned much from many great American sportswriters, including Jimmy Cannon, Dan Daniel, Shirley Povich, Red Smith, and Jim Murray. I poured over statistics now available from websites such as *baseball-reference.com* and *baseball-almanac.com*. I devoured article after article written by the many authors for the Society of American Baseball Research (SABR) on baseball leaders, players, and teams. I interviewed former players and family members, and I watched (and listened to) scores of World Series broadcasts. I also poured over the writings of Bill James, the king of modern sabermetrics, statistics which have now been at least partially retrofitted to seasons as early as 1876, baseball's first year of what is now generally accepted as the major leagues.

I was particularly inspired by Ken Burns' PBS series *Baseball*, first shown in 1994. I learned a great deal from multiple prominent baseball authors and historians, including Robert Cramer, Norman Macht, Lawrence Ritter, Burton and Benita Boxerman, and David Halberstam, and to the more recent writings of Richard Ben Cramer, Jon Pessah, Paul Zingg, Jane Levy, David Falkner, and Talmage Boston. I gained extraordinary insight from authors who have focused on specific dynasty teams: Norman Macht who wrote extensively on Connie Mack and his Philadelphia A's; Bruce Markensun's and Chip Greene's writings on the A's of the Charlie Finley era; Tom Verducci's writings of the great Yankees' teams at the end of the 20th century; and many other authors who wrote about specific seasons including Cait Murphy on the season of 1908, Spatz and Steinberg on 1923, and David Halberstam on 1949.

Other authors' writings, such as Larry Tye, Mark Ribowsky, Lawrence Hogan, John Holway, James Bankes, Roger Kahn, and Jeremy Beer, were insightful and pleasurable. In his *Baseball* documentary, Ken Burns did fans everywhere an amazing service by introducing the modern world to many great Black stars, including the remarkable Buck O'Neil. O'Neil has probably done more than anyone to teach the people, teams, and stories of the Negro Leagues to subsequent generations. His insights and attitude on life are a vital part of this book—and no doubt contributed to the decision in December 2020 by MLB to give the Negro Leagues from 1920 to 1948 "major league" status and incorporate them, including their records and statistics, into MLB history.

I have set out to present the dynasty teams in a way that their stories are more likely to be useful to anyone in leadership or any team, group, or organization. It is thus different than the typical baseball book in that there is not much detailed tracking of a team's performance from game to game and within games (e.g., it was the bottom of the seventh with two outs and men on second and third). But there are more profound descriptions of key individual seasons, specific games, and moments illustrating the more significant human drivers that made the difference for these teams. This book is also different from the typical business book in that there are very few references to financial information or other standard metrics found in business books. This book is instead about the impact of people on the game and on other people. My goal is that while learning more about the great baseball dynasties, you find the path to excellence with your own group, team, or organization.

CHAPTER 1

Greatness in the Moment

I want to thank the good Lord for making me a Yankee.
—Joe DiMaggio

The New York Yankees won the World Series six times in seven years between 1947 and 1953. The five in a row they won from 1949 to 1953 are unmatched by any major league history team. A "Five-peat"—not done before, and not done since. The Yankees' run of success occurred during an extraordinary time for baseball and America. The Allied Forces had just defeated Germany and Japan. U.S. soldiers came back. The baby boom generation began. Soldiers who played Major League Baseball had sacrificed their baseball careers to serve their country. Some of the greatest players in history served our nation during their prime years.

Integration of the major leagues started with Jackie Robinson in Brooklyn and with other stars in other cities. Black men had fought for our freedom and freedom worldwide, and they were belatedly allowed to play in our American game in 1947. Baseball was now indeed the American pastime. The majors included the same 16 teams (eight in each league) that had been in the game since 1902. New York, with three strong teams, was the epicenter of the game.

Mel Allen, Red Barber, and Ross Hodges called the games there. There was one announcer at a time and no advertisements, pop-up ads, or even a score appearing on the screen for TV broadcasts. World Series games took less than three hours, and most other games took around two. Players did not wear batting helmets or other protective gear, and most still left their gloves on the field when their team went in to bat.

The Yankees' streak run from 1947 to 1953 occurred right in the middle of a significant stretch of turnover in key talent. The year 1951 was the last year of Joe DiMaggio's career and the first of Mickey Mantle's.

While both DiMaggio and Mantle were great players—neither was in his prime during this multiyear championship run—and both missed significant playing time with injuries. Other key players (Tommy Henrich and Charlie Keller) left during this period, and others (Gil McDougald and Billy Martin) arrived. To win the American League, the Yankees had to annually contend with, among others, Ted Williams' Boston Red Sox and Bob Feller's Cleveland Indians. And on four occasions after winning the American League pennant, the Jackie Robinson led Brooklyn Dodgers were waiting for them to play in the World Series.

So how did the Yankees of this era perform at such a consistently high level for seven whole years (a baseball eternity) during a complete overhaul of talent? What was it about the organization, its leaders, and its players that led to this success?

Whatever the reasons, it was not something that was expected. Even the beat writers, who still traveled with the teams at the time, typically predicted other teams to win. On opening day in 1949, 112 baseball writers weighed in on who they thought would win the American League. Seventy predicted the Red Sox, 37 the Indians, and four the Athletics. Only one writer predicted the Yankees would win even though the team had won three World Series in the last eight years. And while they won each year from 1949 to 1953, the writers did not predict them to win until 1953—the last year of the streak.

One major reason for the preseason lack of respect was, remarkably for the Yankees, the lack of star power. Whitey Ford did not complete an entire year with the team until 1953, so there was no dominant frontline starting pitcher before then. The Yankees' starting pitchers came primarily from other franchises, and none had been particularly dominant before joining the team. While still having a solid leadership presence on the team, DiMaggio was, for the most part, in decline. Mantle did not play regularly until 1952. Henrich, nicknamed "Old Reliable" by broadcaster Mel Allen and an integral piece on the team in the late 1930s and 1940s, retired. And McDougald, a mainstay infielder for 10 years, did not join the team until 1951. Only two day-to-day starters from 1947 remained in 1953—catcher Yogi Berra and shortstop Phil Rizzuto.

Even to this day, the 1947 to 1953 Yankees' teams are left off many of the top 10 "all-time greatest" teams lists and are often left out of the top

20. This is hard to fathom, given they were the only team in history to win five titles in a row and did it inarguably one of the most "golden" eras of baseball. But these Yankees did not let this public perception define who they were. They were too busy being themselves, and doing what they did, consistently winning big games.

Comparing player statistics between the regular season and postseason (which was only the World Series) is very telling. Players not well known at the time, such as Bobby Brown, Gene Woodling, Billy Martin, and Johnny Lindell, hit remarkably better in the World Series. Each raised his batting average by over 50 points.

More impressive was the improvement in their starting pitching. Eddie Lopat, Vic Raschi, and Allie Reynolds, three key starting pitchers of the era, lowered their ERAs by over 50 percentage points in the World Series. And the sample sizes were not small. Lopat pitched 52 World Series innings, Raschi 60, and Reynolds 72. Raschi's ERA alone dropped from 3.72 to 2.24. The common denominator for this pitching success was Berra. He caught each and every World Series inning pitched by the three during the streak and, as it turned out, was the unquestioned most valuable player (MVP) of the team in this era. He studied and learned which pitches they should throw in individual situations and how to focus on what mattered in the moment.

Sometimes, it took taking the blame when the pitcher made a mistake. Berra did this with rookie Tom Gorman after the pitcher had missed a sign leading to a double steal in the 1952 World Series against the Dodgers. While walking off the field after the Yankees lost a World Series game to the Dodgers, giving the Dodgers a 2-1 lead in the Series, Berra pulled Gorman aside knowing he would have to answer to his manager and the press and said, "The pitch was my mistake, got it?" Berra knew that the team was short of pitchers, and he did not want Gordon to lose his confidence. When Berra faced the press, he took the heat, "He (Gorman) didn't cross me up, and don't none of you guys believe him if he says he did. I messed up the play. I wasn't crossed up. I got what I called for—Blame me!"

Berra's handling of the situation with Gorman was an example of how Berra stepped up in the moment as required by the circumstances. Another example occurred a few years later in 1956. When Don Larsen had a perfect game going into the ninth inning of a World Series game, Berra watched him on the bench before going out for the ninth and saw a teammate wrought with anxiety. Berra knew that Larsen was thinking about pitching to three batters and getting three outs. After Larsen completed his warm-up pitches, Berra walked the ball out to the mound, handed the ball to Larsen, and said, "Let's get this guy out." By doing this, Berra refocused Larsen's attention from the next three batters to the one right in front of him. He brought Larsen back into the only thing he could do anything about—that moment. Larsen proceeded to get the first man out and then completed the perfect game—the only one ever pitched in World Series history. Berra used humor to accomplish the same objective with the super intense Raschi. In challenging moments when Berra felt Raschi need to dial it down a bit and concentrate, Berra would make fun of Raschi's receding hairline by calling him "onion head."

In spite of being past his prime, the unquestioned leader of the team was still Joe DiMaggio. DiMaggio was a great hitter, a great fielder, and was the best base runner of his era. He played with a style and elegance that was unmatched. He rarely showed emotion on the field. Over the 13 years Joe DiMaggio played in the major leagues, his Yankees' teams played in 10 World Series and won nine of them. While he was past his prime by 1949, DiMaggio's presence in the clubhouse was still vital to the team.

Author David Halberstam believed Joe DiMaggio was the most famous athlete in America at the time of his retirement and described an evening when he went to a prize fight with friends including Ernest and Mary Hemmingway. After getting DiMaggio's autograph, one kid took a look at Hemingway and said, "You're somebody too, right?" Even Hemingway, at the height of his own fame, could not compete with DiMaggio.

DiMaggio was famous for his shyness and disdain for small talk. By and large, he kept to himself. It was said during his playing days that while the team was on the road, he "led the league in room service." DiMaggio also had the ability to focus in the moment as well as any other player in baseball history. And he would hold informal talks with other players on the team hours after the game when he could finally relax. DiMaggio would recall specific events of the game that he would turn into teaching moments. From way out in centerfield, he would notice when the pitcher was "pushing" the ball rather than loosening up and throwing it. He would speak directly to the player about it that day in clear and direct sentences.

In addressing why many of the Yankees did so well in pressure situations, Henrich believed that part of it was the ability to concentrate; an equal part was pure adrenaline. The best analogy he knew was driving a car heading for an accident. Suddenly, your reflexes were sharper, you saw better, and you had quicker reactions. Some people fell apart under pressure; others could use it constructively. The Yankees' culture of playing "in the moment" was an integral part of their success—one game, one pitch, and one at-bat at a time. By reframing each moment to the present and eliminating thoughts about the future, the team shed much of the anxiety that can occur in big moments and was better equipped to succeed.

Another element of the 1947 to 1953 teams' success was the historic success of the franchise. Beginning with the Babe Ruth and Lou Gehrig teams in 1927 through 1946, the Yankees won the World Series nine times. Many players from earlier teams were still around, serving in coaching and leadership roles in the 1940s and 1950s. They pushed themselves and each other. The Yankees' players, not the managers, became the keepers of their tradition. It was a very tough team. Gene Woodling later said, "It was a team where everyone demanded complete effort. It was not a team where anyone ever said 'nice try' when you made a long run after a fly ball and didn't get to it. I played on a lot of teams, and they (the other teams) all did that."

These Yankees were like the third generation of a family led by a great patrician grandfather, strong parents, and many uncles and aunts, all of whom loved and supported you but would not tolerate lack of concentration. Their love never strayed, but neither did their honest and straightforward communication and criticism. There was no place to hide, and there was no going off the record. You were held accountable for everything you did. There was simply no other option but to stay on the straight and narrow. They loved you so much that they wanted you to experience your absolute best. A simple but outstanding recipe for generational success.

Another key trait, of not just these Yankees but all of the dynasties in this book, is that they had at least one player who, while not a star, was a solid and stabilizing force in the clubhouse, a clutch player on the field, and an extraordinary gentleman off it. These players had a great deal in common—they came from strong, nurturing families, were well educated, never in trouble, and it is virtually impossible to find a negative word written about them. They served in the military if able during war times. They subjugated their games to the stars of their teams and embraced the role of doing so. They were selfless to a fault and did not care who got the credit. But they often turned out to be the stars of the most important games that had to be won to advance. They were leaders on and off the field. They were not only successful in baseball but also successful in life. And when they were really needed, they showed up. The Yankees were fortunate to have at least two of these players during this era, and both played in their infield.

The first was Phil Rizzuto. Except for three years of service in World War II, Rizzuto was a mainstay at shortstop for the Yankees from 1941 through 1954. When he first tried out for baseball in high school, he stood 4 ft., 11 in. Fully grown, he was 5 ft., 6 in. and 150 lbs. Rizzuto was regularly rejected at each stage of his career because of his size. At his first major league tryout, he was told he was too small to play, and instead, he should "make a living by shining shoes." He even had trouble being accepted as a major leaguer. When trying to get into Ebbets Field for Game 3 of the 1947 World Series, a police officer told him, "Go on, beat it, you can't even play for a midget team."

But Rizzuto somehow willed himself into a great major league career. He learned to master the details that didn't show up on the stat sheet. Rizzuto had excellent hands and became a consistent fielder at shortstop, he mastered the bunt, and he was excellent at the hit and run. By embracing the constant taunts from opponents regarding his size, he became the most popular player on the team. Others noticed, including the baseball writers who voted him as the MVP in the 1950 season, despite hitting only seven home runs and batting in 66 runs—the lowest for an offensive MVP in the award's history. He became known for having the "intangibles" to play winning baseball. During the remarkable streak of successive championships from 1949 to 1953, he played more games than any other Yankees player.

To more recent generations, Rizzuto may be better known for what he did after playing baseball. He became the New York Yankees radio broadcast voice, describing exciting moments with his catchphrase, "Holy Cow."

And that voice of the baseball announcer in the background of Meat Loaf's 1970s hit "Paradise by the Dashboard Light" is none other than Rizzuto himself. All in, Rizzuto contributed 53 years of his life to the New York Yankees. The team retired his No. 10, and in 1994, he was inducted into the Major League Baseball Hall of Fame by the Veteran's Committee—an honor typically reserved for players with great statistics. But for Rizzuto—his career, and indeed his whole life, was about the intangibles.

The second under the radar player for the Yankees was Bobby Brown. Brown played third base for the Yankees and was a particularly good hitter. He was best in the clutch and hit extraordinarily well in World Series games. His .439 World Series batting average is second all-time to David Ortiz for players with 40 or more plate appearances. Henrich said of Brown, "For a million dollars in a tough situation, Bobby Brown will not choke. He might cut down his swing a little bit, he might protect the plate a little more carefully, but he would also become more determined." This is classic Yankees' culture, clutch complementing clutch.

Brown's life—before, during, and after his years with the Yankees—was extraordinary. So jam-packed with service and accomplishment, it isn't easy to summarize it in any coherent chronological fashion. I thank Dallas author, lawyer, and longtime Brown friend, Talmage Boston, for doing so in his book *Baseball and the Baby Boomer: A History, Commentary, and Memoir.*

While in high school, Brown finished first in his class, was class president, and was a nationally sought-after baseball recruit. He was heavily perused by many major league teams, including the Cincinnati Reds. While Brown was still in high school, the Reds invited him to their home park for workouts, gave him a uniform, and Brown traveled with the team to Chicago for a series against the Cubs.

But Brown planned to go to medical school and resisted signing with the majors out of high school. He instead started college at Stanford in 1942, where he studied premed. Toward the end of his freshman year, Brown and some friends witnessed a plane crash out in the water close to a beach. They swam out 400 yards in icy waters and saved the pilot's life, who was flying a Coast Guard patrol plane looking for Japanese submarines. For his efforts, Brown received the U.S. Coast Guard's Life-Saving Medal for Bravery.

Brown enlisted in the Navy that summer and, due to his military service obligations, changed schools to UCLA, where he completed his premed studies. Upon a military transfer, Brown began attending medical school at Tulane University in 1944. He averaged nearly .500 across all three schools, and is now in the sports hall of fame of each one.

After his military discharge following World War II, Brown was sought by many major league teams but ultimately signed with the Yankees. His contract provided for pay of $52,000 over three years, equal to the largest rookie contract ever at that time.

Brown spent most of his first year with the Yankees' minor league team in Newark, where he finished second in the Independent League's batting race to another emerging star—Jackie Robinson. Brown was called up to the majors on September 22, 1946, with Yogi Berra. During this stretch of greatness, he was on the team except for parts of 1952 and 1953 when he joined the Army and served in the Korean War. Brown left baseball on his own terms—retiring in the middle of the season in 1954 to begin his medical residency in California.

One of the most remarkable of Brown's accomplishments was that he attended medical school at Tulane in the off-season while playing in the major leagues. He did this by arranging a deal with the medical school dean and the Yankees—he would stay at school during the winter holidays volunteering at New Orleans' hospitals. The arrangement also required Brown to remain in school through the beginning of the baseball regular season, and, thus, he missed the benefit of spring training altogether each year he played. But as noted by Arthur Daley in *The New York Times*, Brown also had additional obligations during the season when he had to continue to study by reading his medical texts and spending his mornings in New York hospitals doing observation work. Daley also observed that Brown's bright future as a doctor was "… like a sword of Damocles over the heads of Yankee authorities." It allowed him leverage over his employer that his teammates did not have before free agency and the players' union. He could walk away from the game whenever he wanted.

Following his playing career, Brown became a practicing cardiologist in Fort Worth, Texas, for 25 years. During his days of practice, he took a brief leave of absence to serve as the General Manager for the Texas Rangers. Following his retirement, Brown served as the American League president for 10 years. He was a close second to Bart Giamatti when Giamatti was chosen as commissioner.

When interviewed for this book in December 2019, Dr. Bobby Brown discussed the reasons for the tremendous success of the Yankees of this era.

First, said Brown, the Yankees' scouting team was second to none. Paul Krichell was the Yankees' head scout for decades and was critically important in finding and signing great talent, from Lou Gehrig to Whitey Ford, and many in between. Krichell's approach to scouting went deeper than hitting statistics, footspeed, arm strength, and size. He placed a high value on how a player performed under pressure, even if that player lacked other qualities typically relied upon by scouts. He signed Tony Lazzeri, who had epilepsy and whom no one else would touch. He signed a then 5 ft., 6 in. shortstop Whitey Ford and convinced him to learn to throw a curveball and pitch. And Krichell was the one who discovered and signed Phil Rizzuto. All three, whom other teams passed over, became Hall of Famers.

Krichell also looked to personal qualities such as education and intelligence. He was one of those responsible for bringing "college men" to the game. The Yankees were the primary beneficiary. The pitching staff of the Stengel Yankees reflected Kirchell's preference for college-educated players. Two of the three key pitchers of the era—Vic Raschi and Allie Reynolds—attended college. The Yankees also created an environment where the college-educated players worked alongside players such as DiMaggio, Henrich, Berra, and Mantle, none of whom had any formal schooling after high school, and in the case of Berra, none beyond the eighth grade (if that).

Krichell also looked beyond players who "looked the part." He didn't make decisions based on first impressions or first interviews. He thought more deeply about the player, and the person behind the player, and what each could offer. Through innovation and planning, the Yankees of this era found players that others missed.

Brown's second reason for the team's success was the culture. No one was to be ostracized or excluded by a teammate. Brown himself received no ill treatment from his teammates for being one of the first "bonus babies." Brown noted that when traveling with the team, he could go down into the hotel lobby at night and be confident that any teammate he might find would join him to go see a movie. There was no hazing of the type common of the times. Rookies were not treated poorly by veterans. Instead, they were brought into the fold and treated as equals. Rizzuto recalled the abuse suffered by rookies when he came up in 1941 with the example of a veteran holding a letter addressed to a lonesome rookie at spring training and then tearing it up into tiny pieces and throwing it into his locker. Baseball in those days had been a brutal fight for survival; players became very territorial when they saw a player with talent that might take their job. But Rizzuto saw steady improvement in the Yankee culture over the decade of the 1940s, and by the end of the decade, things were different, and it translated into success. By the time of this Yankee dynasty, even heckling opponents from the dugout was disallowed. The clear difference was the influence of DiMaggio, who put an end to this behavior. On his team, players would behave with class, and they would win.

The third reason for their success, said Brown, was that the Yankees proactively sought players capable of clutch performances and then fostered that ability among players on the team. Krichell and his team looked at batting averages and home runs and how players did in clutch at-bats in the late innings, difficult plays in the field when the game was on the line, and pitchers getting batters out when it mattered most. It took time to do this analysis but making an effort to uncover this level of detail made a difference with the Yankees. They were simply the best in the business at deciding which players to hire.

When Brown came up to the majors, with him came his roommate, Yogi Berra. Berra is, of course, famous for his "Yogisms"—some of which he actually said, some which he didn't, and for some we don't really know. But Brown had first-hand experience with many of them. Early in their careers, Yogi told Brown, "Don't expect to hit balls very far in Florida." When Brown asked why, Yogi explained that "the humility is too damn thick down there." When Berra was forced to give a speech before a large crowd, Brown counseled Berra to make it short and thank the crowd for making this day possible. When Berra gave the speech, he ended by saying, "thanks for making this day necessary."

Berra made a fortune in the soft drink Yoo-Hoo over his career and actively promoted it. When asked whether the name Yoo-Hoo was hyphenated, Berra responded, "Hell no, there's not one bubble in that stuff." When Brown and Berra were roommates, they often read before going to bed at night—Brown medical journals and Berra comic books. One night before snapping off the light, Berra asked Brown, "How did yours turn out?"

While loved by his teammates and ultimately by most everyone in baseball, Berra did not look the part—not only as a Yankee but also as a baseball player. He was 5 ft., 7 in. and 185 lbs. with long arms and an odd gait. When he tried to break into the league, most scouts ignored him. Other teams passed on him. And early in his career, he endured endless abuse about his appearance. Everything was fair game—his large nose, heavy eyebrows, dark skin, thick neck, and low guttural voice.

During batting practice before a game in 1947, Senators' pitcher Ray Scarborough hung from the top of the team's dugout with one hand, scratched his armpit like a monkey, and loudly asked Berra how he liked sleeping in a tree. During a game with the Cardinals, Enos Slaughter told Berra his face looked like it was hit with a shovel. Players on opposing teams threw bananas onto the field when Berra came up to the plate. Once, after Berra hit a home run, a particularly disagreeable Detroit Tigers pitcher chased Berra around the bases screaming at him. Later, when Berra was asked what the pitcher was saying, Berra responded that the pitcher repeated, "run on all fours like you're supposed to, run on all fours like you're supposed to." Bucky Harris, Berra's manager in 1947, publicly referred to Berra as an "ape." Even the sportswriters played along. Dan Daniel referred to him as "nature boy" in *The Sporting News*.

Berra appeared to be unaffected by the abuse. He had an extraordinary ability to let the comments roll off his back and remain 100 percent locked in on the job he had to do. This allowed his undeniable talent to shine. Like Rizzuto, Berra's capacity for vulnerability, self-deprecating humor, and ability to laugh at himself turned out to be instrumental for the Yankees in the many pressure games they played throughout their streak. Instead of fighting back (as they rightfully could have done), each chose to take himself less seriously and go along with the ribbing. It turned out to be the right move for them and the right move for the team.

These right moves also contributed to lessening the tension which invariably accompanies winning baseball. When other teams tightened up, the Yankees stayed loose. The ability of Berra and Rizzuto to allow others to poke fun at them was another ingredient in the success of the

Yankees' team. It was okay to be yourself. It was acceptable to admit imperfections. And both men became true leaders during this Yankees' era.

Berra, like DiMaggio, is an excellent example of authentic leadership emanating naturally from the right person at the right time and under the right circumstances. He grew up poor in a tough place on "The Hill" in St. Louis and was part of the United States' D-Day invasion of Normandy. He had been through tough stuff in life, and he constantly had to prove himself as a player. But this background was instrumental in preparing Berra for the greatness that awaited him with the Yankees.

The Yankees of this era cannot be fully understood without looking at Casey Stengel, who managed the Yankees from 1949 through 1960. While he was affable with the press and prone to his famous "Stenega-lese" (to wit: "There comes a time in every man's life, and I have had plenty of them"), he was disliked by some of his players—most notably DiMaggio and Rizzuto. After winning the title in 1949 (which happened to be Stengel's first), Stengel became loud and sarcastic and criticized his players in the press when things went wrong. Rizzuto told one writer during an interview, "You or I could have managed and gone away for the summer and still won those pennants." DiMaggio ignored Stengel from the time of Stengel's arrival in 1949 until DiMaggio's retirement.

Despite the negatives, Stengel did do a number of things that con-tributed to the team's success. He was one of the first to see the talent and genius of Berra. He brought in former Yankees' catcher Bill Dickey to teach Berra to be better behind the plate. He also, in his own odd way, was able to strike something of a leadership balance. He did a good job of putting players in positions where they would succeed, but none seemed ever to be totally comfortable. Stengel motivated and nurtured his players but kept them at arm's length and on their toes—which somehow translated into success. Like other leaders of baseball's most prominent dynasties, Stengel's leadership struck a balance of order and chaos that translated into wins.

Stengel's sense of humor was unmatched. When Stengel went out to the mound to take a pitcher out, the pitcher said, "I'm not tired," to which Stengel replied, "Well, I'm tired of you." On another occasion, Stengel went into the dugout and sat next to the Yankees' player Bob

Cerv. He looked at Cerv and said, "Nobody knows this, but one of us has just been traded to Kansas City." When a reporter asked Stengel a question, and Stengel proceeded to talk for 40 minutes. The reporter said, "You haven't answered my question," to which Stengel responded, "Don't rush me."

This gets to the very essence of one of Stengel's most significant contributions to the Yankees: he was able to keep his teams relaxed and loose—especially in the most important games and in the most demanding situations. He did this with his sense of humor and his sometimes bizarre behavior on the field. This took attention from his players and focused it on him, another way of easing the pressure on the team. The teams played so well that the primary job of their manager became not getting in the way of success. Stengel appeared to have this figured out during his time with the Yankees.

The 1952 World Series television broadcast illustrates this. The network broadcast recordings of Games 6 and 7 of that Series still exist and are believed to be the oldest of their kind in available today. The film quality is remarkably good, and there are many good shots of the team managers and dugouts. Going into Game 6, the Yankees were down three games to two to the Brooklyn Dodgers with both final games (including Game 7, if necessary) to be played at Ebbets Field in Brooklyn.

Based on the players' body language in the two dugouts, one would think the Yankees were ahead, and the games were in Yankee Stadium. The Dodgers' players generally appear tense and stiff, while the Yankees appear to be relaxed and enjoying themselves. Stengel appears frequently waving his arms and yelling—often for no apparent reason—catching the attention of the cameramen, the broadcasters, and the fans. There were many points in both games where the Dodgers threatened and could have jumped ahead, but they never could get over the hump. And when it came time for clutch hitting late in both games, the Yankees surged ahead. The Dodgers appeared to have the better team, but the Yankees' more relaxed approach to the game seemed to make the difference.

The 1947 to 1953 Yankees' team teaches us much about organizational success. True leaders aren't those with titles but those who lead naturally from wherever they are in the organization. The most effective among them lead by example and not by words. Tradition matters and acts as a force that holds individuals accountable and together. No attention was given to outside naysayers, and naysayers within were not tolerated. All players gave their attention to performing in the moment and not on what might happen in the future. The team was innovative in finding and signing the best talent. Players were not judged by their appearance but by merit. Players were versatile and able to play different positions. They played great defense and did the little things right. The team had multiple examples of unselfish high-character players who were unconcerned about who got the credit, and stepped up when needed most. And amid extraordinary pressure, the players found that perfect balance of relaxation and focus. This Yankee team won more championships in a row than any team in the history of the major leagues.

CHAPTER 2

Dynasty in Technicolor

Charles O. Finley is a self-made man who worships his creator.

—Jim Murray

The 1971 to 1975 Oakland A's won five straight American League West Division titles and three World Series championships. The three they won occurred in consecutive years—1972 to 1974. The A's are the only franchise since 1900, other than the New York Yankees, to win three in a row.

The A's streak occurred in the final years of the Vietnam War during the Nixon presidency. The nation had been through the 1960s, a time of significant societal change. Authority was questioned. Claims for individual rights became commonplace, and it was the age of "Up with People." Strides were made in gender and race equality, but there were still miles to go. Many looked for something new, something different, and even a new identity. With their bright green and gold colors, players with beards, mustaches, and sideburns, and a roster brimming with Black and Latino players, these A's provided all of this and then some.

Most fans discovered the A's through color television, which was in an increasing number of homes. Playoff and World Series games were beginning to be played at night, which created a wider audience and greater TV revenue. The new age of television made for a more vibrant and entertaining viewing experience—especially when watching the A's with their very modern bright green and yellow colors. It was a perfect confluence of a broad change in culture, search for self, and technology, which collided with the talented A's at the height of their greatness.

The A's owner was Charles O. Finley. Finley grew up loving baseball, but his work ethic and general business sense put him in a position to afford a major league franchise. Since he was young, he had been an extraordinarily hard worker—mowing lawns, selling magazines, and later making and selling cheap wine in the prohibition era. He had more recently worked five years in a steel mill and sold insurance on the side.

In 1946, Finley contracted tuberculosis, almost died, and spent over two years in the hospital. But while in the hospital, Finley used the time to develop a plan to sell life insurance to doctors. After being released from the hospital, Finley started his own company to sell his new insurance product. The company was wildly successful and became one of the largest of its kind. In a few years, Finley was a millionaire.

Over the 25 years before Finley assumed control of the A's in 1960, the team had few, if any, true stars. Finley knew that had to change. But rather than try and acquire great players immediately (which was difficult to do anyway before the advent of free agency), he plotted out a long-term plan to assemble an excellent team for the future. Much like how Finley used his time in the hospital to plan for his insurance empire, he used the years when the A's were at their worst to put in place a plan to build a championship baseball team. In doing so, he would sacrifice possible success in the short run for a dynasty in the future. While Finley is known today mainly for his bizarre, meddlesome, and often mean-spirited behavior, his planning and business acumen was the primary motivating reason behind the A's dynasty's success. And make no mistake about it, but for Charles O. Finley, there would have been no A's dynasty in the 1970s.

Unlike some other clubs of his era—particularly in the American League—Finley had no problem signing minority players and putting them on the field. Once a scout and the team identified a prospect and decided to pursue him, Finley would meet personally with the player to do what Finley did best as an insurance salesman—persuade. And unlike the prior A's owners, Finley had the cash to pay for this talent. During the same era when he signed the core players of the A's dynasty, his insurance business was doing so well that he was looking for expenses to off-set profits. His baseball team provided those expenses in signing bonuses that he paid liberally to his top prospects. In 1964 alone, Finley paid out $650,000 in signing bonuses, a sum higher than the annual payroll that year for the entire team.

Finley focused on finding a full lineup for the future. Players were told that there would be opportunities for significant playing time sooner rather than later. The plan worked. Between 1961 and 1967, the A's last year in Kansas City, eight key position players and four of the five top pitchers of the A's of the early 1970s were identified and signed. The list now looks like an American League All-Star roster:

1961—Shortstop Bert Campaneris—Signed as a free agent from Pueblo Nuevo, Cuba.

1963—Catcher Dave Duncan—Signed as a free agent out of high school in San Diego, California.

1964—Outfielder Joe Rudi—Signed as a free agent out of high school in Highland Park, New Jersey.

1964—Pitcher Jim (later "Catfish") Hunter—Signed as a free agent out of high school in Hertford, North Carolina.

1964—Pitcher Rollie Fingers—Signed as a free agent out of high school in Upland, California.

1964—Pitcher John "Blue Moon" Odom—Signed as a free agent out of high school in Macon, Georgia.

1965—Catcher and First Baseman Gene Tenace—Drafted in the 20th Round out of high school in Lucasville, Ohio.

1965—Third Baseman Sal Bando—Drafted in the Sixth Round out of Arizona State University.

1965—Outfielder Rick Monday—Drafted in the First Round out of Arizona State University.

1966—Outfielder Reggie Jackson—Drafted in the First Round (second overall) out of Arizona State University.

1967—Pitcher Vida Blue—Drafted in the Second Round out of high school in Mansfield, Louisiana.

These players turned into the core of the 1971 to 1975 A's. Collectively, they would make 56 All-Star Game appearances over their careers. Three—Reggie Jackson, Catfish Hunter, and Rollie Fingers—would be elected to the Hall of Fame.

The A's leadership did not get blinded by the negativity and fan hysteria surrounding their bad play in Kansas City. Instead, the A's focused their resources on evaluating and acquiring talent for the future. They did not panic in tough times by succumbing to public pressure to "win now," but instead aimed higher and came up with a long term plan of action that turned the entire organization around.

Knowing the team did not have a future in Kansas City, a small market with few revenue opportunities, Finley attempted to move the team elsewhere. He spent very little money on promotions which might have better connected the team to the city. He refused to sell radio and television rights. Instead, he promoted on the cheap in a weak effort to get fans to come to the stadium. These included cow-milking contests, greased-pig contests, a sheep pasture behind right field, and a zoo behind left. He hired Miss USA as the batgirl. A Yellow Cab brought pitchers in from the bullpen. He released helium balloons with game tickets inside them. And he bought a mule, named him "Charlie O," and had him brought to the stadium to serve as the team's mascot.

Finley could not obscure his plan from the fans in Kansas City, who effectively turned on him by choosing not to buy tickets, and Finley signed a letter of intent to move the team to Oakland, California. The other team owners confronted Finley about his efforts to move the team and threatened to expel him from the league. Finley responded by agreeing to cooperate in the short term in 1963 by signing an extended lease at Municipal Stadium in Kansas City through the 1967 season. But he redoubled his efforts to sabotage the team in Kansas City, and the four years before the team moved were some of the leanest years during Finley's ownership of the team. In 1965, the team averaged less than 6,000 fans per game in a stadium with a seating capacity of over 30,000.

Finley ran the A's from his insurance office in Chicago. But he seemed to do both jobs full time and simply outworked the other owners. Much of his time was spent developing new ideas for the game, many of which took hold. Finley is generally credited today with introducing the following ideas to Major League Baseball: World Series and All-Star games at night; the designated hitter rule; giant outfield scoreboards with cartoons and graphics; interleague play; and realigning the leagues to feature more local rivalries. Finley as an innovator was unparalleled in baseball history.

He also came up with plenty of ideas that were not accepted. These included a shortened season, the designated runner, allowing active players to be inducted into the Hall of Fame, an air jet contraption which would dust off home plate, the three-ball walk, orange baseballs, colored bases, and pink foul poles. But Finley constantly kept at it—always thinking, tinkering, and trying.

Finley also built a brand based on his team's colors. Before Finley's days as an owner, the uniforms in baseball appeared dull—especially on television. In contrast to the more colorful uniforms in football, they were typically white and gray with some blue and red trim. It was difficult to tell the teams apart. Finley called the colors of the old uniforms "eggshell white and prison gray," and broke new ground in baseball by establishing uniforms with bright green and gold colors for his team.

The new uniforms were the essence of a "brand"—something that creates a psychological affinity for one's product. Virtually anyone who paid attention to Major League Baseball in the 1970s associated bright green and yellow with the Oakland A's. Suddenly, team colors mattered to fans—particularly the young ones. And other teams followed suit. Finley dramatically changed the way the game looked by introducing bold color into it.

By the end of the 1967 season, Finley finally had support from the other team owners to move the team to Oakland for the 1968 season. As the moving vans traveled westward from Kansas City to Oakland, the A's, and perhaps the major leagues as a whole, went from black and white to technicolor. Charlie Finley's vision of a brand-new look for the game would come to life in Oakland and transform the appearance of the game.

Before the 1968 season, Finley brought Joe DiMaggio back to the major leagues. DiMaggio needed two more years of service in baseball to receive the maximum pension, so Finley offered him a job as Executive Vice President and Coach for the next two seasons. The investment immediately paid dividends.

Third baseman Sal Bando, a great fielder, was struggling at the plate in his early years. DiMaggio taught him to close his stance and keep his head down. Bando turned into a key power hitter and was one of the most consistent hitters for the A's during the early 1970s. As sabermetricians learned when they started to retro-fit their many metrics to past times, Bando had the highest WAR (wins above replacement, a statistic that sums up a player's total value to his team) rating of anyone in the American League for five straight years, from 1969 to 1973.

Another DiMaggio contribution led to the development of outfielder Joe Rudi. Rudi struggled with the larger outfields in the major leagues, and DiMaggio taught him how to go back on balls by turning his back to the plate and then turning his body back into the ball's flight to make catches. Rudi would become an All-Star left fielder who won three Gold Gloves. He made a spectacular catch in the 1972 World Series against Cincinnati that turned the tide toward the A's and then credited DiMaggio in a postgame interview.

DiMaggio also mentored the A's brightest star, Reggie Jackson, who struggled at the plate early in his career. DiMaggio worked daily for months with Jackson in 1968, teaching him how to make better contact with the ball. By the All-Star break in 1969, Jackson had hit 37 home runs, on pace to break the single-season home run record held by Roger Maris. Jackson fell short of the record that year but went on to be the A's leading power hitter during the dynasty period and hit 563 home runs in his career.

During the Kansas City years, the A's had constant management turnover. In 1961, Finley's first general manager resigned in the first year of an eight-year contract due to Finley's constant meddling. That general manager sued Finley. Finley would hire three new general managers, but they had the job in title only. Finley himself performed the general manager duties and finally made it official in 1968 by hiring himself. Finley was even worse with his on-field managers. The first, former Yankee great Joe Gordon, was fired after 60 games. Gordon would be one of nine managers fired by Finley before he hired Dick Williams in 1971. Williams would hang on for three years, including the first two championships in 1972 and 1973, but would resign before the A's third championship in 1974.

One of the reasons for Finley's discord with his general managers and managers was that he meddled in virtually everything, including changes in the lineup (before and after the games started), in-game strategy decisions, deciding the menu for the press room, and instructing radio announcers on what to say during game broadcasts. Finley even brazenly asked them to mention his name more often. Finley constantly fiddled with the dimensions of the ballpark in an effort to help his team, and he even scripted the song list for the stadium organist.

He also tried to create nicknames for his players. For example, "Catfish" Hunter, at which he succeeded, and Vida "True" Blue, at which he did not. Finley tried to pay Blue $2,000 to adopt the nickname, but Blue refused. Despite Blue's objection, Finley caused the "True Blue" nickname to be added to the stadium scoreboard and instructed announcers to use the nickname on the radio and television broadcasts. Finley micromanaged like he invented the term and resisted delegating authority of any kind. Said columnist Jim Murray, "Charles O. Finley is a self-made man who worships his creator."

Finley also battled with his new young players over pay. During the late 1960s and early 1970s, as the players in the major leagues began to organize, A's players objected more strongly to Finley's salary offers. In response, Finley chose to make salary disputes public in ways designed to humiliate his players. When Captain Sal Bando pushed for a higher salary, Finley publicly chided Bando by stating he was already in decline and was a lousy fielder. Finley had similar disputes with others, including Reggie Jackson in 1970 and Vida Blue in 1972, each having spectacular seasons. Finley's public abuse of each player likely impacted their performance the following year, and in the case of Blue, it may have affected him for the rest of his career. The game was changing, but Finley was not changing with it. Finley's poor handling of the compensation demands of his players and the players' attempts to increase player rights would ultimately lead to his undoing as a baseball owner.

With the A's accumulation of talent in the 1960s, things started to change on the field when the team moved to Oakland. In 1968, the A's won more games than they lost (82-80) for the first time since 1952. The young players were starting to come into their own. The 1969 and 1970 teams won 88 and 89 games, respectively, and finished second each year in the American League West Division.

In 1971, Finley's long-term plan would begin to bear fruit. Dave Duncan, Sal Bando, Bert Campaneris, Joe Rudi, Rick Monday, and Reggie Jackson were everyday starters. Vida Blue, Catfish Hunter, Blue Moon Odom, and Rollie Fingers were key pitchers. All had been pursued in their teenage years by Finley and his scouts while in Kansas City in the 1960s. By 1971, each was in or near his prime. Finley had built his dynasty.

But managing and maintaining the dynasty was another thing altogether. The chaos that was the Finley A's also manifested itself in fights on the field and off, with players on other teams and even between teammates. Reggie Jackson was part of many brawls, including one that occurred on the field with the Twins pitcher Dick Woodson after Woodson threw at him. Jackson also got into it in the clubhouse with his own teammates—once with Mike Epstein in a dispute over the use of game tickets and another time in the shower with Billy North over a discussion about Jackson preferring white women. Bob Locker recalled having to pull Jackson off more than one teammate.

Jackson credited Finley as the ultimate cause of the fighting, noting Finley's legendary cheapness left the players tough and hungry. Bando, the chairman of the team's "morale committee," said, "Total candor in the clubhouse is a tradition with us ... The owner screams at the players, and the manager screams at the players, and the players scream right back." In the parlance of today, it was definitely a "hostile work environment." Jackson believed that the fighting helped them be tougher on the field and contributed to their winning. Some thought the fighting was a result of the culture created by Finley—who also never seemed to take action against the players after the altercations.

Finley had a way of getting crossways with everyone—his players, managers, other league owners, the league leaders, and the fans. There was constant turnover on the team, including 19 separate trades in 1972 alone. Manager Dick Williams was typically not consulted and would find out about the trades when he came to the ballpark. The 1973 opening day roster had 12 (of 25) players who were not on the team during the World Series championship year before. Over the three championship years, 75 separate players played at least one game for the team. Seventeen different players played at second base alone.

But there was at least an arguable method to the turnover madness. The great majority of the many acquisitions and trades Finley made involved fringe players and were essentially low-risk efforts to improve the team. Reliever Bob Locker, for example, was purchased by the club in the 1970 season and contributed to the American League pennant in 1971 with a record of 7-2 and a 2.86 ERA and to the World Series winning A's in 1972 with a record of 6-1 and an ERA of 2.65. Finley then traded Locker before the 1973 season and tried to bring him back in 1974, but Locker could not play due to an elbow injury. Finley constantly tinkered with his team, but the record shows it worked out for the better more often than not.

Nearly 50 years after his playing days with the A's, Locker harbored no animosity toward Finley. Instead, Locker seemed to have reverence for him and gave Finley credit for Locker's opportunity to play on a World Championship team. "It was all about Charles O. Finley," he said. He was a "promoter extraordinaire and laid the groundwork for all of us." Locker also gave Dick Williams credit for being "ahead of his time in using the bullpen." In 1972 and 1973, Locker had become something of a "set-up man" and thrived on the continuity of coming in to set the table for Rollie Fingers. Locker's performances in 1971 and 1972 were instrumental in getting the team into the World Series.

While many baseball owners are criticized for decisions they make, money they did not spend, and the price of tickets, Finley was criticized— righty so—mainly for the way he treated people. But the players rallied around one another by viewing Finley as the first baseman Mike Epstein aptly described him: "A common enemy." Third baseman Sal Bando said, "I would say all but a few of our players hate him. It binds us together."

When Williams first met the press as the A's manager, he calmly stated that there was no reason the team could not win the American League West Division. Williams wanted to instill confidence in his young team from the beginning, and he did. His delicate balance between tough love and encouragement in leadership resonated with the A's young players. Dick Williams turned out to be the perfect on-field leader to get the team over the top. Finally, after many failed attempts, Finley made the right leadership choice with the on-field management of his team.

Williams' most formidable challenge was dealing with Finley. There was a telephone in the dugout, and Finley would constantly call Williams, often from his insurance office in Chicago. Nothing was off-limits— lineup changes, pitching changes, anything, and everything. While in Kansas City, Finley famously fired his manager during a game and had the in-stadium announcers communicate the change over the loudspeaker to the replacement, who was playing right field at the time. Finley berated both players and Williams, but Williams learned how to shield the players from it. He learned to defuse, deflect, and when necessary, ignore him. No one knows how many times Finley fired and rehired his managers over the years but suffice to say George Steinbrenner had nothing on Charles O. Finley.

In 1971, the A's broke through and finally won the American League West Division, going 101-60. Remarkably, no regular player hit above .277. But the A's won the old-fashioned way—with great pitching and defense. The team ERA and fielding percentages were each second in the league. It was the year of Vida Blue, who went 24-8 with an ERA of 1.82 and made the cover of both *Sports Illustrated* and *Time* magazines. Dick Williams was named the American League Manager of the Year.

The A's were not yet quite good enough to get to the World Series and lost to the Baltimore Orioles in the 1971 American League Championship Series. Baltimore swept the A's 3-0, scoring five runs in each game. Baltimore also had more strong pitchers—a lesson that Finley took to heart. In the off-season, Finley traded one of his core players from the acquisition of talent in the 1960s, Rick Monday, to the Cubs for Ken Holtzman. Finley was not afraid to make changes and again chose correctly. And this trade, unlike so many of the others, was for a frontline player. Holtzman turned into a postseason difference maker.

In 1972, Finley expanded his brand of green and gold colors from trim to single-color solid pullover jerseys. The colors popped even more. Finley also unintentionally added even more to the team's brand. In the early 1970s, most teams, including the A's, had strict policies that facial hair, except mustaches, was not allowed. But Reggie Jackson's skin began to get aggravated when he shaved, and well, he was Reggie Jackson, so he started growing a beard. When told by Finley to "shave it," Jackson told Finley, in essence, to "shove it." Realizing that he would not win this battle with his best player, Finley encouraged everyone on the team to grow facial hair and paid $300 to each who did so by Father's Day. Everyone joined in the fun, and each team member succeeded—thus, creating a "look" that further defined the team itself. The mustaches and sideburns became as much of the A's public brand as the team's colors, and many felt it had something to do with unifying the team for their championship runs.

Catcher Gene Tenace was one of the original core players signed in the 1960s who did not turn into an everyday player. He wanted to play baseball so badly in his early years that by force of will, he became a major league player despite developing stomach ulcers along the way as a result of his father berating him while he played. Tenace's role with the

A's was to back up another 1960s signee Dave Duncan. Duncan was great with the pitchers, and after his playing career, he became baseball's most sought-after pitching coach and a crucial part of the St. Louis Cardinals 2011 World Series Championship. Tenace did not have a great year in 1972 and struck out a lot. But better times lay ahead.

The A's made it to the 1972 World Series but were faced with playing the powerful Cincinnati "Big Red Machine." Due to the Reds' traditional look and brand, it was dubbed the "hairs against the squares," the "liberals vs. conservatives," and "the bikers vs. the boy scouts." The Reds gave the A's no respect before the Series and made it clear in the press. Pete Rose said that the "real" World Series was the Reds' defeat of the Pirates in the National League championship game, and Reds' manager Sparky Anderson uncharacteristically made public his opinion that the National League played at a higher level than the American League. Worse yet, team leader Reggie Jackson had a badly pulled hamstring from the 1972 American League championship game and was ruled out for the World Series.

Enter Gene Tenace. Tenace was put into the starting lineup by Williams as the seventh hitter in hopes that his presence would generate more offense than would Duncan. It did. Tenace hit two home runs in Game 1, accounting for all the runs in a 3-2 A's win. He then hit a home run in each of Games 4 and 5. He batted in a total of nine runs in the Series.

Except for Game 6, which the Reds won 8-1, the A's pitchers Blue, Fingers, Hunter, Odom, Locker, and new acquisition Holtzman shut down the Reds' offensive juggernaut. A spectacular Joe Rudi catch against the wall in Game 7, using techniques learned from Joe DiMaggio, cemented the Series win. The A's bested the Reds in a thrilling four games to three, with six of the seven games decided by one run. When things got tough, the Reds tightened up and couldn't hit. In contrast, the rollicking A's powered through. Over the course of the Series, the Reds hit a paltry .209. The Oakland A's were World Champions, and Gene Tenace was the World Series MVP.

There was even drama in the stands in the 1972 World Series. A fan in line for tickets before Game 6 heard another fan say, "If Gene Tenace hits a home run today, he won't walk out of the ballpark." The fan who heard the statement reported it to the police, and the team ordered extra security. A man carrying a loaded gun and a bottle of whiskey was arrested during the game. Tenace was not told of the threat until after the man was arrested.

Great pitching and defense continued to carry the A's over the next two years—winning championships in 1973 and 1974. The pitching was again led by Hunter, Holtzman, and Fingers, who were a combined 10-3 in the World Series over the three-year championship run with a remarkable average collective ERA of 2.02. The ERA numbers were at least .50 below their regular-season numbers. The A's were either first or second in team ERA in all three championship years, and their great pitchers got even better when it mattered. Like most dynasty teams, the pitchers were able to increase their concentration levels during crucial games and in the postseason.

But even during good times, Finley could not help himself. In the 1973 World Series against the Mets, reserve Mike Andrews made two errors in the 12th inning of Game 2, and the A's lost. Following the game, Finley kicked Andrews off the team and attempted to get him to file a false statement that he was injured and could not play. The team rallied around Andrews by each wearing his number as a patch on their uniform for the next game, and the fans booed Finley incessantly. It took the Commissioner to change the decision and put Andrews back on the team. Despite winning the World Series, manager Williams resigned at the end of the year—at least in part due to how Finley handled Andrews. Andrews never played in the major leagues again. And perhaps also in response to the way the team responded to Finley's treatment of Andrews, Finley went cheap on the championship rings, which Catfish Hunter called "horsemeat" and "[not] even as good as a high school ring."

After the 1974 season, Finley failed to make a contractual payment to the team's pitching ace Jim Hunter. The withheld amount led to an Unfair Labor Practice Charge and an arbitration proceeding. The arbitrator voided Hunter's contract, and he became a free agent. Shortly after hitting the market, Hunter signed with the New York Yankees for $3.2 million over five years and a $1 million signing bonus. In 1975, without Green and Hunter, the A's were good enough to win the Division but were swept by the Boston Red Sox in the American League Championship Series. Hunter would lead the Yankees to World Series championships in 1977 and 1978.

Finley then proceeded to run headlong into the most successful labor movement in American sports history. The Players Association, led by Marvin Miller, had gained increasing ground during the A's Championship years. They had become more effective in negotiating with the owners, and by getting the owners to agree to salary arbitration, set the table for more advancement. But the players still had a significant hurdle—the so-called reserve clause, which appeared in each player's contract. That clause had been interpreted for over 100 years to mean that each player's service was tied to the team for the next year and then for successive years after that. This interpretation gave owners all the bargaining power and the players none. But Miller had his own interpretation of the clause and viewed it as applying for one year only, not for successive years.

Miller had salary arbitration and a new idea on the reserve clause, but he needed a test case. In 1975, pitchers Dave McNally with the Orioles and Andy Messersmith with the Dodgers gave it to him. Neither player signed their contract for that season but continued to play out the entire year. At the end of the year, they declared themselves free agents and sought salary arbitration. This gave Miller the chance to argue his interpretation of the reserve clause, and in an opinion handed down by impartial arbitrator Peter Seitz on December 23, 1975, Seitz agreed with Miller. Free agency was born.

Some owners had done an excellent job with player relations over the years and were well situated to keep their players for longer periods. Charles O. Finley was not. His tight-fisted, manipulative, and abusive behavior toward his players resulted in the end of the A's dynasty. One by one, Finley's key players left the team, including Jackson to Baltimore in 1975, Bando to Milwaukee and Campaneris to Texas in 1976, and Tenace and Fingers to San Diego in 1977. Every one of the team's key stars over the 1971 to 1975 run was gone by 1978.

In assessing the success of this team during their dynasty run, it is critical to note that they mastered clutch situations, which were commonplace for the A's. In their three-year run of championships, the A's played in 12 World Series games that were decided by one run. What were the key ingredients to their ability to win in these three years? Part was the clutch pitching. Fingers said that due to Finley's tight-fisted ways, "We needed those World Series checks." But the historically great pitching performances by Hunter, Holtzman, and Fingers, in particular, were monumental for the A's.

The team was accustomed to pressure and being on edge due to the omnipresence of Finley. Was that a positive for them in big games? It may very well have been. They seemed to thrive on chaos. Reggie Jackson would later say that the A's were better than all the teams (including the World Champion Yankees) for whom he played in the later 1970s. At least one of the A's World Series teams (usually the 1974 team) is included on most all-time top 10 teams' lists.

There are many leadership takeaways from the A's dynasty of the 1970s. While the team was horrible when Finley purchased it in 1960, Finley hunkered down and planned ahead in a way that was not popular with his team or the A's fans in Kansas City. He then stayed the course and let the plan play out. Finley demonstrated that in even the darkest of times, plans for the future could be made. Some of those plans will take longer than others to materialize, and there may be more dark days to endure. But if the plan is sound, it can lead to dramatic success. Finley and his scouts spent significant time and effort evaluating not just how a person would perform right away but 3, 5, or 10 years down the road. Finley also hired people like Joe DiMaggio to help develop his young players. Even after finding the core of the team, Finley continued to look for additional pieces that would make it better. Finley's ability to remake his team was at the heart of his team's ultimate success.

Finley was also a fearless innovator. He was not afraid to try new things—especially things that were potentially transformative, like the team's bright colors. Finley rebranded a team that had been historically bad for 25 years and turned it into a spectacular success in 10 years. He tinkered with the roster until he had the right people in place, and then made one more significant change by trading Rick Monday for pitcher Ken Holtzman. He also repeatedly changed his manager until he had the one that could lead the A's to a championship. And in doing all of this, Finley worked harder than any other major league owner.

But Finley was also a micromanager and did not allow others to lead. He mistreated his players, and they disrespected him for it. The credit goes to the player leaders and manager Dick Williams for getting the team to rally together despite Finley's bad behavior, and turn that bond into a formula for success. But when free agency came into being in 1975, Finley's core players—who were still relatively young—finally had options. The game changed, and Finley did not change with it. As a result, his players went elsewhere. Ultimately, Finley's mistreatment of his players caused the downfall of the A's dynasty. Had Finley better navigated changes in the game and demonstrated even common decency with his team, the A's dynasty might have lasted throughout the rest of the 1970s and beyond. Instead, once he had to bargain with free agent players as equals, the dynasty fell apart. In the end, the manner in which Charlie Finley treated others destroyed his franchise.

CHAPTER 3

Competition, Survival, and the Emergence of More Powerful Forces

I was right on time.

—Buck O'Neil

In the new Bill James' *Historical Baseball Abstract*, historian James does perhaps the most thoughtful, thorough, and inclusive list of the Top 100 baseball players of all time. He considers all professional baseball players since the organized game began in the 1870s. Many teams who won a World Series title are not represented on the list by any players. The best-represented team is not the Yankees, Cardinals, Dodgers, Reds, or A's, or a major league team of any era—but by a team near Pittsburgh not named the Pirates. The players ranked 4th, 9th, 17th, 52nd, 65th, 76th, 86th, and 95th were all on the 17-man roster of the Homestead Grays during the 1930s.

The players' names, in order of where they appear on the list, are Oscar Charleston, Josh Gibson, Satchel Paige, Smokey Joe Williams, Buck Leonard, Cool Papa Bell, Willie Wells, and Martin Dohigo. Three more who were not on the list, Ray Brown, Bill Foster, and Judy Johnson, all played on the team in the 1930s and were later elected to the Hall of Fame. There are no major league teams who had anywhere close to this level of all-time talent on one team during any era.

The Homestead Grays joined two other Negro League teams from the 1930s and 1940s—the Pittsburgh Crawfords and the Kansas City Monarchs—as great professional dynasties. All three teams won multiple championships and absolutely must be discussed among the greatest baseball dynasties of all time.

It is essential to put the Negro Leagues in context with major league white baseball by pointing out the differences in addition to the players' skin color. As noted in the previous chapter, until 1976, the standard major league player's contract included the "reserve clause" that tied a player to his team from year-to-year. The clause artificially depressed player salaries and left players with almost no negotiating leverage. This clause harmed the players and ultimately harmed the teams for which they played by depressing revenues and limiting true competition.

The Negro Leagues had the opposite problem. There were multiple leagues, and players could change teams from year to year and even change teams within a year by joining a team in another league. If a player received an offer from a team in another league to play a weekend series, that player could accept. Owners and managers in the Negro Leagues were constantly looking to add key players to their teams and were likewise guarding against other teams raiding theirs.

Since the beginning of the 20th century, Major League Baseball teams have played a fixed schedule with a fixed number of games each year and some type of championship (since 1903, the World Series) scheduled to occur at the end of the season. From 1901 to 1960, teams had a set schedule of 154 games. In 1961, the schedule increased to 162. Conversely, the Negro Leagues did not have a fixed number of games from year to year, and teams within those leagues played a varying number of games. The number of official "in league" games teams played each year varied widely (sometimes of the magnitude of 40–80). Teams also played just as many games against teams outside their leagues. These nonleague games were against a wide variety of competition ranging from local semipro teams to teams of major league all-stars. There was regular turnover from year to year with which teams played in which leagues. And the leagues themselves came and went.

The Negro League postseason involved a series between the top Eastern team and the top Western team in some years. In other years, the team with the best record in the first half of the season would play the team with the best record in the second half. In some years, no championship series was played. Whether a championship series occurred depended on business realities the major leagues did not face—such as whether a stadium was available, how much revenue could be generated by the games, and the fact that the players could often make more money barnstorming with newly constructed teams.

In the major leagues, teams have helped one another financially when necessary to stay afloat, share revenues with one another, and are exempt from antitrust laws. The Negro League teams had no such advantages. They faced largely unrestricted competition in its purest form, and only the strong teams survived. Some of the best teams, and even the leagues they played in, failed.

So, given significant differences between White and Black leagues and the fact that after integration, the Negro Leagues disbanded for good, why study the Negro Leagues at all? The question is best answered by another question: How many modern businesses, teams, organizations, and groups operate under a system where all the competitors are known, the dates and times for events are scheduled before the year begins, participants cannot freely resign and join competitors (or start a new organization), the competition ends on a date certain which is also scheduled months in advance, and antitrust laws do not apply? Exactly. The way the Negro Leagues operated and competed is, from an organizational standpoint, more like the teams and groups of today.

The primary sources for the Negro Leagues' statistics are newspaper stories and box scores. Many of the papers that covered the games came out weekly and did not include the detail to which we are accustomed today. Some game accounts were incomplete or inconsistent with another newspaper's version of the same game. There were even inconsistencies between the written article for a game and the box score provided with it. So, while historians have made great strides in reconstructing Negro Leagues' statistics in recent years, details about specific games and player performances are still fuzzy. And mythology has crept in. For example, some believe that the best hitter from the Negro Leagues, Josh Gibson, hit nearly 800 home runs. Satchel Paige, often referred to as the leagues' best pitcher, claimed he pitched in 2,500 games and won 2,000 of them. Unfortunately, the statistics that were kept do not support these claims. Separating fact from fiction in assessing the history of the Negro Leagues is important and difficult to do.

This said, the press more closely covered the dynasty teams, so there are more first-hand (and more likely accurate) accounts of how these teams played, how their players interacted, and the challenges they all faced. There were also many "exhibition" games between the best Negro League teams and major league teams that were more often covered by the mainstream press and where the players themselves were quoted discussing one another. These quotes are very helpful in assessing the relative quality of play in the different leagues, and the quotes about individual players are outright fascinating.

Organized Black league play began in 1920 with the Negro National League created by Andrew "Rube" Foster, himself a great player. Three leagues were created over the decade of the 1920s, but as the economy declined and the stock market crashed in 1929, all three leagues failed. The powerful force of the Great Depression dramatically affected the Negro Leagues. A few independent teams survived, but most did not.

Following the Great Depression, three teams emerged as dynasties: the Homestead Grays, Pittsburgh Crawfords, and Kansas City Monarchs. All three teams would experience stretches of superiority and greatness while competing against each other and other teams in the leagues. They would also compete for the same key stars, many of whom are on Bill James' Top 100. And as it turns out, many great players moved between these three teams—making the study of the dynasties that were the Grays, Crawfords, and Monarchs best done together.

The Homestead Grays, the team on which so many players on Bill James' Top 100 played, were among the most successful and long-lasting franchises in the Negro Leagues' history. The team was formed in 1912 and existed until 1950. The team's founder and owner, Cumberland Posey, was college-educated and from a prominent Pittsburgh family. The largest Black-owned business in Pittsburgh—the Diamond Coke and Coal Company—was owned by his father. His team was very successful in 1930 and 1931 while an independent team, and then between 1937 and 1945, they were a part of the recreated Negro National League. The Grays were based in Homestead, Pennsylvania, but played many of their home games in two major league stadiums: Forbes Field in Pittsburgh and Griffith Stadium in Washington, DC.

The Pittsburgh Crawfords came into being in the mid-1920s and became wildly successful from 1932 to 1936, during which time they won four championships. They were owned by Gus Greenlee, whose primary business endeavors included bootlegging during Prohibition and the "numbers racket," a lottery game where participants put down a "half penny" with a minimal chance for it to pay off big. Greenlee built and owned the Crawford Grill, one of the best jazz clubs in the east in Pittsburgh's famous Hill District. In addition to his bootlegging and gambling endeavors, Greenlee was happy to be of service to provide loans to people in need of paying for rent and food—thus adding loansharking to his empire. Greenlee was one of the wealthiest businessmen in Pittsburgh for a while and used that wealth to purchase the best baseball talent money could buy.

Perhaps, the Black baseball franchise that is best known today is the Kansas City Monarchs. They were a charter member of the Negro National League in 1920 and remained a league team through 1931. When the league failed in 1931, they survived and played as an independent team from 1932 to 1936. They joined the new Negro American League that formed in 1937 and continued to be a league member until the Negro Leagues ended in the 1950s. The Monarchs were created and owned by J.L. Wilkinson, one of the few white owners in the history of the Negro Leagues.

The Monarchs won 10 championships and multiple Black World Series, including the first such contest played in 1924. The Monarchs were well funded and known to pay and treat their players well. They were very innovative and carried with them a portable lighting system. This allowed for games under the lights well before the major leagues provided them. The Monarchs produced more major league players than any other franchise. One of them was Jackie Robinson.

The Negro League teams faced almost insurmountable odds to stay in business. The teams often played two or three games per day, each in a different city, to provide enough revenue to survive. Teams typically traveled in cars or old buses. The Homestead Grays traveled in two Buicks, each of which would carry nine men. The vehicles had equipment boxes on the back and a luggage rack on the top. They traveled over bumpy and sometimes treacherous country roads, and the players were often denied access to hotels and restaurants. They were even denied the use of restrooms when they stopped for gas. Team rosters typically included 17 players or fewer, and there was no injury or disabled list. If a player was on the team, he played. If a pitcher started a game, he finished it. Playing with physical pain and constant fatigue while battling unrelenting racism was part of the job.

Oscar Charleston, who is fourth on the Bill James all-time best list, started in Black professional baseball in 1915 and played until 1941. He played for 10 separate teams. He also played in Latin America in the off-season. Charleston could do it all on a baseball field—hit for average, hit for power, run, field, and throw—all at an elite level. His recorded statistics in official Negro League games (those played in the 40–80 game seasons) included a lifetime batting average of .352, an on-base percentage of .446, and a slugging percentage (a statistic that captures power hitting) of .574. Compared to similar statistics in major league history, he would be fourth in batting average (behind Ty Cobb, Rogers Hornsby, and Shoeless Joe Jackson), sixth in on-base percentage (wedged between Lou Gehrig and Barry Bonds), and ahead of Mickey Mantle in slugging. Charleston's combined abilities to hit, get on base, and hit for power were among the best in baseball history.

Charleston's speed and defensive ability were also elite. He would commonly position himself right behind second base in the shallow outfield to serve as a fifth infielder but would chase down and catch balls hit into the outfield over his head. Buck O'Neil, Negro League player, manager, and Negro League spokesman until his death at 94 in 2006, played against Charleston and watched Willie Mays (number 2 on James' list) for Mays' entire career. O'Neil believed Charleston to be the better overall player. O'Neil, who also saw Ty Cobb, Babe Ruth, and Tris Speaker play, and actually played against them in exhibition games, believed Charleston's skill set encompassed the best attributes of all three.

John McGraw, one of the greatest major league managers of all-time, said Charleston was the best player he ever saw. Honus Wagner, who many at the time believed was the best player ever (and was number 3 on James' list behind Ruth and Mays), said, "I've seen all the great players in the many years I've been around and have yet to see one any greater than Charleston." Major League Hall of Fame pitcher Grover Cleveland Alexander called Charleston the best ever.

Charleston also had a temper and a propensity to get into fights on the field. And he was fearless off it. After one game, Charleston and teammate Cool Papa Bell were confronted by Ku Klux Klan members in full regalia. As Bell told the story later, Charleston snatched off one of the "white hats" and the klansman backed off. On another occasion when Charleston walked into a restaurant, a waitress said, "We don't serve N———s," to which Charleston responded, "I don't plan to order one." While there appears to be no direct evidence that Jackie Robinson learned his on-field fierce and combative ways in the face of discrimination from Charleston, there are several similarities between the two men. Charleston fought some of the same racist battles Robinson did—20 to 30 years before him. If Charleston's leadership and his overall contributions to the game are considered in determining who was the all-time greatest, his star rises even higher.

There is no definitive way to compare Charleston to the all-time great major leaguers. But like comparisons made for those who played in the major leagues across eras, we can look at anecdotal evidence like statements above from his contemporaries. We can also look at the historical records of games between White and Black professional teams. In Ken Burns' acclaimed documentary *Baseball*, it is noted that in the exhibition games that were played between the Negro League and major league teams, the Black teams won almost 2/3rds of the games. So, while Charleston never played in the major leagues, it is pretty clear he could have if given a chance, and he may have become an all-time great.

In 1931, the Grays and Monarchs were probably the only teams that made money. Posey cut the entire Grays' team's payroll to $600 per month. He trimmed travel expenses and per diems. He also worked hard to maintain the image of his team and his players by requiring them to wear collared shirts and ties when on the road. He had to schedule extra exhibition games to keep the team afloat, so the Grays were often exhausted when on the field. The Monarchs' owner Wilkinson was able to lease out his portable lighting system to make ends meet. Despite the challenges, the Grays went 143-29-2 in all games played that year. Some historians believe they were the best baseball team, of any league, of all time.

While Charleston, at 36 years of age and still a great player, was the undoubted leader of the Grays' team, the MVP was Josh Gibson. He was a 6 ft., 1 in. and a 220-pound catcher and was to go on to become the greatest power hitter in the Negro Leagues. Gibson won nine Negro League home run titles in his career. Some writers of the time compared Gibson to Babe Ruth as a hitter. Some called Gibson the "Black Babe Ruth" while others called Ruth the "White Josh Gibson." Ruth was reported to be honored by the comparison. Many of Gibson's home runs are legendary. *The Sporting News* credited him with hitting a 580-ft. home run that hit the bleacher wall of Yankee Stadium two feet from the top. Gibson is also credited with hitting .351 against white major league pitchers.

Unfortunately for Posey and the Grays, they faced strong competition in their own backyard. In the late 1920s, Pittsburgh gambler and racketeer Gus Greenlee founded a new franchise called the Pittsburgh Crawfords. Greenlee had a constant flow of cash due to his dubious businesses, and his financial wherewithal gave him a significant leg up on the Grays and other teams. He built a brand-new 7,500 seat stadium with showers and dressing rooms for both teams, amenities they were not allowed to use in the major league stadiums in which they played. He bought a large new Mack bus with leather upholstery in which his players traveled.

Crawford could also afford to pay top dollar for baseball talent, and he raided the Grays' players. The first was Charleston himself, who was hired as "player manager." Within days of being hired, Charleston had received commitments from several great players, including a few of the Top 100 on the James' list: Satchel Paige, Josh Gibson, Judy Johnson, Jud Wilson, and others. As a result, the Crawfords became the new dominant team.

Satchel Paige is number 19 on the Bill James' list and is considered one of the all-time best pitchers in all of baseball. He was 6 ft., 4in. and rail thin with many pitches, including a dominant fastball. He was one of the most prominent players who would jump teams and leagues for better opportunities. He played for teams all over the country, from California to Maryland to North Dakota, and elsewhere including Cuba, the Dominican Republic, Puerto Rico, and Mexico. Paige was vague about his age—claiming the "goat ate the Bible with the Birth Certificate in it." It was later determined that Paige was born in 1906 and would have turned 26 his first year with the Crawfords. As Charleston aged and Paige came into his own, Paige became the top gate draw among the Negro teams.

The lack of accurate and complete statistics is particularly unfortunate for Paige, as his true greatness cannot be accurately quantified. But like Charleston, Paige received many compliments from well-known major league stars. After playing against Paige in an exhibition game, Joe DiMaggio called him the "best and fastest pitcher I ever faced."

In 1932, the Crawfords competed as an independent team, and in 1933, they competed in the new Negro National League, which several owners, including Greenlee, formed. The Crawfords became the dominant team with the best stars and were league champions in 1933, 1935, and 1936. In 1933, Paige pitched to an overall record of 31-4. Then, he abandoned the Crawfords to pitch for a team in Bismarck, North Dakota, who paid him $400 per month, $150 per month more than Greenlee would pay.

Charleston's biggest challenge as a manager was reigning in Paige who never played with anything but his own interests in mind and was easily distracted by not only higher pay from other teams but also women, fishing, and other extracurricular activities. Charleston was responsible for making sure Paige showed up, especially when Paige was being advertised as the main attraction. These efforts by Charleston—and his leadership in general—provided even more support for Charleston being the all-time greatest. In this area, his efforts far exceeded Ruth, who was really more like the nonteam-oriented Paige with his selfish behavior that included drinking, carousing, and stretches of his career where he simply couldn't play due to being out of shape.

Going into spring training in 1937, the Crawfords looked unbeatable. Gibson and Paige were in their primes and Charleston had developed into an outstanding manager. The league had largely recovered from the Depression and the economics looked better. But enter the emergence of another powerful force—Dominican Republic Dictator Rafael Trujillo.

Trujillo was putting together a team for a politically charged baseball series against a rival, reportedly to decide an election, and initiated a full-scale raid on the Crawfords. Trujillo's representative contacted Paige first and offered $30,000 to find nine players to play on the team. Paige was allowed to keep what he could of the cash. Before Greenlee knew what had happened, Paige, Gibson, Cool Papa, Bell, and six others vanished from spring training and were off to the Dominican. The series was reportedly very close, and when Trujillo realized he might lose after paying all that cash, he placed a large part of his army (armed with bayonets) in the packed stadium to help "motivate" his team. At the moment that they won the series for the island championship, the American players made a mad dash from the stadium to the airport and were able to return to United States safely. Their fears were well-founded. In the fall of that same year, Trujillo had over 15,000 Haitians killed in an act of "ethnic cleansing."

Owner Greenlee did not handle the mass departure well. When the players returned from the Dominican in July 1937, he and other owners tried to ban them from the league, and Greenlee tried to ban Paige for an extended period. Posey viewed the treatment of Paige differently and more wisely stating publicly, "to punish him severely by baseball law is like chastening a child that was brought up wrong."

Without their stars, the Crawfords' attendance predictably plummeted, and the team that manager Charleston had to scrape together did not do well on the field. Greenlee was forced to move the team, and it then folded in 1940. The stadium Greenlee built was torn down and replaced by a housing project. Greenlee's dynasty had died the same way it was born—at the hands of a full-scale raid on talent. Had he played the long game, recognizing that the players would return and continue to need to play to make a living, he would have likely been able to put his team back together. But he whiffed on the opportunity.

Posey's Grays had not done well on the field after the exodus of the star players to the Crawfords in 1932. However, Posey did a much better job maintaining relationships with his stars after they left his team. As a result, Posey was able to bring back Gibson and others, and the Grays returned to prominence. From 1937 to 1945, the Grays won eight of nine Negro American League Championships and three World Series titles in the four years when the series was played. Posey's steady hand and patience through the depression years and Trujillo's raid were rewarded by the top stars wanting to return to play for his team and then winning on the field.

Paige would ultimately have the opportunity to pitch in the major leagues and did so from 1948 to 1953, beginning when he was 42 and ending when he was 47. He pitched in 179 games and had a lifetime ERA of 3.29—impressive statistics for a man in his 40s. Few pitchers in history pitched this well into their mid-40s. The only two who are near Paige's level are Warren Spahn, who pitched in 143 games and had an average ERA of 4.01 over the last five years of his career—ending when he was 44; and Nolan Ryan, who pitched in 129 games and had an ERA of 3.62 over the last five years of his career ending when he was 46. Paige pitched for Cleveland in a World Series game in 1948, the year the Indians won the world championship. Paige was also part of one of the most extraordinary publicity stunts in the history of baseball by pitching three innings for the Charlie Finley Kansas City A's in 1965 at the age of 59.

Josh Gibson's career did not finish nearly as well. By the mid-1940s, Gibson was drinking heavily and had begun to suffer from headaches. He began behaving erratically and his weight ballooned. He died in 1947 at the age of 35 and never played in the major leagues.

In the later 1930s and into the 1940s, another emerging powerful force was at play—the increasing public pressure to integrate the major leagues. Integration in baseball was part and parcel of a broader movement to eliminate discrimination in housing, the workplace, and other sectors of society. There were also boycotts against retail businesses that refused to hire African Americans. The Black press played a prominent role in this effort, and in the late 1930s, the white press started to add their support. In a poll of major league players taken during this time, 80 percent said that they had no problem playing with, and against, Negro League players. The emergence of Jessie Owens, Joe Louis, and successful Black athletes in other sports added fuel to the fire. But the major league owners—led by Commissioner Kenesaw Mountain Landis—ignored these efforts while pretending there were no organized forces to keep Blacks out.

At least one major league executive, Branch Rickey of the Brooklyn Dodgers, did not share the views of the mainstream owners. In early 1943, the Dodgers' president and general manager began quietly scouting Black players with the end goal of integrating the major leagues. Paige and Gibson were early suggestions but were quickly rejected due to a selfish nature (Paige) and being subject to the "temptations of the nightlife" (Gibson). Two years passed and Rickey had not found the right player to be the first to integrate. His biggest hurdle was that his scouts could not show up at Negro League games without arousing suspicion, and thus, he could not get the inside story on a player's background and character.

Enter Gus Greenlee and Oscar Charleston. In 1945, Greenlee was working on starting yet another Negro League, and Charleston was slated to manage a team. Rickey got wind of the plan and saw an opportunity. He would enter his team, the Brooklyn Brown Dodgers, in the league and get the cover he needed to scout Black players properly. While Rickey's main goal remained integration, he also hoped to build organizational ties with the Black community and make some money at Ebbets Field while the major league Dodgers were away. When the new Black league was announced, the now pro-integration public exploded in outrage because the new league looked precisely like the segregated leagues that had existed before.

The new league started and immediately began to flounder, but it gave Rickey the cover he needed. At Charleston's recommendation, he began to meet with certain players, including catcher Roy Campanella. Why Campanella was not chosen to be the first player to integrate baseball other than Jackie Robinson is somewhat unclear. While there are conflicting reports, it may have come down to a misunderstanding between Rickey and Campanella. When Rickey asked Campanella "[would] you like to play for me?" Campanella understood that Rickey asked Campanella to play for the Brown Dodgers and not the major league club. Because Campanella was already making a good living with his current Negro League team, he rejected the offer. Rickey apparently did not notice the failure to communicate between the two men.

Shortly after his meeting with Campanella, Rickey met with Jackie Robinson and extended the invitation to him. Robinson, understanding what was being asked of him, accepted the offer. Campanella learned of this while playing cards with Robinson a few days after his meeting with Ricky. He then realized his mistake—he could have been the first player other than Jackie Robinson to integrate Major League Baseball. Had he not misinterpreted Rickey's question and became the first, Oscar Charleston would have been credited with making the recommendation.

The Kansas City Monarchs' first baseman, manager, and driving force during their championship run in the 1930s and 1940s was Buck O'Neil. Considering O'Neil's impact as a player, manager, and spokesman, he may have been the most valuable contributor to the Negro Leagues in their history. O'Neil's grandfather was a member of the Mandingo tribe of West Africa and came to the United States on a slave ship. O'Neil himself grew up in the Sarasota, Florida area, and worked in the celery fields where his father was a foreman. He wanted to go to Sarasota High School and was devastated when told he couldn't because he was Black. O'Neil served in World War II in the Mariana Islands and then in the Philippines in a Stevedore Battalion. He was a Boatswain First Class responsible for a dozen men. He was once complimented for his leadership skills by a military officer, "If you were white, you'd be an officer by now."

During O'Neil's playing and managing days which stretched from 1937 to 1943 and after the war from 1946 to 1948, he was known as an excellent teammate, leader, and brought positivity and a big smile every day he came to work. His presence in the clubhouse made a difference as the Monarchs dominated the Negro Leagues during the time he played and managed.

After 1947, Jackie Robinson's first year in the major leagues, the Negro National League folded. The top stars in the Negro Leagues (including Roy Campanella) began moving to the major leagues. The Monarchs kept going and were still successful into the early 1950s by wisely selling their best players to (and even scouting for) major league teams. O'Neil excelled at this, too, and later became a scout for the Chicago Cubs. O'Neil identified many future stars, including Elston Howard, Ernie Banks, Lou Brock, Lee Smith, and Joe Carter. The ingenuity shown by the Monarchs and O'Neil in the face of the force that would most certainly end the Negro Leagues was extraordinary. But that force and its impact, while way too late, was the right thing to happen.

Beyond O'Neil's playing, managing, and scouting accomplishments, his greatest achievement was promoting the Negro Leagues. He became the main driving force behind creating the Negro Leagues Hall of Fame and served on the Hall of Fame's Veterans Committee sponsoring the induction of many Negro League players. He was tireless in carrying on the league traditions by recalling stories about Charleston, Paige, Gibson, and others. He was a contributor to Ken Burns' *Baseball* and may have stolen the show—demonstrating his in-person way of communicating and connecting that no doubt fueled the extraordinary impact he had on others.

It is hard to describe the pride and joy O'Neil conveys during his interview regarding his personal experiences with men like Charleston, Gibson, Paige, Jackie Robinson, and others. His recollection of teams, games, the racism they faced and felt, and his understanding of what the leagues meant and would mean to America was remarkable. It was as if O'Neil knew that it was his duty to pass the torch that would enlighten generations to come about Black baseball and seized the opportunity to do so.

Buck O'Neil died on October 6, 2006. At his memorial service, many of his words were recalled including these which he said many times when asked whether he wished he had been born later and been able to play in the majors: "People ask me: How do you keep from being bitter? Man, bitterness will eat you up inside. Hatred will eat you up inside. Don't be bitter. Don't hate. My grandfather was a slave. He was not bitter. I learned that from him. And you know what? I wouldn't trade my life for anybody's. I've had so many blessings in my life. I don't want people to be sad for me when I go. You shouldn't feel sad for a man who lived his dream. You know what I always say? I was right on time."

There is much to learn from the Negro Leagues generally, and the Grays, Crawfords, and Monarchs in particular. Organizations should prepare for emerging powerful forces because they can and will come. This goes beyond saving for a rainy day—it's keeping a watchful eye toward the larger forces that potentially impact your organization and being ready for what might come. Create contingency plans suitable to your organization. And be aware of the fact that not all of these forces are bad and that some may be for the greater good—even transformative as was the integration of the major leagues.

These dynasties also teach to build relationships with key individuals and try and build incentives for them to stay when tempted by the competition. And if they leave, leave the door open for them to come back. If you are running your organization the right way, they left because they found a better situation for themselves, not anything you did. Be the organization that people want to be part of and will come back to. Find talented individuals and good people to lead your organization and make them part of your public image. Character matters—include it in your clubhouse. Make your group's core "team first" people but understand that you may need to have a talented individual or two who may not always share those values. In this event, set up the right kind of leadership and oversight where the individual can contribute and the organization is protected. Constantly try and build your dream team but know that loading it with only all-stars is likely not the recipe for success. Include servant leaders and people who don't really care who gets the credit. Always play the long game, and don't get discouraged with short-term losses. And remember the words Buck O'Neil learned from his grandfather, "Don't hate … and don't be bitter, it will eat you up inside." As this book was going to press in 2022, Buck O'Neil was finally inducted into the Major League Hall of Fame.

CHAPTER 4

The First Dynasty

A leader is one who knows the way, goes the way and shows the way.
—John Maxwell

The first decade of the 20th century saw the first mass production of the automobile and the widespread application of the combustion engine. It saw the advent of low-cost photography and the concept of the snapshot. The typewriter was invented. These and other technological advances fueled the expansion of Major League Baseball to the masses in America. The American League, an outgrowth of the former minor league called Western League, was created and recognized by the National League as a major league. The World Series was born. Attendance increased dramatically in the decade. Even though there were not yet teams west of St. Louis, Major League Baseball indeed became our national game.

The first 20th-century major league dynasty was the Chicago Cubs. In 1906, the Cubs' record was 116-36, a winning percentage of .736, the best in the history of Major League Baseball. In 1907, the Cubs went 107-45 with a winning percentage of .704, thus completing the best two-year run in the history of Major League Baseball. (The team only played 152 games of a 154-game schedule because their lead was so large they did not need to play make-up games that were canceled.) In 1908 to 1910, the Cubs won 99, 104, and 104 games, respectively—ending the best three-, four-, and five-year runs in the history of Major League Baseball. The Cubs also set the records for winning percentage over a 6-, 7-, 8-, 9-, and 10-year stretch. All these records stand today.

The Cubs won four pennants in five years between 1906 and 1910, and they won the World Series in 1907 and 1908. During this run, the Cubs had tremendous competition, including the Honus Wagner-led Pittsburgh Pirates, who won the National League Championship in 1902 (before any World Series was played) and the World Series in

1909. The Cubs also had to compete with the John McGraw and Christy Mathewson-led New York Giants, who won the World Series in 1905; the Ty Cobb-led Detroit Tigers in the American League; and a burgeoning dynasty in the American League, the Philadelphia A's. The Cubs did not officially become the Cubs until 1907. The team had previously been known as the White Stockings, Colts, and even the Orphans, but by 1906, the Chicago *Daily News* was referring to the team as the "Cubs" due to the number of young players on the team, and they were generally referred to as such by their fans.

While most writers and historians referred to the first 20 years of the 20th century as the "dead ball" era, the ball itself (at least until 1910) was the same one that was used at the end of the 19th century. What had changed were the rules. Before 1901, a foul ball was not a strike. A hitter could continue to foul off pitches one after another without impacting the ball and strike count. In 1901 in the National League and 1903 in the American League, a new rule was put into place that foul balls would count for strikes one and two. The new five-sided home plate was introduced, giving a pitcher more corners to pitch over than the former diamond-shaped foot-square plate. Strikeouts went up by 50 percent and batting averages fell from near .280 to the range of .240 to .250. Power hitting was reduced as hitters became more cautious with two strikes on them. Fielding improved as players began using larger gloves and the infields became better maintained by groundskeepers.

It did not help the hitters that the umpires continued to use as few balls as possible in each game. And each pitcher would try and dirty up the ball to make it easier to manipulate, curve, slide, and drop. Pitchers also scuffed and cut the ball, used their belt buckles, bits of an emery board, or a razor blade tucked into their gloves. Outright mutilation of the ball was supposed to be against the rules, but the umpires typically did nothing about it. Pitchers could also legally employ the spitball, making the ball swerve and spin in even more mysterious ways. Later in games, the ball would become black and misshapen—making it hard to hit very far. On cloudy days and as dusk approached (all games were played in the afternoon), the ball became more difficult for hitters to see. Home runs were rare in this era. From 1906 to 1909, the most home runs hit in a season by the entire Cubs' team was 20.

During the dynasty years, the Cubs played at their old park—West Side Grounds. Wrigley Field was not completed until 1916. West Side Grounds seated 16,000 at its largest capacity, and beams obstructed at least one third of the seats in the park. Built with wood, the park was very susceptible to fire. Similarly built stadiums had burned to the ground in Boston, Philadelphia, St. Louis, and Cincinnati. Players were called into duty to help fans out of the grandstands. Fortunately for the Cubs, there were no fires of significance at West Side Grounds.

Beginning later in the decade, teams began to use concrete and steel to construct their parks. The dimensions of the West Side Grounds were cavernous, including 560 ft. to center field, far longer than any modern stadium. When large crowds required it, the Cubs seated overflow fans on planks laid down behind home plate and along the foul lines from home plate to just past the edge of the outfield turn. Fans also stood behind a rope in center field when the regular seats were sold out. There were no dugouts, and team benches sat at field level, which directly exposed players to additional dangers of the game. Wicked foul balls took a toll on players who weren't paying attention.

Major League Baseball during this era was not for the faint of heart. Fights on the field, in the stands, and the dugouts were commonplace. Fans baited players, players baited each other, and everyone tried to bait the umpire—who during that time often ruled the game solo, with no help from another umpire on the field. Making unpopular calls before home crowds was a dangerous thing, and on many occasions police had to accompany umpires off the field and out of the stadium. There are many accounts of glass bottles and other objects being thrown at men on the field. And there were reports of guns in the stands—particularly on the Fourth of July. It was a game played, managed, and watched mainly by men who smoked (thus the concern about fires), drank, and didn't mind a good fracas. For the most part, women did not come to the park.

The Cubs did not have all-time great players. What the Cubs did have were very good players at every position, great pitching, and an even better defense. They also had virtually no turnover of players during their dynasty run. Except for one position, where two players platooned, and in one year where they lost their regular catcher, the Cubs' regular day-to-day lineup included the same players between 1906 and 1910. The core pitchers also remained the same. In all five of the dynasty years, the team's pitching ERA was first in the National League, and its fielding percentage was either first or second. The Cubs had consistency, and they had balance. But the team had to overcome many obstacles to win—including a devastating loss to a cross-town rival, an ongoing feud between two core players that prevented them from speaking to one another, and the most controversial pennant race in the history of baseball.

The Cubs' manager, first baseman, and unquestioned leader was Frank Chance. Chance was also known as "Husk" (short for "Husky") or "the Peerless Leader" ("PL" if you were stretched for time). Chance was hard-nosed and stubborn. He bowled over opponents at every opportunity and was tough on his own team—fining them for so much as shaking hands with an opposing player. Chance was known to say to them, "You do things my way, or you meet me after the game." Given that Chance spent off-seasons working as a prizefighter and was called "the greatest amateur brawler of all time" by boxing legend John L. Sullivan, his teammates usually complied with his instructions. But he was also great at his craft, and he was liked as much as he was respected.

Chance was hired during the season in 1905 when the team finished in third place, 13 games behind the Giants, who won the pennant and the World Series that year. Before the 1906 season, Chance convinced team owner Charlie Murphy to bring in three new players, all of whom made big contributions that year: third baseman Harry Steinfeldt who led the league in hits, pitcher Jack Pfiester who went 20-8, and outfielder Jimmy Sheckard who was excellent at taking walks and getting on base. Once the season started, Chance brought over two additional pitchers who also became key contributors: Orval Overall and Jack Taylor. Each went 12-3 for the Cubs in 1906. Chance's boldness in quickly turning over the roster paid off. When a new leader takes over, there is a window of opportunity to make changes. Some leaders are hesitant to do this—waiting too long to make necessary changes to personnel, perhaps out of a desire not to rock the boat. Chance realized he had an opportunity to change the team's makeup, and he seized the opportunity. All five of the new players would make key contributions over the coming years.

Chance was remarkably good at evaluating talent. He valued speed, defense, and smarts. He encouraged small stakes poker as a way to stir the mental juices, sometimes joining a game to see how well a player thought under pressure. If a player did not play cards well, he was not trusted by Chance. And his decisions on which players the Cubs would have on their team were as good as any manager's in the game's history.

Chance was also a perfect manager for his era, a time when planning, strategy, and teamwork were more critical. Chance employed bunt hits and run plays, stolen bases, and stealing opponents' signs to take advantage of scoring opportunities. He and second baseman Johnny Evers carefully cataloged the pick-off motions of opposing pitchers, the quality of opponents' throwing arms, and circumstances when opposing teams used a pitchout or a hit and run. Chance and Evers were also very careful in positioning their defense, and the Cubs may have been the first ball club to use the shortstop to cover second base when a left-handed batter was up with a runner on first. Chance could work the margins with the best of them.

Chance was also an excellent first baseman and a great base runner. He stole 67 bases in one season and 401 in his career, both outstanding for a first baseman. He was also known for digging in and getting hit by pitches. Chance did this to his ultimate detriment as determined a decade later that he had sustained severe head injuries caused by beanings. But Chance used all the tools available to him to gain an advantage. For example, a common Chance strategy was to intentionally get hit by a pitch, act as if he was injured by limping to first base, and then surprising the pitcher by stealing second. Upon completing the steal, he was known to stand on the base and proclaim to the pitcher, "Hit me again, asshole. See what it gets you?" His skill set of toughness, planning, thoughtfulness, speed, and bravado was unique and was one of the key ingredients of the team's success.

Chance's 1906 Cubs were brilliant at home, going 56-21, but even better on the road—60-15. Over the last 63 games of the season, they finished 55-8. They were first in the National League in team batting, pitching, and fielding. Waiting for them in the World Series was their cross-town rival, the Chicago White Sox, known as the "Hitless Wonders" due to their season batting average of .228, the lowest regular-season batting average of any team who played in a World Series in history. The Series looked like David against Goliath. Unfortunately for the Cubs, it ended like the Biblical version. The White Sox won four games to two and surged ahead in Game 5 and Game 6 by, ironically, actually hitting—scoring eight runs per game. The White Sox also relied on their top pitcher Ed Walsh, whose go to pitch was spitball. Chance was not pleased with the result of the World Series but quickly turned to the following year. Like many of the dynasties studied in this book, 1906 was a "stairstep" season where the team excelled during the regular season but did not win the championship.

The Cubs' middle infielders were Johnny Evers at second base and Joe Tinker at shortstop—thus forming the double-play combination of "Tinker to Evers to Chance" as described in Franklin P. Adams' poem "Baseball's Sad Lexicon." The three were the most significant contributors to the Cubs' defensive prowess, which was by far the best in the National League during their dynasty. This is supported by their team fielding percentage and a statistic called "Defensive Efficiency." Defensive Efficiency is a rating of how many balls hit into the field of play (in other words, balls hit that aren't foul balls) are turned into outs. The Cubs' Defensive Efficiency Rating over their five dynasty years was first in the National League in four of those years and second to the Pirates in one year. This wasn't happenstance but was driven by Chance's focus on fundamentals and having his fielders in the right positions for each individual batter—a precursor to the modern-day "shift." Chance understood a critical metric that was not widely known or studied at the time—and his focus on it made a difference. He was ahead of his time in doing the little things right.

Evers and Tinker played so well together that they were called the "Siamese twins of baseball because they played the bag as if they were one man, not two." But while they worked together on the field, they did not get along off it. Prior to a game in 1905, Evers took a cab from the players' hotel to a game. Tinker was supposed to join but was late, requiring him to pay full freight for the next cab. This turned into a dispute, which in turn led to a brawl on the field between the two men on September 14, 1905. After the brawl, they did not speak to one another for the entire dynasty run. The reality is that some people will simply not get along. It happens in groups, teams, companies, and families. Chance and the Cubs were able to rise above this and were successful. Not all groups can do the same, and it typically takes a strong leader to overcome it.

Cubs' pitcher Mordecai Brown's life changed as a five-year-old. While working at his family's farm in Indiana, he got his right index finger caught in a machine designed to separate the grain from stalks, and the finger was sliced off. The next year, he fell while chasing a rabbit—and was left with a permanently bent middle finger and a paralyzed little finger, both also on his right (pitching) hand. Brown loved baseball, and when forced to pitch in a semipro game because of an injury to the team's regular pitcher, he learned the deformity allowed him to throw a devastating curveball. The rest is history. Brown became the Cubs' best player on their dynasty team—winning 127 games and *averaging* a 1.41 ERA over the five-year period from 1906 to 1910. Brown was often called in to pitch by Chance in pressure situations and almost always came through. While Brown is 83rd on Bill James' Top 100 list, he is likely No. 1 on the list among players with a physical disability that impacted the on-field performance. Brown's nickname given to him well in advance of the Americans with Disabilities Act and without any sensitivity to people with physical limitations was "Three-Finger Brown."

The greatest pitcher of the age was probably Christy Mathewson with the New York Giants. Mathewson, known as the "Christian Gentleman," was one of the most revered athletes of the time. Mathewson and Brown had many pitching duels in crucial games. In 1912, Mathewson wrote a book called *Pitching in a Pinch or Baseball From the Inside* in which he recognized the greatness of Brown: "Brown is my idea of the almost perfect pitcher … . He is a finished pitcher in all departments of the game. Besides being a great worker, he is a wonderful fielder and sure death on bunts. He spends weeks in the spring preparing himself to field short hits in the infield, and it is fatal to try and bunt against him." During the Cubs' dynasty run, Brown outdueled Mathewson more often than not.

Many believe the Chicago Cubs of 1907 was the greatest team of all time. They played to a record of 107-45 and sailed through the regular season, besting the Pirates by 17 games. The Cubs then dominated the Detroit Tigers in the World Series, winning four games and losing none (with one tie). Each of the Cubs' five main pitchers had ERAs under 1.70, and the team ERA was an astonishing 1.73. The team's Fielding Percentage was .730, over .20 ahead of any other team in the National League. This Cubs team prevented the other team from scoring runs better than any team in the major leagues since the beginning of the 20th century.

The path to victory in 1908 was far more difficult. It occurred during the biggest year for pitching in a decade of great pitching. The collective batting averages of the hitters in both leagues was .239, both record lows. Only one of the 16 major league teams had ERAs over 3.00. Seven pitchers threw no-hitters, and seven of the all-time lowest ERAs occurred that year. It was the age of the spitball, and the pitch was used liberally, most notably by Ed Walsh, who won 40 games in the 1907 season. The wealth of pitching produced two of the closest and most exciting pennant races of all time: a three-team race in the National League between the Cubs, New York Giants, and Pittsburgh Pirates; and a four team race in the American League between the Detroit Tigers, Cleveland Indians, Chicago White Sox, and St. Louis Browns.

The Cubs and the Giants were rivals. The Giants and their manager John McGraw had a strategy similar to the Cubs—relying on toughness, "inside" strategy, and doing everything they could to outthink their opponents and gain an advantage. McGraw was also a master at baiting umpires. The games between the teams had historically involved fights, chicanery, and raucous fans. While the Giants won the National League and the World Series in 1905, the Cubs were better in 1906 and 1907. On the morning of September 23, 1908, the teams were in a virtual tie for first place in the National League, and the season was coming to a close.

The game they played on September 23 in the Giants' home stadium, the Polo Grounds, was critical to the pennant race and turned out to be one of the most controversial games of all time. The stands were packed, and the crowd was as raucous as ever. Consistent with the style of the times, pitching and defense dominated the game.

The score was tied 1-1 in the bottom of the ninth. The Giants had men on first and third base. The man on first base was Fred Merkle, a young college-educated player who was not a regular starter for the Giants but had played well thus far in the game, including hitting a single that put him on base. The crowd had been riding the Cubs all day and were now delirious, needing just one hit and one run to win. The hitter, Al Bridwell, delivered that hit into right field. The runner on third ran home, and the fans jumped the low fences and rushed onto the field to mob the players. Merkle started running toward second base but saw the crowd bearing down on him and instead turned and ran toward the Giants' clubhouse. Unfortunately, he had forgotten one of the most basic rules in baseball that there was a force play at second base, and if the ball were thrown to a fielder who touched second base before he arrived there, he would be out, and the run would not count.

Cubs' second baseman Johnny Evers saw what was going on and called for the ball in the midst of the madness. The Cubs' centerfielder picked up the ball and rifled it toward Evers. But a Giants' coach saw what was going on and, in fighting through the midst of sheer chaos on the field, either intercepted the throw or picked it up after it had been intercepted by someone else. He then threw the ball into the stands. Evers continued to call for the ball at second, jumping up and down on the base. Another Cubs' player ran into the stands and either found the ball (or, depending on whom you believe, found another) and threw it to Tinker, who relayed it to Evers, who touched second base and screamed "he's out." The plate umpire Hank O' Day saw the play as the crowd circled around him and confirmed that Merkle was out because he had not touched second base. Chance also saw what was going on and yelled at the umpire to clear the field because if the run didn't count, the game was still tied 1-1. But the police would not let O'Day stay on the field and began to escort him toward safety. Both managers, Chance, and McGraw with rings of police around them chased the umpire screaming at him, trying to influence the call. In all of the madness, Merkle never did touch second base. It took multiple police paddy wagons to get the Cubs' players and the umpires away from the field and to safety.

In 1908, there was no film of the games, no radio broadcasts, and apparently no photographs showing what actually occurred during the play. Merkle later acknowledged he had not touched second base but claimed that the other umpire, Howard Emslie, saw the crowd coming and waived Merkle to the clubhouse, saying, "You have the game." But the key was that the main umpire called Merkle out. Part of the reason that Evers, the Cubs, and umpire O'Day were aware of the situation was that the same thing had happened less than three weeks before in a game in Pittsburgh, and they were ready.

It took three days to sort things out. After a league decision and multiple appeals, it was finally decided that the game would be ruled a tie, on account of darkness, to be replayed at the end of the year, if necessary, to decide the National League Championship Series. It was true that the game could not have continued due to the mob on the field and darkness. Games in these times usually took less than two hours and often finished within 90 minutes. As such, the game started at 4:00 even though the sun was to set at 5:52. And in 1908, there were no lights in the Polo Grounds.

Of course, "if necessary" happened, and the teams met again in the Polo Grounds on October 8, 1908, before a howling mob of more than 30,000 fans. Thousands more watched the game on the surrounding bluffs and elsewhere. It was probably the most notable sports event in the nation's history up until then. Large portions of the fence at the Polo Grounds were broken down by patrons who insisted on gaining entrance. Most of the New York police force was present to keep order. Giants' manager John McGraw reportedly tried to bribe the umpires before the game but was unsuccessful. Two fans who tried to perch themselves on an elevated railroad structure to watch the game fell to their deaths. Seven fans were taken out of the stadium "stark raving mad." A fan hit Frank Chance with a thrown glass bottle damaging cartilage in his neck.

The play in the game earlier in the season haunted Merkle for the rest of his life. Even the man who got the hit on the play, Al Bridwell, regretted it. "I wish I'd never gotten that hit that set off the whole Merkle incident. I wish I'd struck out instead. It would have spared Fred a lot of humiliation." By the time of the game on October 8, Merkle had lost 20 pounds. His eyes were hollow, and his cheeks sunken. He had begged McGraw to send him down to the minor leagues. During the game, he sat in the dugout cowering behind the water cooler.

As the Cubs went on to the field before the game, the crowd was unmerciful. "I never heard anybody or any set of men called as many foul names as the Giants' fans called us that day from the time we showed up until it was over," said Mordecai Brown, who pitched for the Cubs that day. But Brown was magnificent, and the Cubs won the replayed game 4-2 to win the National League Championship. It took armed police officers to get the Cubs safely out of the Polo Grounds. The Cubs then won the World Series four games to one against Detroit.

Despite the Cubs' record-setting performance on the field, no one player stood out. If they had a MVP, it was probably Mordecai Brown who was disabled in the very part of him that mattered most for his craft—his pitching hand. For the Cubs, the whole was truly greater than the sum of the parts. Even deep studies of why they were successful don't turn up much other than great leadership, great balance, and great team play. They were consistent and stayed on the field, avoiding injury. As shown by how the team was built and how they won the Merkle game, they knew the rules of the game cold. They studied, and they prepared. They were smart and played smart. They did the little things necessary to win—not just once in a while but seemingly every time. They were able to put personal differences aside on the field. They found a special gear when it mattered, which generated a combination of great pitching and defense, and simply would not let opponents score runs when they needed to most.

The Cubs epitomized the notion of a great team *emerging* from a collection of individuals. No single player stood out as a superstar, but there were also no weaknesses. Frank Chance set a very clear and uncompromising standard, and the players learned to embrace it. They understood and believed what their leader was trying to do, and they bonded and rallied around that mission. They also policed each other and learned to live with clear and regular communication that was direct and sometimes included tough messages. Chance also knew when to shake things up, tone it down, and let players find their own way through challenges. The Cubs of this era are on nearly every list of the all-time greatest teams.

CHAPTER 5

As One of Nine Men

Joe DiMaggio played the game at least a couple of levels higher than the rest of baseball. A lot of guys, all you had to see to know they were great was a stat sheet. DiMaggio, you had to see. It wasn't only numbers on a page—although they were there too—it was a question of command, style, grace.

—Jim Murray

At the beginning of 1936, the United States was still in ravages of the Great Depression. The unemployment rate was nearly 20 percent. The summer of 1936 was the hottest on record in the United States. Eight states experienced temperatures of 110 degrees or greater, including over 120 degrees in North Dakota, South Dakota, and Kansas. As many as 5,000 Americans died from the heat. The dust bowl battered the southwest. Black Sunday, the worst "blizzard" of the Dust Bowl occurred on April 14, 1935; by the end of that year, experts estimated that 850,000,000 tons of topsoil had blown off the southern plains.

From October 2, 1935, to November 1, 1939, fascist Italy invaded, conquered, and annexed Ethiopia and then signed a treaty of cooperation with Nazi Germany. In 1937, Japan invaded China. In the coming months and years, Adolph Hitler began his march across Europe and had started to make threats to conquer the world. Americans awoke daily to read about these events in the newspapers and saw newsreel footage of them in movie theaters. Anxiety and worry were everywhere. More than ever, Americans needed something to take their minds off a constant barrage of troubling news and a future rife with dreadful possibilities.

Americans needed distractions, and they needed heroes. Enter the world of sports. American Jesse Owens won four Gold Medals in the 1936 Olympic Games in Berlin right in front of Adolph Hitler and a large crowd which included many applauding Germans. In June 1938,

American heavyweight boxing champion Joe Louis defeated German Max Schmeling by knockout in just over two minutes. Schmeling had previously beaten Louis, and when Schmeling arrived in New York City for the fight, a Nazi publicist accompanied him. The publicist announced before the match that Schmeling planned to demonstrate Aryan supremacy by winning the fight, and then donating the prize money to build tanks for the Nazis.

In 1938, the Tigers' great first baseman Hank Greenberg gave chase to Babe Ruth's then single-season home run record of 60. He did not quite get there but still hit 58, a remarkable accomplishment by any measure. Greenberg was Jewish and said that when he hit a home run that year, he felt like he was hitting it against Hitler. Greenberg was one of the first players to later enlist in the military during World War II. He saw combat and served his country for four years during the prime of his playing career. Many other baseball stars, including Bob Feller, Ted Williams, Yogi Berra, Stan Musial, Joe DiMaggio, and Jackie Robinson, also served.

The 1936 to 1941 Yankees also gave Americans something to cheer for. They won five American League pennants and five World Series championships in a six-year period. In the five years they won the World Series, the Yankees went 20-4 in World Series games after winning 102, 102, 99, 106, and 101 regular season games in an era when teams played only 154 games each year. In the five winning years, they won the American League by an average of 15 games over the second-place teams.

The 1930s was an era of sluggers, and these Yankees were the best sluggers of them all. They led the American League in home runs, runs batted in, and runs scored each year during the dynasty years. In 1936, they hit 182 home runs—59 more than the second-place Cleveland Indians and twice as many as most of the teams in the league. They scored 1,065 runs that year, an average of nearly seven per game. The team got extraordinary production out of virtually every position—including catcher, second base, and third base, positions that at the time were not known for high offensive contributions. Lou Gehrig's and Joe DiMaggio's personal statistics were some of their best ever—each batting in 125 or more runs multiple times. Gehrig won the MVP award in 1936, and DiMaggio won it in 1939 and 1941.

The Yankees' manager was Joe McCarthy. He had a calm but direct style, preferring to provide pats on the back and words of encouragement rather than riding players. He established very clear expectations. He did not like characters, loudmouths, or oddballs. He wanted players who did the little things right and stuck to business at all times. When traveling, he expected players to show up for breakfast at 8:30 a.m. in the hotel lobby dressed in coats and ties. Appearance and image mattered. Only baseball could be discussed in the clubhouse. No outsiders. No shaving. No radio. No card playing. No pipe smokers. "This is a clubhouse," said McCarthy, "not a club room."

Moderate drinking was not prohibited, but excess drinking was, and McCarthy could tell the difference in how a player performed on the field. Players were required to prepare for games, be ready at all times, and go full speed—whether the game was tied or the Yankees were 10 runs ahead. Mental errors were not tolerated. If a player did not meet these expectations, he was shown the door. McCarthy balanced the right level of discipline with the players he had and found a way to get their best.

The years of this Yankee dynasty marked the intersection of the end of Lou Gehrig's career and the beginning of Joe DiMaggio's. Gehrig and DiMaggio were integral parts of other Yankee dynasties—Gehrig as part of the 1920s Murderers' Row teams and DiMaggio as part of the Yankees later in the decade through his retirement after the 1951 season. Gehrig had great years in 1936 and 1937 when he was 33 and 34 years old. The slightly better one was 1936, during which he hit 49 home runs, batted in 152 runs, and hit .354. Over a period of 14 plus years, Gehrig played in 2,130 consecutive games—earning him the nickname "The Iron Horse." That record stood until 1995 when broken by Cal Ripken.

But Gehrig's on-the-field performance declined precipitously toward the end of 1938. In spring training in 1939, Gehrig became a shell of his former self. He mishandled balls at first base and began to stumble and fall. He dragged his left foot when he walked. Gehrig missed easy pitches during batting practice and would get exasperated in the locker room with his shirt buttons and trouser belt while dressing. Once an excellent bridge player, he began to struggle when shuffling the cards, and then reached a point where he could no longer do it.

On May 2, 1939, Gehrig took himself out of the lineup, ending his consecutive games played streak—stating it was for the good of the team. Gehrig had amyotrophic lateral sclerosis (ALS), a noncurable neurological disease that affects nerve cells in the brain and spinal cord causing loss of muscle control. Gehrig went public with his condition, and America watched while he fought it. But he succumbed to the disease and died on June 2, 1941. Gehrig left a mark on the game and the world. Eighty years after the end of Gehrig's career, he is still widely regarded as the best first baseman to ever play the game. ALS now bears his name: Lou Gehrig's disease.

There is still no medical certainty on the cause of ALS. Gehrig himself was in extraordinary health until he began to experience symptoms. He was raised in a good home by loving parents. He was well educated during his youth and had entered Columbia University before being signed by the Yankees. He ate well and rarely drank. He got plenty of sleep. He married his first serious girlfriend, Ellen Twitchell, and remained happily married until his death. There is movie footage of Gehrig swinging a bat while not wearing a shirt which shows a man with remarkable upper body strength and muscle definition, despite not having the benefits of the weight training of athletes today. Gehrig had lived an extraordinarily healthy life and looked to be the personification of good health before ALS took its toll.

But Gehrig had also been the victim of multiple beanings by pitched balls during his professional career. The worst occurred in an exhibition game in 1934 in Norfolk, Virginia, decades before players began wearing batting helmets. Gehrig took a direct hit to the head from a pitch, and the ball bounced high and banged against the side of the press box. Gehrig dropped as if he had been shot, passed out, and was down for five minutes. At least one player on the field thought he was dead. The next day, he awoke to throbs in his spine that seemed to radiate through his entire body. The hospital x-rays showed no fracture, but he did have a concussion and an enormous welt about two inches above his right eye.

Two weeks later, Gehrig began complaining of a backache. After hitting a single in the game that day, he could no longer stand up straight. Through it all, Gehrig managed to get in the lineup every day and continue his consecutive game streak. While Gehrig continued to play for five years and kept his streak alive (including playing the day after the beaning in Norfolk), it is entirely possible that the beanings contributed to the cause of his death. As the science of brain trauma in sports has advanced, experts have determined that repetitive head trauma in sports can cause death later in life; and some have speculated it may have led to Gehrig's.

Joe DiMaggio grew up in San Francisco and did not show much aptitude for anything except baseball. He left high school in his freshman year and never returned. But his meteoric rise as a baseball prodigy was remarkable. In two years—from 1931 to 1933—he went from playground games to the AAA level in the minor leagues, one step from the majors. In 1933, while with the AAA San Francisco Seals, DiMaggio hit in 61 straight games—a longer streak than the major league record of 56 he would set in 1941. He concluded the year hitting .340 with 169 runs batted in. DiMaggio was heavily pursued, not just by the Yankees but by several major league teams. In spite of his low level of education, DiMaggio himself negotiated his contract with the Yankees—a first-year salary of $8,500, up significantly from the Yankees' initial offer of $5,625.

While many regard the "Murderers' Row" Yankees' teams of the 1920s and early 1930s as one of the greatest teams ever, the Yankees had won only one World Series in the seven years before DiMaggio's arrival. The win occurred in 1932, Babe Ruth's last good year. Ruth's productivity declined substantially beginning in 1933, causing most to believe that the Yankees would become "Gehrig's team." But despite Gehrig's greatness, the team did not win the World Series in 1933, 1934, or 1935.

After falling short again in 1935, the New York sportswriters were all over the Yankees—calling McCarthy "second-place Joe." They claimed that Gehrig could not lead the team to the title as the lead player and concluded that the team had lost the magic it had in the 1920s. The mainstream New York press referred to it as "the pennant problem." And the New York Sun did not mince words in a headline that read: "Yanks Pin Hopes on Rookie." Yankee general manager Ed Barrow counseled DiMaggio "don't get too worked up" and "don't pay too much attention, don't let it get to you … ." DiMaggio interrupted, "I never get excited." Against the backdrop of events in the nation and the world, Yankee fans' hopes had been dashed three years in a row. But the fans knew about the arrival of a confident 21-year-old rookie from San Francisco and had hope.

The impact that Joe DiMaggio had on the New York Yankees from 1936 to 1941 cannot be overstated. He arrived to a team that was essentially unchanged from the previous years of falling short. The primary pitchers and core everyday players were substantially the same. Red Ruffing and Lefty Gomez pitched roughly a third of the team's innings before DiMaggio's arrival and after he arrived. Lou Gehrig had manned first base for over a decade before DiMaggio arrived and continued to play until he fell ill in 1939. Bill Dickey had been the Yankees' regular catcher and remained their regular catcher through 1941. Second baseman Tony Lazzeri had been the Yankees' regular second baseman since 1926 and remained so through 1938. The shortstop and third base combination of Frank Crosetti and Red Rolfe was in place before DiMaggio's arrival and remained the same until the 1940s. And even one of the other outfielders—George Selkirk—stayed in place from before DiMaggio's arrival in 1936 into the 1940s. While a great team, the Yankees had still finished second by an average of five games from 1933 to 1935. Without DiMaggio, there was nothing to indicate that their fate would change except to experience the usual decline as their players aged.

But everything did change upon the arrival of DiMaggio in 1936. In May and June of his first year, he played so well that he became the first rookie ever to start in the mid-summer All-Star Game. DiMaggio took Ruth's old spot in the lineup hitting third. He was an immediate star. On July 13, DiMaggio appeared on the cover of *Time* Magazine. For the year, rookie DiMaggio hit 29 home runs with 125 runs batted in and a batting average of .323.

In the 1936 World Series, DiMaggio made a key play which led to the championship. Up three games to two in the World Series against the New York Giants, the score was tied in the ninth inning. DiMaggio hit a single and made it around to third. The batter hit a sharp grounder to the Giants' first baseman. The first baseman did the right thing. He looked at third to freeze DiMaggio. The problem was at the crack of the bat DiMaggio had already broken for home but stopped dead in his tracks between third and home, thus putting all the pressure on the first baseman who was still holding the ball. The first baseman elected to throw the ball to third and DiMaggio broke for home. The third baseman caught the ball and threw it home to the catcher who caught it and braced for a collision with the charging DiMaggio. But DiMaggio didn't run into the catcher. He didn't even slide. Instead, he launched himself into the air—headfirst, over the tag and over the catcher—and in the air, DiMaggio twisted his body and landed behind the plate with his hand on it. The Yankees won. This would be just one of many "instinctive plays in a critical moment" by DiMaggio.

In Game 2 of that same Series, the Yankees were ahead 18-4 late in the game. Fans were starting to leave the stadium, but the public address announcer asked them all to stay in their seats so one special fan—President Franklin Delano Roosevelt—could get to his open limo and ride on the field out of the stadium through the center field gates. The Giants were up, and their batter hit a rocket shot to straight centerfield. DiMaggio was off before the crack of the bat could be heard in the stands. He turned his back and ran for the deepest curve in the horseshoe-shaped Polo Grounds. He was 475 ft. from home plate when he made the impossible catch, over his shoulder while running full speed. He was going so fast he couldn't stop when he reached the stairs going up to the clubhouse in deep center field, so he just ran up the stairs.

When he reached the top of the stairs, he turned around with the ball in his hand to show he had caught it. He had forgotten about Roosevelt's planned exit, and as he looked down on the field, he saw Roosevelt's limo heading straight toward him to drive out the gates below where he was standing. He immediately stood straight with respect. Roosevelt looked up into the stands and caught DiMaggio's eye, smiled with his famous cigarette holder in his mouth, put his hand to the brim of his hat, and saluted Joe DiMaggio.

The Yankees followed their championship that year with championships in 1937 and 1938. At some point—likely in 1937—DiMaggio took over as the team's leader. There has been very little printed on this, likely because of Gehrig's professionalism in allowing it to occur, but it clearly did happen. It appears that Gehrig continued to be cheerful, patient, and supportive of DiMaggio, which he had been since DiMaggio's arrival with the Yankees. Gehrig also complimented DiMaggio publicly. In 1937, Gehrig was quoted saying, "Joe is the best defensive outfielder in the game. Once he is told where to shift for a certain batsman, he never has to be reminded." In 1938 when DiMaggio took over the coveted cleanup batting spot from Gehrig, with Gehrig moving down to fifth, there was no public complaining by Gehrig. Part of Lou Gehrig's legend was the quiet encouragement of leadership succession on the team. There was no public rivalry as there had been when Gehrig began to take over for Ruth in the early 1930s. Having seen how Ruth mishandled the transition, Gehrig knew better.

During the championship years of this Yankee dynasty, DiMaggio averaged over 136 runs batted in each year. He had over 600 plate appearances each year except one; but struck out an average of 26 times per year. His home run total during this period was 167. DiMaggio's ratio of strikeouts to home runs during the championship run was .78, and for his career, it was 1.02. These ratios are substantially better than virtually any other slugger of his generation and far better than those who came later. Babe Ruth hit 714 home runs and struck out 1,330 times, a ratio of 1.86. Gehrig had 493 home runs and 790 strikeouts, a ratio of 1.60. Ted Williams, whom many believe was the greatest hitter of all time—with an outstanding eye for the strike zone—was better, 521 home runs and 709 strikeouts for a ratio of 1.36 but still paled in comparison to DiMaggio. And how about the great sluggers of the last 20 years? Barry Bonds is 2.10, Alex Rodriquez is 3.29, Reggie Jackson is 4.61, and Mike Trout, as of this writing, is at 3.77. Joe DiMaggio holds the all-time record for the number of seasons with more home runs than strikeouts at 7.

The 1939 Yankees are regarded by many as the best baseball team of all time. In historian Talmage Boston's book *1939 Baseball's Tipping Point*, he lays out the many reasons for this, including DiMaggio's impact, the team's many other great players, the team's impressive statistics, and the fact that the team had no weak links. He also notes the many writers and historians who have shared his view that this team was the all-time best; among them Dan Daniel, Charles Alexander, Richard Tofel, Rob Neyer, and Eddie Epstein. Of the many remarkable things about this team is the fact that Gehrig had retired at the very beginning of the year, and while supporting the team from the dugout, he was not on the field for the great majority of the games that season.

DiMaggio's 56 game hitting streak in 1941 stands today as one of the unlikeliest records in professional sports to be broken. It is 25 percent better than Pete Rose's second-longest streak of 44. From May 15 through

July 16, DiMaggio got a hit in every single game. When the streak began in May, the Yankees were in fourth place. When it ended in July, they were in first. The streak lifted the play of the team and the players on it. The team had a streak of its own of 14 wins embedded in the larger story of DiMaggio's consistent hitting. The nation followed DiMaggio on his daily hit journey, and a regular greeting as someone entered a diner or bar anywhere in America that summer was "did he get one today?" There was no need to mention his name. The story moved from the sports pages to the front pages. Radio stations broke into regular programming to announce DiMaggio's at-bats. DiMaggio had become a true American hero at a time when the country needed it the most. When the 56-game hitting streak ended, another began, and he would get a hit in 72 of 73 games. In 622 plate appearances in 1941, DiMaggio struck out a grand total of 13 times.

Over the course of the streak, things were going badly in England. After a rampage across Europe, the Nazis invaded the Soviet Union. England was now in the Nazis' crosshairs and the Nazis were bombing the U.K.'s harbors, museums, palaces, and even the Houses of Parliament. On May 27, 1941, Roosevelt addressed the nation on radio, "It is unmistakably apparent that unless the advance of Hitlerism is forcibly checked now, the Western Hemisphere will be within range of Nazi weapons of destruction." Roosevelt declared an "unlimited national emergency." By this time, over 16 million Americans had been called to the military to prepare for battle and 750,000 more were soon to sign up. As Hitler continued to threaten the world, Joe DiMaggio became the world's hero.

But under the pressure of the streak, DiMaggio began to have stomach pain. DiMaggio said that when the pain came on, "it was like dying inside." It likely didn't help that DiMaggio was smoking two packs a day of unfiltered Camels (of which the company sent him carton after carton for free). He had started smoking in grade school. He was also drinking large quantities of coffee. The Yankee clubhouse manager, who himself would get coffee for DiMaggio, said DiMaggio would drink 23 half cups in a day. He was ultimately diagnosed with stomach ulcers. At 26 years old, DiMaggio was aging far faster than most men his age and made his heroism much more difficult. But he powered on.

The Yankees won the World Series again in 1941—their fifth win in six years. After sailing through the regular season and winning the American League by 17 games, they faced the Brooklyn Dodgers in the World Series. After the Yankees took a two games to one lead, the critical inning of the entire Series occurred in Game 4. The Dodgers were ahead 4-3, and the Yankees were down to their final out in the ninth inning. Tommy Henrich was up and swung and missed on strike three. But the catcher dropped the ball, and Henrich made it to first base. DiMaggio was up next and hit a single, moving Henrich to second. The next Yankee batter hit a ball to the wall in right field. Henrich came around third and scored the tying run, and DiMaggio never slowed down running from first. He reached home plate just behind Henrich and was going so fast his slide took him six feet past the plate. The Yankees won the game and completed the Series with a win the next day. The team followed their tradition and sang the Beer Barrel Polka in the locker room.

Those who saw DiMaggio play say he earned his title as "The Greatest" the old-fashioned way—play-by-play, game by game, and season by season. Teammate Charlie Keller remembers watching the veins in DiMaggio's neck bulge as he waited, his entire body coiled in anticipation for a pitch from Bob Feller, one of the best pitchers of that generation. Tommy Henrich said even DiMaggio's slides were ferocious. "He was the roughest, hardest slider … and he would hit the ground harder than anybody else." DiMaggio seemed to have an extra gear when needed—at bat, on the base paths or in the field. While in these moments, his strength, speed, awareness, and focus all seemed to rise to extraordinary levels allowing him to accomplish superhuman feats. During these times, DiMaggio seemed to become the main character in his favorite comic book—Superman.

Yankees' manager McCarthy noted that centerfield in Yankee Stadium was the largest and most difficult to play in baseball. That is why he put DiMaggio there. The great writer Roger Angell said of DiMaggio, "No one else brought such presence and quiet command to the hard parts of the game, or is remembered by all who saw him play as being engaged in a private vision of his work that was offered daily for our pleasure." DiMaggio's caliber of play not only impressed others but also inspired them. "Without saying a word, he led the Yankees to championships year after year after year," said former teammate Jerry Coleman. "We wanted to perform like DiMaggio," he said, "Because of that … you push your-self harder." Coleman's comment captures the essence of why DiMaggio's Yankee *teams* performed better. His actions, and not his words, inspired them. They wanted to play *like* him. They pushed harder *because* of him. DiMaggio modeled to his teammates *how to play* the game and did so as well as anyone who ever played.

"He's the most complete ballplayer I've ever seen," McCarthy said. "He can hit, hit for power, run, throw and play the outfield." When asked by a reporter if DiMaggio could bunt, McCarthy replied, "I'll never know"—meaning there was no possible situation where the great DiMaggio would be asked to do so. Yogi Berra said DiMaggio had no weaknesses. Ben Cramer described him as "the most determined, most ferocious, most hard-knuckled spikes in your face winning ballplayer we had ever seen." Ted Williams himself said, "Joe DiMaggio was the greatest all-around player I ever saw. His career cannot be summed up in numbers and awards. It might sound corny, but he had a profound and lasting impact on the country." Stan Musial said, "Joe was the best, the very best I ever saw." Bob Feller agreed, "Joe DiMaggio was the best all-around ballplayer."

DiMaggio was legendary for never throwing to the wrong base, get-ting thrown out on the base paths, or misjudging a fly ball. Many said he ran from first to third faster than any other player. His manager, Joe McCarthy, said DiMaggio could have easily stolen 60 bases a year, "He just didn't need to do so for the team to win." DiMaggio was as great a defensive player and base runner as he was a hitter. McCarthy said, "He did everything so easily. You never saw him make what appeared to be a great catch because he didn't fall down or go diving for balls. He didn't have to. He just knew where the ball was hit, and he went and got it."

DiMaggio's 13-year career was shorter than that of many great stars, in part because of his three-year service in the war. In the printed ver-sion of Major League Baseball's All-Century Team, it is estimated that DiMaggio sacrificed more than 60 home runs, 300 RBIs, and 500 hits during the three years of service between 1943 and 1945. DiMaggio also played in an unfriendly field for right-handed power hitters. Left center-field, where right-handed hitters would hit most of their home runs, was called "Death Valley" due to its dimensions. Ruth and Gehrig were both left-handed hitters and benefited tremendously from the short porch in right field in Yankee Stadium. In the 1991 *The Elias Baseball Analyst*, it is estimated that Yankee Stadium reduced home runs 37 percent for right-handed hitters. DiMaggio suffered even more. He hit 65 more home runs on the road (213) than he hit at home (148)—the most considerable disparity of any player in major league history. Numbers alone do not tell large parts of the true DiMaggio story. One has to look beyond those numbers to discover the true impact of this great player.

For years after his retirement in 1950, Joe DiMaggio was regarded as the "best living ballplayer" (which would have excluded Ruth, Gehrig, Cobb, Honus Wagner, and the great pitcher Walter Johnson who had all died). He was introduced as such into the 1990s even though many past stars such as Ted Williams, Mickey Mantle, Bob Feller, Willie Mays, and Henry Aaron were still alive. While DiMaggio himself insisted on this introduction when he made appearances, no one seemed to object. And it was true DiMaggio was generally regarded in the top six players at that time.

As late as 1999, DiMaggio's greatness still seemed to be in the memories of historians. That year, ESPN did a television series on the all-time greatest athletes across all sports. DiMaggio finished 22nd overall and fifth among baseball players. But at about that same time, DiMaggio started to slip in the all-time best player rankings. The *Sporting News* listed DiMaggio at number 11 in 1998. Bill James (who included the Negro Leagues) listed DiMaggio 13th in 2001. In 2011, the *Bleacher Report* ranked him at 24. In the last two years, *The Baseball Scholar* dropped him to 41 and SB Nation dropped him to 56. On all of these more recent lists, certain players who themselves acknowledged that DiMaggio was the best or greatest they had ever seen (Mantle, Williams, and Musial) appear ahead of him.

While DiMaggio appeared flawless on the field, he was flawed off it. Until his death, he was intensely private. His marriages to actresses Dorothy Arnold and Marilyn Monroe were each short and ended in divorce. He had one son, Joe Jr., from whom he became estranged and remained as such until his death. Joe Jr. died within six months of his father—as a result of a drug overdose. By the time of DiMaggio's death, he had also become estranged from his brother, Dominic, a key player for the Boston Red Sox in the 1940s and 1950s. Friends came and went, and most were out of DiMaggio's life by the time of his death. He would not always give the writers what they wanted, and some resented him for it. He held out for more pay in 1938 and was booed by fans and treated poorly by the press. From that point forward, DiMaggio became more distant and less trusting. DiMaggio's self-image was that of the superhero, and he guarded it to the exclusion of all other forces in his life. He absolutely loved the adulation he received, but to maintain his self-image, he had to remain a great baseball player, an endeavor into which he poured virtually all his energy. Unfortunately, those close to him paid part of the price for his greatness. But the fans, who were desperately in need of heroes in DiMaggio's time, got what they needed.

Sabermetrics have not been kind to Joe DiMaggio. It may be due to his shorter career and related lower home total. More likely, those doing the rankings simply do not give DiMaggio enough credit for what he did under pressure in big games, nor do they give him enough credit for greatness in the many areas not captured by numbers—including super-human catches, throws, and base running. But for whatever reason, these modern views of DiMaggio are unfair to him and ignore the essence of why DiMaggio was great. Worse than that, they ignore the absolute number one factor that should be considered above all in analyzing who was the greatest player of all time.

The ultimate goal in baseball and any other sport is to win. The purpose of any player should be to do all in his power to contribute to that winning. Almost to a person, athletes in team sports, baseball, and beyond will talk about their goal of "winning it all." The New York Yankees had won one World Series in seven years before Joe DiMaggio arrived in 1936. Their last World Series title was in 1932. In the three interim years, they finished the year an average of 5.5 games behind the first-place team in the American League. They did not even qualify for the World Series. Following Joe DiMaggio's arrival to the Yankees, a team that was otherwise basically unchanged from what they were before, the Yankees won five World Series titles in the next six years after winning the American League by an average of 15 games. No team in the history of baseball made such a dramatic improvement and then played at a championship level as long.

But the one who said it best was Connie Mack—maybe the best manager of all-time—who said, "As one of nine men, DiMaggio is the best player that ever lived." *As one of nine men*—that is the key. DiMaggio's direct and incontrovertible contributions to the Yankees increased their standing by at least 20 games per year (from an average of over five behind to an average of over 15 ahead) for five years in six. No other team in the history of professional baseball has even come close to this level of dominance.

Much of DiMaggio's greatness does not show up in the statistics—modern or otherwise. Demonstrating that greatness cannot be displayed with a few statistics, a short paragraph, or anything short of a very thorough analysis of *all* his contributions to the Yankees. In an age of increasingly shorter attention spans, it is more difficult to explain DiMaggio's greatness. To truly appreciate him, we must consider big plays in big moments: like the great leap over the catcher to spur the Yankees on to win the 1936 World Series against the Giants; the catch and run up the clubhouse steps in that same World Series that led to a salute from President Roosevelt; and the heads up base running play in the 1939 World Series against the Reds where his remarkable slide made the difference in the game. DiMaggio had his own great statistics—MVP awards and other credentials—but his true greatness lies not in those statistics but in that extra gear, that extra awareness he had when it mattered. Joe DiMaggio absolutely charted the Yankees' course for greatness, and then led them to victory time and time again. He did this during a time when America needed heroes, and he delivered. If one accepts the fact that the true measure of a player is found in his contributions to the success of his *team*, Joe DiMaggio is second to none as the greatest player in baseball history.

This Yankee dynasty demonstrates that one player can make the difference between first and second, and in the team being very good and becoming an all-time great. It also shows us the optimal kind of leadership and teamwork that surrounds that one great player. This included the prior leader of the team stepping aside and allowing the new leader to succeed him—textbook leadership succession. This team also reveals the more profound cultural components of winning—continuity of people, team play, selflessness, focus, tuning out distractions, team-oriented discipline (but still enjoying humor), and a burning desire not to lose. These principles must become ingrained in the fabric of the team and each of the players that make it up. It takes not only a boss to lay down those rules but also a lead player to adopt and demonstrate them. When that great player is going through a stretch of great individual success, it should impact others on the team. In turn, they will find a way to raise their own individual performances. Above all, that one great player's greatness cannot be found so much in his own personal success (which he still may have) but in how his great play translates into the success of the team.

CHAPTER 6

The Forgotten Elephants

Success is not final, failure is not fatal: it is the courage to continue that counts.

—Winston Churchill

The Philadelphia A's in the first half of the 20th century put two separate dynasties on the field. The first occurred from 1910 to 1914 during which they won four pennants and three World Series. The second took place from 1929 to 1931 during which the A's won three pennants and two World Series. These teams were both managed by one of the greatest managers of all-time, Connie Mack. Mack managed the A's for 50 years from 1901 to 1950. He also owned at least part of the team for his entire time with the A's. Mack served as owner, general manager, and the on-field manager; a combination of jobs no single person has held since, and the holding of which at the same time is now prohibited by major league rules. Connie Mack is one of the most fascinating figures in baseball history.

Mack, whose given name was Cornelius McGillicuddy, was born in 1862, as the Civil War was raging. His father was away serving in the Union Army the day Mack was born. Mack played catcher in professional baseball in the late 1800s and became the A's manager in 1901, the year they (and the American League) were formed. When he became the A's manager, he was 38 years old. When he retired in 1950, he was 87. No one manager has come close to managing for that long, let alone serving consistently for the same team the entire time. Connie Mack won more games, lost more games, and managed more games than any manager in baseball history.

He was tall, lean, rarely used profanity, and almost never did so on the field or in the dugout. He called his players by their formal first names, for example, Albert instead of Al, and expected to be called "Mr. Mack."

He was one of the very few managers in baseball history that didn't wear a uniform during games. Instead, he dressed in a three-piece suit, tie, and shined dress shoes. He sometimes took off the coat and rolled up his sleeves (while not taking off the tie) on hot days. Mack believed dressing in this fashion created a distance between himself and his players which he believed necessary to achieve their respect. He almost never argued with umpires during games. Of 7,792 games he managed in his career, he was never thrown out of a game.

Mack coached his players not only on baseball but also on life skills. He encouraged marriage for players and encouraged them to save their money and invest it wisely. He felt that the players had a great opportunity to make an exceptionally good living in professional baseball, and they should cut out all bad habits to play at their best each day. This wisdom was designed to put the players in a position where they had peace of mind so they would have clarity of thought. He valued quick thinking and believed it to be a critical skill on the field.

As written in the *New York Times* when Mack passed away: "The old-time managers ruled by force, often thrashing players who disobeyed orders on the field or broke club rules off the field. One of the kindest and most soft-spoken of men, [Mack] always insisted that he could get better results by kindness. He never humiliated a player by public criticism. No one ever heard him scold a man, even in the most trying of times of his many pennant fights."

To keep his A's teams in business, he was not afraid to make tough decisions—and would sell his players to other teams when necessary. He was frugal with salaries. He understood as well as anyone that professional baseball is, above all, a business.

But Connie Mack was not perfect. He made a few poor decisions and lost more games than he won over his long career. For a brief time between 1913 and 1916, a rival startup league called the Federal League challenged the National and American Leagues. The owners of the Federal League offered higher salaries to players, thus giving them actual negotiating power with teams in the major leagues. When his players considered offers from the new league, Mack took it personally. In some respects, Mack handled this challenge like one of his successor owners of the A's, Charles O. Finley, handled free agency in the mid-1970s. Each addressed the challenge of a new economic order by drawing a clear line in the sand with players. And each had his great dynasty team completely self-destruct, almost overnight. Mack could not have been more different than Charlie Finley, but they handled competition for their players similarly in some ways.

Mack also had to learn about the negative impact of high maintenance superstars. Early in his managerial career, Mack brought in two players who were extraordinarily talented—and are now regarded as all-time greats. But each had flaws that held back their teams, and each is now remembered as much for his bizarre behavior and involvement in scandal as for his great talent.

The first was Joe Jackson, or "Shoeless Joe Jackson" as he was called due to a time in the minors where he played without shoes after developing blisters trying to break in a new pair of shoes. Jackson ultimately became well known for two things: (1) a career batting average of .356 which is still third highest all-time; and (2) being on the Chicago White Sox team that was accused of conspiring with gamblers to throw the 1919 World Series against the Cincinnati Reds. Jackson, along with seven others on the White Sox (nicknamed "Black Sox" because of the dirty uniforms the players wore due to their owner being too cheap to pay to have them washed), was banned from baseball because of his alleged involvement in the World Series scandal.

While Jackson ultimately did become an all-time great hitter; he did not show it in 1908, the year Connie Mack brought him up to the major leagues. Jackson played well in the minors with the A's minor league team in New Orleans. But Jackson was from the South and was uncomfortable in Philadelphia. On multiple occasions, he hopped a train to go back to the South to be with his family. His teammates razzed him about his lack of sophistication, southern accent, and inability to fit in. Jackson was completely uneducated and illiterate. Mack went as far as to "Arrange for a more literate boy to join the team at the same time to be sure that Joe would always have a pal and to read him the menus and also the reports of the games." But Jackson never did do well with the A's, and Mack ultimately traded him away right before the A's began their dynasty run from 1910 to 1914. Jackson then had a historically great 10-year career before being banned for his role in the scandal.

The second player was perhaps the most bizarre superstar in the history of Major League Baseball—George Edward "Rube" Waddell. Waddell was the best left-handed pitcher in baseball from 1901 to 1909 and may have been the best left-hander the game had ever seen until Sandy Koufax in the 1960s. Waddell played for Connie Mack's Philadelphia A's for parts of the 1902 to 1907 seasons. Waddell had an extraordinary fastball and a devastating curve. He established the record in 1904 with 349 strikeouts in one season while also winning 27 games and pitching to a 1.48 ERA. The strikeout record stood until Koufax broke it in 1965. The problem with Waddell was that Mack never really knew when Waddell would show up, and when he did show up, what version of Waddell he would get. To put it mildly, Waddell was an interesting *bunch* of guys.

Waddell (who was born on Friday the 13th and died on April Fool's Day) was fascinated by a number of things other than baseball, among them: shiny toys, puppies, fire wagons, fighting fires, fishing, alcohol, and women. Opponents knew of Waddell's fascinations and that he could be distracted. Tigers' manager Hughie Jennings would go to the dime store before games against the A's and pick up little toys like rubber snakes and when Waddell was on the mound, Jennings would distract Waddell by setting the toys out on the field and yelling "Hey Rube, look!" Teams would also bring puppies to the games and hold them up in the dugout and from the coaching boxes while taunting him. Waddell was known for dashing off the mound to chase a passing fire wagon and to accompany the fireman to the fire to fight it. He was rumored to have actually saved several people from burning buildings. "I'm a peach at a fire," said Waddell, "There is nothing I'd rather do than fight fires." Waddell's off the field adventures were legendary—performing in vaudeville shows, leading marching minstrel bands, wrestling alligators, riding ostriches, and once punching a lion at an animal show which led to the beast swiping Waddell's arm with his paw and wounding him.

Waddell was an alcoholic and tended bar during the season which allowed him to drink more easily before the games he pitched. He would enter the stadium through the crowd and demand that the fans share their food and drink with him. After walking down through the grandstand, he would then walk across the field toward the clubhouse while disrobing—whether he happened to have underwear on that day or not. The only underwear he seemed to own were the red shorts that firemen wore under their firefighting gear. Before games, Waddell would pour ice water on his shoulder to cool down his arm lest he "burn up the catcher's glove." He would turn cartwheels and back somersaults, his back to the dugout, when he struck out the other side. He often made farm animal noises from the mound and kept up a running dialogue with opposing players and the crowd while pitching. When he won his first game in Philadelphia after giving up just one infield hit, he shouted to the fans, "It's all over, go home." The fans carried him off the field on their shoulders.

He was prone to disappearing for days during the season, usually to go fishing, to pitch for a team in another league, or to spend time with a woman. During one off-season, he was staying at the home of one of his sets of in-laws while that wife was inexplicably staying somewhere else. When Waddell came home drunk, his father-in-law asked him for his part of the rent. Waddell's response was to pick up a flat iron and beat his father-in-law in the head, knocking out six of his teeth. When his mother-in-law intervened with a broom, Waddell beat her over the head with a chair. The family dog finally got to Waddell and sunk his teeth into his pitching arm. After punching the dog, Waddell jumped on a train and skipped town.

Mack tolerated Waddell in large part because he was a great draw for the fans. Waddell was equal parts superstar and showman, and people would flock to stadiums all over the country to see him play. Mack assigned a team employee to be Waddell's "keeper"—to keep an eye on him. If Waddell were able to slip away to a bar, the keeper would sweep in behind him to pay the tab. Once when Waddell took a train to the west coast to pitch for another team, Mack sent Pinkerton detectives out to pick him up and bring him back. When traveling with the team, Mack made sure Waddell slept in the berth above him on the train. The team did not pay Waddell his salary but piece-mealed out one or two dollars here and there when Waddell really needed it. Mack would try and send part of Waddell's pay to his wife, but determining who that was at the time was a challenge.

As Waddell continued to drink and self-destruct, things got worse. Waddell had helped the A's win pennants in 1902 (before the World Series was played) and in 1905. But controversy surrounded Waddell when he failed to pitch for the A's in the 1905 World Series. There are two separate explanations for his absence: either he hurt his shoulder on a train with a teammate in a tussle over a straw hat, or he was paid large sums by gamblers to fake the injury. In either event, the A's lost that World Series. Waddell became even less punctual and reliable beginning in 1906. Mack was more often having to pick Waddell up in person, pay off his debts, and deal with legal claims and charges against Waddell, and was tiring of town fathers telling him that they were glad he was going. Waddell was also increasingly injured—often times from off the field antics such as horse and buggy accidents and getting slammed to the ground by world wrestling champion Frank Gotch after Waddell had challenged him to a match. The A's players finally forced Mack's hand, and after the 1907 season, Waddell was traded away.

Mack's experiences with Jackson and Waddell affected the qualities Mack looked for in players going forward. He began to emphasize intelligence and spent more time looking at players on college campuses. Many of the players on his first dynasty from 1910 to 1914 were college educated—for example, Eddie Collins from Columbia, Jack Coombs from Colby College, and Jack Barry from Holy Cross. Mack continued to emphasize the education of player prospects going forward. In 1914, Mack was contacted by Jack Dunn who owned an International League team in Baltimore. Dunn offered one of his best players, an impressive left-handed pitcher who could also hit. Due in part to the fact that Mack's dynasty was imploding, he did not have the cash to purchase the player. The player, like Waddell and Jackson, was uneducated. The player was ultimately signed by the Boston Red Sox and was later traded to the New York Yankees. Due to the poor state of the team's finances at the time and his emphasis on education, Mack passed on Babe Ruth.

Above all, the most important imperfection to know and understand about Connie Mack is that while he raised up two great dynasties, his teams lost at a rate and at a level unprecedented in baseball history. In his 50 years of managing, his teams finished *last* in the American League 16 times including one stretch of seven straight. Overall, Mack *lost* 3,948 games, over 1,500 more than the next most losing manager in Major League Baseball history.

By 1910, the first title of the first A's dynasty, Mack had balanced the ship with talented (and stable) players. Their pitching was extraordinarily strong and was led by Albert Bender. Bender was a Native American and a member of the Ojibwe tribe. He was dark-skinned and if he had been classified as African American, he would have been banned from Major League Baseball. There was never an explanation as to why Native Americans did not suffer the same fate as the Black players, but Bender got to play and he played well. He did so while putting up with constant acts of discrimination such as fans shouting racial statements at him, crowds whooping in parody of supposed Indian like behavior, and of course, being called "Chief."

The A's could also hit, and in a year when stadiums were still too large for a player to hit many home runs, the A's led the American League in triples with 105. The A's faced Frank Chance's Chicago Cubs in the 1910 World Series. The Cubs had won four pennants in five years and were favored. But Bender and Coombs shutdown the Cubs en route to a 4-1 Series victory, and the A's began to take over for the Cubs as the new dynasty on the block.

In 1911, the A's repeated as American League champions and faced John McGraw's New York Giants in the World Series. In the early 20th century, after the American League was formed, McGraw worked hard to discredit the new league referring to the teams as "losers" (and worse). He took particular aim at the A's—stating that the A's initial majority owner Ben Shibe's investment was a "white elephant, sure to become a financial drain." The phrase white elephant was a phrase used more commonly in those times meaning "useless, troublesome or expensive to maintain." When Mack heard about McGraw's statement, he immediately adopted the white elephant as the A's logo and displayed it prominently on the team's jerseys. It remains a symbol used by the team to this day.

Due to bad weather in Philadelphia, there was a delay of six days between Games 3 and 4. It remains the second-longest delay between games in World Series history. The only longer one was the earthquake that caused a 10-day delay in the 1989 World Series between the same two franchises—which by then were the Oakland A's and San Francisco Giants. Then, an event took place in Game 5 of the Series which provided a glimpse into the mind and judgment of Connie Mack. The A's were up three games to one and looking to close out the Giants in the Polo Grounds in New York. As the sun was going down in the bottom of the tenth, a Giants player slid home for what was counted as the winning run. However, the player slid wide of the plate and the umpire did not make the "safe sign." Giant fans stormed the field, and Mack made the decision *not* to challenge the play—in spite of the fact that he could have, and probably would have, prevailed. Mack felt that if he challenged the call, the fans would have instituted a mass riot. Instead, he let it go. It proved to be the right call. The A's clinched the Series by winning the next game 13-2. Mack's patience in that moment and focus on the bigger picture carried the day.

The A's finished third in the American League in 1912, and another forming dynasty, the Boston Red Sox, won the American League and the World Series. But the A's came back to win the pennant again in 1913. Just as in 1911, they faced the John McGraw led New York Giants, again shut down the Giants' hitters (this time to a team average of .201), and again beat them four games to one. Home Run Baker shined with nine hits, seven runs batted in, and a home run.

The A's infield was extraordinary, and the sportswriters of the time referred to them as "the $100,000 infield." They were led by second baseman Eddie Collins, an all-time great who is regarded by some as the best second baseman to play the game. The infield also included first baseman John "Stuffy" McGinnis, shortstop Jack Barry, and third baseman Frank Baker. Unfortunately for the players, the total of their salaries was nowhere close to $100,000. In the view of historian Bill James, they were the best infield in the history of baseball.

Jack Barry was an under-the-radar star. He did not have great hitting statistics and was not fast or particularly athletic. But he stepped up when it mattered. Ty Cobb referred to Barry as "the most feared hitter on the A's" and Tiger manager Hughie Jennings once said, "I'd rather have Barry than any .400 hitter in the business."

In 1914, the A's won the American League pennant but lost the World Series to the upstart one-year-wonder Boston Braves. Mack was becoming increasingly concerned about his team that year because winning was beginning to take a back seat to the quest for higher salaries. Six members of his team were contacted by the IRS for not reporting their World Series' bonuses. Fans were also becoming complacent with winning, attendance was off the pace of past years, and team revenues were down. By the end of 1914, the team had a deficit of at least $60,000. Mack was also losing players to the newly created Federal League, and as noted, refused to adjust player compensation to compete with them.

In 1915, Mack's team went 43-109 and drew a mere 146,232 fans to the park—an average of less than 2,000 per game. The following season was even worse. In 1916, the A's finished 36-117, 40 games behind the *next-worse* team, the Washington Senators. In an article published in 2016 (partially titled, "The Pathetics"), the 1916 Philadelphia A's were recognized by *Sports Illustrated* as the worst team of all-time. Beginning with the 1915 season, the A's finished last in the American League seven straight years.

Mack used the time after the end of his first dynasty to revamp his core philosophies in relation to his next dynasty. But he resisted the temptation to take the easier route and go halfway. Instead of using his scarce resources to bring in mediocre players (and put a mediocre team on the field), he waited until he found great players. And he began to better discern which players those were. Based in part on his past failures, he began to identify specific criteria that he followed in acquiring players. This began with intelligence. Mack realized the value of player intelligence in contributing toward winning teams.

Mack also had certain types of physiques and physical skill sets in mind. He looked primarily for bigger men who could run, hit, and throw with equal skill. His core players would have the right *balance* of these qualities rather than being dominant in any one of the three. Mack's ideal physique for a player was 5 ft., 10 in. to 6 ft. in height and 175 to 185 pounds in weight, with a body built in proportion. This build was necessary, said Mack, because "baseball can be a somewhat rugged sport where endurance counts and, under those circumstances, size and muscle pay off." Mack also preferred tall pitchers because he believed that they had an advantage over hitters.

As Mack neared 60 years of age, the sportswriters of the day were questioning whether he had what it took to build another great team. Mack thought otherwise, and he began to map out his next dynasty. He knew that he needed to spend money to make money. Toward that end, he acquired three new young position players: catcher Mickey Cochrane (after whom Mickey Mantle was named), outfielder Al Simmons, and first baseman Jimmy Foxx. Mack also spent money to renovate Shibe Park. The changes included bringing in the outfield fences to make it even easier for his new young hitters to hit home runs. Mack also put together a great pitching staff led by Robert "Lefty" Grove and Rube Walberg who both stood 6 ft., 2 in. Grove was offered to Mack by Jack Dunn, the Baltimore owner who had offered Babe Ruth to Mack over 10 years before. This time, the price was much higher—over $100,000—but Mack gladly paid it. The new dynasty was starting to come together. Mack rounded out his new team with veteran players who he believed could still help his team win. These included two key players from his first dynasty: 42-year-old Eddie Collins and 45-year-old Jack Quinn. Mack knew the team would go through moments when veteran leadership would be required to lead the team through. This was especially important as Mack aged. He would be 67, 68, and 69 in the three primary years of the second dynasty.

The result of Mack's efforts in reassembling his team was the creation of one of the best teams in baseball history. The A's ascension from the bottom started slowly moving up to seventh place, sixth place, and then fifth place over the three-year period from 1922 to 1924. In 1925, the A's rose to second. From 1926 to 1928, they gave the "Murderers' Row" New York Yankees as much as they could handle during the Yankees' dynasty period—and the A's got progressively better winning 83, 91, and 98 games. The A's broke through and overtook the Yankees in 1929 to 1931 during which time they were a dynasty of their own—winning 104, 102, and 107 games. The 1929 A's team won the pennant by 18 games over the Yankees and then bested the Chicago Cubs in the World Series four games to one. The 1930 A's team beat the St. Louis Cardinals four games to two. And perhaps the best of the three A's dynasty teams—the 1931 version—was upset by the St. Louis Cardinals four games to three.

Catcher Mickey Cochrane won the American League MVP Award in 1928 and hit .320 lifetime. He was the inspirational leader of the team and earned the nickname "Black Mike" for his horrible disposition after the A's lost. Left fielder Al Simmons knocked in at least 125 runs in each dynasty year, with 157 in 1929. Simmons' batting averages over the three-year dynasty run were .365, .381, and .390. He hit .334 for his career. Foxx was a power hitter coming into his own as the dynasty began. Foxx hit 23, 33, and 30 home runs over the three-year dynasty run and, the next year, 1932, Foxx hit 58 home runs and drove in 169 runs. Simmons' and Foxx's World Series statistics over the three-year period were also extraordinary. Simmons hit .329 with an on base plus slugging percentage of 1.037 and Foxx hit .334 with an on base plus slugging percentage of 1.034. The career on base plus slugging percentages of the two men are some of the best in postseason history.

But the unquestioned MVP on the A's team was pitcher Lefty Grove. He won 20, 28, and 31 games during the three-year run. In 1931, Grove went 31-4 with an ERA of 2.06. Grove's career postseason ERA was 1.75 over 51.1 innings. Over his career, he won nine American League ERA titles and won 300 games against only 141 losses, a winning percentage of .680—the highest among all pitchers who won 300 games. Grove was just as intense as Cochrane. On days he pitched, he arrived with a scowl. If a photographer tried to take a picture of him, he would throw a ball right at the photographer's camera lens. If Grove lost, he was known to tear off his uniform and then tear up the clubhouse.

In spite of their intensity level, there was harmony on the team. Third baseman Jimmy Dykes noted, "We ribbed each other but also helped each other on and off the field. We had no cliques, no factions, no holdouts [although Simmons did hold out for a time before the 1930 season], no nonsense." Shirley Povich, the sports editor of the *Washington Post* agreed: "The A's had a collection of players whose chief interest was baseball. That's all they concentrated on. There were no other involvements. No divided attention. Above all, they played to win." Like their manager Connie Mack, the players balanced mutual respect and (for the most part) professionalism with a strong inner competitive spirit.

In 1932, Mack's second dynasty ran square into the effects of the Great Depression. The $750,000 Mack borrowed for renovations to Shibe Park was due. His payroll had grown such that every one of his players was paid over $10,000. As budgets tightened, there was far less disposable income and attendance went down even after Mack reduced ticket prices. And Mack, now in his 70s, was left with only one option—to again sell his top talent to other teams. The A's would not win another pennant until 1972—after the team had moved twice, from Philadelphia to Kansas City in 1954 and from Kansas City to Oakland in 1968. Mack remained on with the team until October 18, 1950, when he retired.

Connie Mack III was 15 years old when his grandfather passed away in 1956 and was nearly 80 when interviewed for this book in 2020. Mack III has memories of going to games at Shibe Park in Philadelphia to watch his grandfather manage the A's in 1947 and 1948 and learning to keep score from his mother (Mack's daughter-in-law). Mack III also recalls his grandfather, dressed in his traditional suit and tie, taking him and his brothers down to the clubhouse and introducing them to the players. In spite of his many roles with his A's teams, Mack clearly found time for his family, and was as much a leader there as he was with his team.

Mack III also recalls accompanying the team to the A's spring training site in Ft. Myers, Florida. Mack III's mother and father so liked the Ft. Myers area that they ultimately moved their family from Philadelphia to Ft. Myers. That move placed Connie Mack III in the state where he would later serve in the U.S. House of Representatives from 1982 to 1989 and in the U.S. Senate from 1989 to 2001. Even while serving in Congress, Mack III felt that people wanted to meet him more because he was Connie Mack's grandson than because of his standing in the House or Senate.

Mack III felt that "carrying the name of his famous grandfather was not a burden but was instead a challenge and an obligation." He was aware of the high level of integrity and character of his grandfather, and maintaining those same standards were instrumental to his very successful political career. Mack III recalled his parents telling him that his grandfather so guarded his own image of integrity "that when traveling with his daughter-in-law (Mack III's mother) on the train from Philadelphia to Florida, he would not accompany her walking from the passenger car to the dining car for fear of the other passengers (not knowing that she was his daughter-in-law) believing he was traveling with a young woman."

Mack told his grandson that his favorite teams were from the era of his first dynasty in 1910 to 1914 and that his biggest regret was trading 21-year-old Nellie Fox to the Chicago White Sox after the 1949 season. Fox would ultimately be elected to the Hall of Fame and is regarded as one of the best second baseman to ever play the game. Mack III believes that "one of the qualities that made my grandfather so successful was his sheer love and enthusiasm for the game." He got up every day excited about baseball. This passion was so strong and authentic that it resonated with his players.

The foremost Connie Mack biographer is Norman Macht. When interviewed for this book in 2021 at the age of 91, Macht recalled meeting an 85-year-old Connie Mack in 1948 when Macht was just 18. Macht was then a "gopher" for announcer Ernie Harwell when Harwell was the announcer for the minor league's Atlanta Crackers. The A's were in town for an exhibition game against Atlanta. Prior to the A's games, the team would place a bench in the outfield on which Mack would sit to watch batting practice. Macht approached Mack while he was sitting on the bench and Mack asked him to sit down and join him. Macht describes Mack as "very gracious and accommodating." He noted that Mack's hands were not beat up with gnarled fingers as was typical with former catchers of the day. Instead, his hands were smooth, and his fingers long and slender. Macht asked Mack a few questions about rumors of infighting on the team. Mack answered them carefully, acknowledging that there had been some team conflict but that it didn't affect their play. Macht then watched as Mack warmly greeted and took the time to talk to opposing players, groundskeepers, scorecard vendors, and concessionaires.

Nearly 50 years after meeting Mack, Macht published his first book of three on Mack's great life in baseball. When Macht first approached his publisher about the work, he envisioned only one. But as he got into the life of Mack, he found there was a much deeper story to tell. Eight years and over 1,900 pages later, Macht completed his third book on the amazing story of Connie Mack. Macht noted that every single player who he interviewed expressed great reverence for Mack. They told stories of Mack as a tough but honest negotiator of salaries. They felt Mack was telling the truth when he said that he was paying them all he could. And if a player wanted to be sent elsewhere, Mack would do his best to trade or sell him. Macht marveled at Mack's longevity—especially given the grind of the travel which was still by train at the end of Mack's career in 1950. Mack seemed to know everyone and would stop and talk to virtually anyone who wanted to speak to him whether in a hotel lobby, restaurant, or on the street. But Macht also felt that Mack stayed in the game a few years too long and had to rely on his players to take over some of the managing duties at the end of his career. Macht also noted that Mack made some mistakes with players in his last years which impacted the team's success.

In Jim Collins' best seller *Good to Great*, he compares companies in certain industries that became great versus those who only became very good. Collins and his team spent years evaluating over 1,000 companies to try to determine the underlying causes for the difference. One thing Collins and his team found was that the great companies had what Collins calls "Level 5 Leaders." The traits of these leaders sound like a detailed description of Mack:

> ... an individual who blends extreme personal humility with intense professional will. They channel their egos needs away from themselves and into the larger goal of building a great company. It's not that Level 5 Leaders have no ego or self-interest. Indeed, they are incredibly ambitious—but their ambition is first and foremost for the institution, not themselves. They found that these leaders cut against the grain of conventional wisdom, especially the belief that we need larger-than-life saviors with big personalities to transform companies. Instead, these leaders were modest and willful, humble and fearless. But those who find such leaders and mistake their modesty and shy manner as signs of weakness found themselves terribly mistaken... and beaten in the end.

Connie Mack was a Level 5 Leader. Never flashy and never calling attention to himself, he did what he thought was best for the team. He balanced humility with an intense will to win. He had ambition, but it was directed to serve the team, not himself. Like Collins' Level 5 Leaders, Mack was modest and willful and humble and fearless. He was also very patient and eschewed the average for the great. He learned from his mistakes, and for the most part did not repeat them. He became disciplined and principled in the type of players he sought. Mack played fairly and modeled good behavior for the men who played for him. He made things better for others.

Baseball has been plagued for its entire history by bad behavior—cheating, selfishness, gambling, moral failure and racism, among many examples. But largely because of Mack himself, his teams had far fewer examples of this than other teams. In choosing its leaders, including its top leader, any organization is well served to consider the life lessons taught by Connie Mack.

CHAPTER 7

Balancing Act

Balance is not something you find, it is something you create.

—Jana Kingsford

By the end of the 1960s, all major league teams had added Black players to their rosters and the quality of competition in professional baseball had improved dramatically. Many teams were at the top of their game in the decade of the 1970s, and Major League Baseball may have been at its all-time competitive best. Becoming a true dynasty was becoming increasingly difficult.

The best team during this era was the Cincinnati Reds, who between 1970 and 1976 won five National League Western Division titles, four National League pennants, and two World Series' championships. Their winning percentage of .592 was the best of the decade. They were known for their great power hitting but were far better in other areas of the game that were not generally recognized at the time. They had great leadership in the front office, in the dugout, and on the field. They took advantage of a new technological advance better than any team during the era. They improved by adding pieces to their team and pulled off what turned into one of the most one-sided trades in major league history. A Cincinnati Reds' player won the National League's Most Valuable Player Award in 1970, 1972, 1973, 1975, 1976, and 1977. And they still had to move some pieces around to find the secret ingredient to get over the hump and win World Series' championships.

The Reds' dynasty team was built by general manager Bob Howsam. By the time he joined the Reds in 1967, Howsam had already built and presided over a World Series winning team in St. Louis. Howsam recognized the value of speed, defense, scouting, player development, and the art of making a deal. Howsam, and the things he valued as a baseball executive, turned out to be ideal for the Cincinnati Reds.

By the time Howsam arrived, the Reds were planning on building a new playing facility called Riverfront Stadium, and Howsam immediately made the decision to install artificial turf. This new playing surface had been used in the Harris County Domed Stadium (later, the "Astrodome") in Houston, as well as in other National League stadiums, and had proven to favor speed, line drive hitting, and truer bounces for defensive players. After making the decision, on the playing surface, Howsam set about to build his team by acquiring the type of players who most benefit from it: fast players with the ability to hit line drives (which produced more extra-base hits that would get through the gaps in the outfield) and players who possessed defensive range which allowed them to get to balls that other fielders couldn't.

Howsam inherited three key players who were or would all become great stars. The first was Pete Rose. By the beginning of the 1970 season, Rose had won the Rookie of the Year award in 1963, had finished in the top 10 for the National League's MVP Award five times, and was a four-time All-Star. In 1969, Rose hit .348 with 218 hits. He was also versatile and would ultimately play second base, third base, left field, and right field over the course of his career. Rose was an exciting and aggressive player and was loved by the Cincinnati fans and his teammates. He was 29 years old in 1970.

The second was Tony Perez who came up to the Reds at the end of the 1964 season. He could play first or third base and had himself been an All-Star three times and finished in the Top 10 for the MVP Award twice prior to 1970. Perez was a power hitter and was also very popular. His sense of humor and ability to keep things loose in the clubhouse proved to be essential to the team. Perez was 28 years old in 1970 and had already begun to play a huge role in mentoring a young Johnny Bench.

The third inherited star was Bench himself who by 1970 at the age of 22 had already been an All-Star twice and had won three Gold Gloves. Even then he was regarded by most as the best catcher in baseball. He was supremely confident behind the plate and had no problem with instructing pitchers on what pitch to throw and fielders where to position themselves in the field. He was also a great power hitter.

Howsam's next major move was to hire Sparky Anderson as the Reds' manager, who in spite of his white hair was only 35 years old in 1970.

Anderson had a short and mediocre career as a major league player and only five years' experience as a manager—all in the lower levels of the minor leagues. Prior to that, he worked on a factory line, stocked products at Sears, and sold used cars. It was not a popular hire in Cincinnati. "Sparky Who?" blurted the local papers. Except for those who played for him in the Reds' farm system, none of the players had heard of him. Bench said, "We all jumped on his credentials." Reds' All-Star Lee May referred to Anderson as the "minor league motherfucker" both to his teammates and to Anderson himself.

But Anderson had a deep understanding of how to motivate teams and bring out their best. He treated his players as professionals and generally dealt with player problems one on one. Anderson could reach and inspire men and show them how to bring out their best in the form of what they could contribute to the team. His impact was felt immediately.

Anderson's first order of business was to make Pete Rose the team captain. Rose had been with the team for eight years, was born and raised in Cincinnati, and was a bona fide star by the end of the 1960s. The move rankled Bench at the time because he felt he, as the catcher, was the field general. While Rose and Bench were actually partners in a couple of business ventures (a car dealership and a bowling alley), they had their differences—some that were well known by their teammates. But Bench respected Rose and recognized Rose's value to the team, "He always led by example [with] that 'Charlie Hustle' spirit from the moment he walked on the field until the lights went out." Bench also admired Rose's concentration. It was "the key to his game, and he keeps it day in and day out .... He was like a kid about it, like that kid in the television spots who tosses his ball hat on the post and sleeps on his glove." "After a game, I'm usually so exhausted mentally and physically that all I can do is unwind some and then go to sleep. Pete will go out into his garage and sit on a stool for hours listening to some far-off game just to see who wins." (When Bench wrote this in 1979, Rose's gambling habit had not yet come to light. Rose's late night following of other games may have had to do with something other than Rose's sheer love of the game.)

The real issues between Rose and Bench were not that they were particularly selfish when it came to the Reds, but that they were both alpha—lead dogs. In the late 1960s and early 1970s, neither was particularly good about subordinating that position to someone else. One of Sparky Anderson's biggest challenges as the Reds' manager was to manage the egos of these two great players.

Personnel wise, the 1970 team was almost identical to the 1969 team which had finished third in the National League West. To the surprise of everyone, except maybe Anderson, almost everything went well through the first four months of the season: hitting, pitching, and defense. The Reds dominated in all aspects of the game and won a remarkable 70 of their first 100 games; and then coasted to the National League West title.

Bench won the National League MVP Award. Perez was third and Rose was seventh. All three made the All-Star team. It was sometime during the 1970 season that Los Angeles sportswriter Bob Hunter named the team the "Big Red Machine." The Reds then proceeded to sweep the Pirates three games to none in the National League Championship Series.

But in the World Series, the Reds would play one of the greatest teams of all time—the 108-54 Baltimore Orioles. Led by Brooks Robinson at third base, the Orioles beat the Reds four games to one. Robinson hit .429 in the Series with two home runs and six RBIs. His most impressive contributions came in the field where he made a series of great defensive plays including three diving stops. Sparky Anderson said of Robinson, "I'm beginning to see him in my sleep … If I dropped this paper plate I'm holding now, he'd pick it up on one hop and throw me out."

The Reds did not handle their success well in the off-season following the 1970 season. The Reds' players were highly sought after public figures in the 1970 to 1971 off-season and spent much of their time on the banquet circuit. As William Leggett noted in a *Sports Illustrated* article published in 1972, the Reds' players were "a cast of heroes gifted with humor and good looks. In addition to being hits on the off-season banquet circuit, they were also hogs. When they got around to spring training, they were overweight and under-eager."

At spring training in 1971, Bench showed up 13 pounds overweight, and his poor conditioning showed on the field in the 1971 season. His home run total dropped from 45 to 27, his runs batted in from 148 to 61, and his average from .293 to .238. According to Bench himself, he went from MVP to MDP (most disappointing player). The Reds failed to make the postseason in 1971.

Re-enter Bob Howsam and Sparky Anderson. Rather than just hope that the Reds would return to their 1970 form in 1972, they took action. In the middle of the 1971 season, the Reds made a trade for a little known outfielder named George Foster who was not playing in San Francisco because he backed up Bobby Bonds (father of home run king Barry), and then in November 1971, the Reds made a blockbuster trade with the Houston Astros giving away the right side of the Reds' infield Lee May and Tommy Helms and receiving in return pitcher Jack Billingham, outfielder Caesar Geronimo, and second baseman Joe Morgan.

The trade did not at all appear one-sided when it was made. Bench said of the trade, "Morgan was rumored to be a troublemaker," and many thought the Reds had given up too much. Bench said that Morgan "took a pretty bad rap about being moody and hard to manage. But after he joined the team, Perez and Rose started needling him, and he gradually began to realize that this team really counted for something." And as history played out, it was clear the Reds made out far better than the Astros. Geronimo, Morgan, and Foster all became part of the "Great Eight," the everyday position players who led the Reds team to World Series championships later in the decade.

Geronimo was installed as the Reds' new right fielder in 1972 and Morgan became the new second baseman. Bench played much like he did in 1970 and put up big numbers. Tony Perez and Pete Rose continued to play at all-star levels. The Reds ran away from the rest of the National League West and went 95-59, 10½ games ahead of the second place Dodgers.

In early September of every year, the Reds put their players through extensive medical evaluations. A routine lung scan of Bench came back blurry and he was asked to retake the exam. The next test revealed a spot about the size of a half dollar. The test for tuberculosis came back negative but the doctors still recommended surgery. Bench and his doctors told no one about the spot, and Bench soldiered on—finishing the season on a tear hitting seven home runs in seven days. He ended up first in the National League in home runs and RBIs.

The Reds again met the Pittsburgh Pirates in the best of five National League Championship Series. The teams split the first two games, and in the fifth and deciding game, the Pirates led 3-2 going into the bottom of the ninth. Johnny Bench came up with the crowd on its feet and scream-ing. Through the noise, Bench heard a familiar voice and turned back into the crowd to see his mother standing in the middle of the center aisle behind the catcher. She smiled and yelled, "Hit a home run." Bench turned back to the pitcher Dave Giusti and on a 1-2 pitch, he smashed the ball over Roberto Clemente's head into the right field stands to tie the game. The Reds proceeded to win the game and were back in the World Series.

The Reds met the Oakland A's in the "Hairs vs. Squares" World Series described in detail in Chapter 2. Both Sparky Anderson and Pete Rose stated to the press that due to the superiority of the National League, the Reds would beat the A's handily. These comments became prime bulletin board material for the A's and were horrible mistakes. Bench said, "A lot was made of what they looked like, and what they supposedly stood for, and in the course of all that, I think a lot of people forgot that they played the game pretty well." They did. The A's won the World Series in seven games.

After the Reds lost the Series in 1972, Johnny Bench checked into Holmes Hospital in Cincinnati to address the spot on his lung. The doc-tors first tried to scan the spot with a probe that was put down his throat, but the spot was on the inside of the lung and the probe could not get to it. So Bench had the spot removed surgically.

The procedure required the surgeon to make a horizontal incision of about 12 in. just under his right arm. He then took the rib bone apart, cut it from the cartilage, and pulled it away. This allowed the surgeon to get into the lung and remove the circle of the growth on the inner lobe. The spot turned out to be benign lesion—probably caused by an airborne fungus. While the surgery was a success, the recovery from the broken rib and damage to Bench's chest was slow and painful. Bench said it was the worst pain of his life. He came back in time for the 1973 season but in large part to the long-term impact of the surgery, Johnny Bench was never the same player again.

The Reds did not fall off the ledge like they did after the 1970 World Series. They won 99 games in 1973 and 98 games in 1974. In 1973, they made it back to the National League Championship Series but lost to the New York Mets. Rose sparkled that year—hitting .338 with 230 hits.

In 1974, the Reds finished a close second in the National League Western Division to the Los Angeles Dodgers who then became the third straight World Series victim of the Oakland A's. While the Reds didn't yet reach their ultimate goal of winning the World Series in either year, they took a number of important steps in that direction.

Joe Morgan had immediately stepped in as the Reds' regular second baseman at the start of the1972 season. But after the Series loss to the A's, he did not feel as though he was playing at his best level. Over the winter between the 1972 and 1973 seasons, Morgan became a fanatical workout warrior. Beginning in December, he started swinging a leaded bat in his garage every day. In February, he started hitting off a tee at a local field. He worked on making his wrists and arms strong and his batting stroke more precise. He worked with team coaches in spring training to develop more of an uppercut swing. He started using videotape of his swing when the technology was still very crude and just beginning to be used by baseball players.

Due to this extra work, Joe Morgan transformed himself into a power hitter. In 1972, his slugging percentage was .435 which was pretty good for a second baseman. In the first season after focusing his training on power hitting, it went up to .493 and his home run total jumped from 16 to 26. Over the next three years, Morgan's slugging percentage was .494, .508, and .576 and his on-base plus slugging percentages were .921, .974, and 1.020—extraordinary power numbers for a player at any position, let alone a second baseman. The 1.020 in 1976 is the best in the history of Major League Baseball for a second baseman. As a result of Morgan's self-created power, Sparky Anderson moved him from second to third in the batting order.

George Foster, the outfielder that couldn't get ahead of Bobby Bonds in San Francisco and for whom Howsam had traded in 1971, also started to come into his own as a power hitter beginning in 1974. In 1973, Foster had eight runs batted in. Over the next four years, he had 41, 78, 121, and 149. By the 1975 season, there was no way to keep him out of the lineup. The challenge was that Foster was really best suited to play left field, but veteran All-Star Pete Rose was firmly entrenched there. Anderson approached Rose about making a move, and Rose agreed to move to third base—his third regular position since his career began in 1963.

Another young outfielder, Ken Griffey Sr., came up to the Reds at the end of the 1973 season and hit .385 in 25 games. He was also impossible to keep out of the lineup but was really best suited to play right field. So, Anderson convinced Caesar Geronimo to move to center. Anderson also made Dave Concepcion, who had shared time at shortstop for four years, the regular starter. Foster, Griffey, Geronimo, and Concepcion all had the type of speed that Howsam sought to excel on the team's artificial turf.

Johnny Bench never had the same explosive hitting statistics he had prior to his surgery. His home run totals dropped from 33 to 28 to 16 over the period of the championship years from 1974 to 1976. But he remained the same strong leadership presence on the field and continued to get clutch hits and throw out runners. As Bench's power numbers declined, others—mainly Morgan and Foster—picked up the slack.

Howsam addressed another area of need, relief pitching. As Bench noted, "We had no real stopper." Howsam brought in two young closers, Rawly Eastwick and Will McEnaney, who immediately improved the Reds' bullpen. And based on his past failures in overworking starting pitchers, Anderson became even more aware of keeping his starting pitchers fresh and began to effectively use six starters instead of five to keep their innings down over the course of the year. Often criticized for being "Captain Hook" with his starters, Anderson actually followed a regular rule which he described as follows, "In the late innings, don't let your starting pitcher face the tying run if there are men on base." That was the system, and it worked.

Anderson had also established some structure and protocols for his stars. He organized the locker room where Bench and Perez were in one corner and Rose and Morgan in another. This "corner office" positioning sent the message that these were the four leaders of the team. He reinforced this message by having the group also take batting practice together. He also required each of the four stars to check in with him in his office each day. This allowed him to monitor their moods and mindsets, and message other players through them. It also allowed Anderson to stay abreast of any problems or issues any of the other players were having, thus allowing Anderson himself to address them which he often did. Anderson's new order of organizational structure provided stability and certainty that the team needed. It also facilitated Rose and Bench focusing less on their individual rivalry and spending more of their collective energies on together leading the team.

Sparky Anderson's single greatest attribute as a manager was probably his ability to keep 25 players focused on the single goal of winning. He had rules and discipline, but he had a unique ability to take the pressure off. He was calm when calm was better for the team. He was loud when the team required it. Multiple players recalled how Anderson handled a long losing streak during the 1972 season, he simply came through the clubhouse after a loss and said, "Let's get dressed and go home. We are going to win the pennant this year." It was a simple statement of fact rather than an opinion, a challenge or hyperbole. It turned out to be true.

An example of the "loud" Anderson occurred when one player criticized a teammate in the press but did not allow the writer to print his name. Anderson addressed the entire team, "Anytime I catch a player criticizing another player on this team, that player is going someplace else … and if you do it, at least have the guts to put your name on it." On another occasion when a reserve player complained that the stars on the team got preferential treatment, Anderson shot back, "You're damn right they do and don't expect me to treat you the same. When you contribute to the team what they do then you'll get the same kind of consideration."

Anderson was not afraid to address his stars if he had a problem with something they were doing. He jumped on Morgan when he saw moodiness. He confronted Rose over his womanizing—not only because of the impact it would have on the players but more importantly on their wives. He got on Bench when he refused to sign autographs or did not sign his name clearly. Bench began giving the same guidance to other players who scrawled their name rather than take the time to sign it well, "You shouldn't be in a hurry. Someone wants that to read it."

And Anderson could be flexible. When he came to the Reds he was staunchly against the baseball tradition of pitchers responding in kind with opposing players when someone on their team was hit by a pitch, "Because they don't have any class doesn't mean that we are gonna play that way." But the team stars pushed back making the point that being hit without retaliation was tantamount to being intimidated, and Anderson reluctantly struck a compromise and allowed pitchers to send a message, as long as the pitch was designed to brush the player's back and not hit him.

Another example of Anderson's flexibility was demonstrated after an assistant coach counseled him on his practice of involving himself with the players' personal problems. Anderson saw that this was taking a toll on him, and he eased back—letting the player first address the problems on his own. In both instances, Anderson invited communication and the issues were addressed and resolved out in the open without sweeping them under the rug.

An incident occurred during the 1973 National League Championship Series in New York against the Mets in Shea Stadium that may have also played a role in cementing the team together. After game two, Ken Harrelson of the Mets was quoted in the paper as stating the Reds had choked. Rose and Morgan took note and made a pact to send a message to Harrelson the first chance they got. The opportunity came to Rose as he attempted to break up a double play while sliding into Harrelson at second base. He slid hard and Harrelson went down hard. Harrelson yelled at Rose and Rose went at Harrelson. The benches cleared and a melee ensued. The crowd got involved. An empty beer can hit Rose and a whiskey bottle barely missed him. Other debris rained down from the stands.

Anderson pulled his team off the field and later said, "Pete Rose has contributed too much to baseball to be allowed to die in left field at Shea Stadium." Rose himself, who thrived on such chaos, said, "I knocked the war in the Middle East right off the front pages of the New York papers." The Mets had to send Willie Mays, Tom Seaver, and manager Yogi Berra to the outfield fences to implore the crowd to return to order. The Reds lost the game and Rose was followed out of the stadium by fans and stalked at the team hotel. He received death threats that night on the phone in his room.

In the next game in the series, Rose went 5 for 5 and hit a home run in the 12th which won the game. He held up his fist as he rounded the bases—silencing the crowd. In the final game of the series, which New York won, New York fans turned into an angry mob as the game went on. It got so bad that the players' wives were brought down to the field level before the last inning to sit in the dugout and leave through the clubhouse. When the game ended, the crowd came onto the field full force. They ripped up chunks of turf, mobbed the Mets players, and tried to strip their uniforms off their bodies. Seats in the grandstands were splintered.

As the surge came toward the Reds, the players grabbed bats in self-defense and locked arms at the front of the dugout while their wives and team personnel exited through the tunnel to the clubhouse. The players were prepared to start swinging if they couldn't get back into the clubhouse and one Mets fan took a Johnny Bench knock to his shins. Finally, the players were able to peel off and get back into the clubhouse. It took over two hours for the area to clear, so the Reds' bus could leave and go to the airport. The Reds did not discuss this incident in the context of their later success, but it is likely that this "brothers in arms (or bats)" experience may have cemented the team together for good.

The 1975 Reds team won the most games in the history of the franchise—108. They blanked the Pirates three games to none in the National League Championship Series, and in one of the most famous World Series of all time, they defeated the Boston Red Sox four games to three. The defining difference of this team was balance.

No one player (hitter or pitcher) had a dominant statistical year, but each of the "Great Eight" and 10 separate pitchers provided solid, and relatively even, contributions. Morgan was voted the National League's Most Valuable Player. Morgan's improvement, the infusion of young talent, and the veteran stars' willingness to not only lead but also allow the young talent to shine made the difference. Suddenly, the pressure was not all on Rose, Perez, and Bench. By continuing to transform the team, Howsam and Anderson finally achieved what the Reds, in spite of their awesome speed and power, had never had—balance.

The most dramatic World Series game that year (and for many, the most dramatic of all time) was Game 6 between the Reds and the Boston Red Sox. After the game was postponed three times by rain, the Reds and Red Sox slugged it out like gladiators until Carlton Fisk's home run in the bottom of the 12th at 12:33 a.m. smashed into the left field foul pole at Fenway Park to win it for Boston. Before Fisk's homer, former Reds' player and weak hitting reserve Bernie Carbo hit a three-run homer in the bottom of the eighth to tie the game. Then, the Red Sox loaded the bases in the bottom of the ninth and were poised to win, but George Foster made a great catch next to the stands on the left field line and threw out a

Red Sox runner who had tagged and tried to score. (The runner later said he heard the third base coach yell, "Go go!" when the coach had really said "No no!")

Before his at-bat in the 10th inning, Pete Rose stepped up to the plate and said to Carlton Fisk who was catching, "This is a great game, ain't it?" Players almost never said things like that to an opponent, but Rose was so excited in the moment that he dispensed with standard protocol. In the 11th, Morgan hit what looked like a two run homer, but the Red Sox's Dwight Evans took off in a dead run toward the right field stands and thrust out his glove at the last moment to catch the ball over his shoulder right at the fence. He then twirled and threw, doubling off a runner for the second dramatic game altering double play of the game. Anderson said it was the greatest catch he had ever seen.

The most famous TV footage from Game 6 was Carlton Fisk waving his arms toward fair territory after he hit the winning home run in the bottom of the 12th. The camera was situated behind the left field wall, and capturing film through a hole in the scoreboard would normally have followed the flight of the ball. But right before Fisk hit it, "a rat the size of a cat" appeared on the camera being run by NBC cameraman Lou Gerard who was stationed there. Not wanting to provoke the rodent, Gerard left the camera pointed at Fisk instead of directing it toward the flight of the ball.

The memorable image of Fisk's gesturing has become the most common visual takeaway of the Series. "It was an amazing aberration that changed television," said John Filippelli, who helped direct the broadcast of the game for NBC, "The focus was on the individual instead of the ball." The capturing of the footage changed the way broadcast film was taken—redirecting the emphasis on filming people and their reactions to key moments. NBC producer Roy Hammerman received multiple Emmy nominations. Left fielder Foster had the presence of mind to actually pick up the famous ball and keep it. Joe Morgan stood on the field among the emerging mob from the stands and made sure Fisk touched every base.

But the Reds came back to take Game 7. After falling behind 3-0, Tony Perez hit a two-run homer to make it close. Morgan had the Series winning hit in the top of the ninth of Game 7, breaking a 3-3 tie. In spite of the great momentum in favor of the Red Sox coming out of their Game 6 win, the Reds came through when it mattered and won the Series. Rose had 10 hits, five walks, and hit .370 in the Series; he was voted the World Series' MVP. The writers, believing that the Reds were going to win the Series in Game 6 before Carbo's home run, had voted to give the award to reliever Rawly Eastwick.

The 1976 Reds' team was probably even better than the 1975 team. While they didn't win as many games (they won a mere 102), they dominated the postseason—sweeping the Philadelphia Phillies 3-0 and then sweeping the New York Yankees 4-0 in the World Series. The Reds are the only team in history to sweep their way through a playoff and the World Series. Balance was again the key. Five players hit over .300 and five players batted in 74 or more runs. Six starting pitchers won between 11 and 15 games. The bullpen, led by closer Eastwick, was solid and balanced. Joe Morgan again won the National League's MVP, and Johnny Bench won the World Series' MVP by hitting two home runs, six RBIs, and batting .533.

The Reds became the first National League team to repeat as World Series champions in over 50 years, the last being John McGraw's New York Giants in 1922. The fact that the 1975 and 1976 World Series' MVPs were won by Rose and Bench, respectively, is telling. Both were able to summon up the energy to excel in October because they didn't have to carry as much of the load during the regular season. Both lineups were almost perfectly balanced from top to bottom, and while there was not one-star pitcher, nearly the entire staff made regular contributions. Sparky Anderson was named Manager of the Year.

Mention the Big Red Machine today to a baseball fan and the immediate thought is of power hitting. While this is partly true, the Reds only finished first in the National League in slugging average twice during the dynasty run—in 1970 and in 1976. And that power hitting became far more effective when it became more balanced across the order.

Far lesser known is the fact that the Reds finished first in the National League in fielding in six of seven years between 1971 and 1977, and in some of those years by a wide margin. They also regularly finished first in the league in fewest errors. The Reds' defense was particularly strong up the middle. From 1974 to 1977, a period of four years, four Cincinnati Reds—catcher Johnny Bench, second baseman Joe Morgan, shortstop Dave Concepcion, and centerfielder Caesar Geronimo, each won the

National League's Gold Glove in his position. The Reds' *defense* during their dynasty period was at least as essential as their hitting. And the core of that essential defense was right up the middle of the field … in perfect balance (and just as Bob Howsam had designed it for the Reds' new artificial turf).

While the real story of the Cincinnati Reds of the 1970s is what they did as a team, the individual success stories are undeniable. Pete Rose's legend as a player has been minimized because of his off the field problems later in his career. He was accused of, and investigated for, gambling— including gambling on his own team. Commissioner Bartlett Giamatti banned Rose for life, which led to his suspension from the major leagues. As a result, Rose is not eligible to be voted into the Hall of Fame. But Rose's gambling issues should not diminish what he accomplished on the field. He has the all-time record for the most career games played at 14,053. He showed up at work like no one player ever has, before or since. More well known is that Rose holds the all-time record for career hits at 4,256. And it didn't matter where he was playing to get his hits— he had 2,123 at home and 2,133 on the road.

Less known is how much Rose's teammates respected him. Said Morgan, "He was a guy who went out of his way to be helpful to others, particularly young players. He used his familiarity with Cincinnati to help younger players find apartments, schools for their kids, the whole thing." Rose regularly looked out for his teammates, including the younger ones trying to make their way in baseball.

Rose made many contributions to bringing his teammates together including providing "champagne celebrations" for each Reds' hitter who experienced the 100th strikeout of his career. This rite of passage was intended to convey that if you stay on the field long enough, you will fail, and that is okay. Rose loved baseball, he loved the men he played with, and they loved him.

Bench was born ready to catch in a major league game. When he was 17 years old, he caught the attention of Yogi Berra. Berra's assessment was, "He can do it all—now." Bench had extraordinary command with pitchers, even as a young catcher. In his second year while catching Gary Arrigo, he realized in a game against the Dodgers that Arrigo didn't have a fastball. So, Bench flashed the sign for Arrigo to throw his curve. Arrigo refused and threw his fastball instead. To demonstrate the weakness of the pitch, Bench caught it with his bare hand and flicked it back to the pitcher from the crouch. This caused an explosion of surprised laughter among the players on the field and among the fans in the stands. Arrigo got the message.

Watching Bench order veterans around the field was a sight to behold. Morgan said,

> With his catcher's gear on, he looked like a gladiator. He was just special when he stood behind the plate or at the mound, and everyone in the ballpark knew it. When he came out firing, he didn't look like anyone else.

An article on 22-year-old Johnny Bench appeared in the *New York Times* on August 30, 1970. Author William Furlong provided some deep insights into Bench's ability and personality. "He'll come out to the mound and chew me out as if I were a 2-year-old," said 30-year-old pitcher Jim Maloney, "But so help me, I like it." Bench was born old. "I call our pitchers 'kid'" said Bench. Even as a rookie, he was able to dominate older and more experienced players. Said Furlong,

> Bench does not subscribe to baseball's unwritten code of modesty, but his is nicely measured about it: Bench will say "I've got a little ability" when he thinks you know better; and to fervid overstatement when he thinks you do not—"I can throw out any runner alive."

When Bench was young, his father trained him to fire a ball 250 ft., nearly twice the length of the throw from home plate to second base, while in a crouched position. Base runners rightly feared him, and he threw out over half that tried to steal when Bench was behind the plate. Many didn't even try.

> Bench's hands are enormous—he can hold seven baseballs in his throwing hand. His ability to throw out runners (and pick them off first base if they get too much of a lead) allows the pitcher to concentrate more on the hitter. Most pitchers want to throw low

and inside to hitters as this is generally the most difficult pitch to hit. But it is also the most difficult pitch to catch and try and throw out a base runner. With Bench, no problem. He was able to turn any pitch into a rocket throw to second base.

Bench was an extraordinarily strong man, but as Bench himself acknowledged, "strength alone is no real indicator of anything. You must have the reflexes, the coordination, to go along with it." The Reds did testing of the players on reflex action, and Bench scored the highest. Bench was above all, a great athlete. Unfortunately, like Berra, Bench was probably asked to catch too many innings early in his career. He broke his thumb and other bones in his throwing hand which led to him becoming a "one handed" catcher, keeping his throwing hand behind his back when the pitch came in.

When Bench sustained a foot injury, the treating doctor noted by an x-ray that three bones in the same foot had previously been broken and healed naturally. Even more than his strength and athleticism, Bench was simply very tough. "And then to top it all," said Morgan, "he had the ease and magnetism about him. John was comfortable in the presence of celebrities and movie stars." From the very beginning of his career, Johnny Bench was the real deal.

Joe Morgan was the catalyst that took the Reds to the mountaintop. He brought power hitting from the second base position and almost never made a mental error in the field. The sportswriters recognized this in awarding him the National League's MVP Award in the 1975 and 1976 seasons. He was also honored with five straight Gold Gloves. Morgan worked at not just the physical aspects of his craft, but how to think through a game, how to anticipate what was coming next, and how to motivate his teammates. He came to a Reds' team that clearly had already made great leaders—Rose, Bench, and Perez—and he somehow improved the leadership mix. Many, including Bill James, believe Morgan to be the best second baseman of all-time. It is hard to argue with him.

After leaving the Reds in 1978, Sparky Anderson managed the Detroit Tigers to a world championship. He is one of only two managers in history (the other being Tony La Russa) to win championships in both leagues. Anderson is on nearly all credible top 10 managers' lists, and some list him in the top five. Bob Howsam's decision to hire Anderson as the Reds' manager for the 1970 season turned out pretty well after all.

The Cincinnati Reds of the 1970s were a classic example of not only the value of sheer power and talent but how to harness that power and talent into winning. Brawn had to become smart. The team built a new stadium and built a plan around it, which included bringing in players with speed and strong defense. Their leadership stayed fixed on that goal and stayed persistent in finding the right players to accomplish it. Their manager did not begin with the respect of the team, but he gave respect to them and then earned it in droves for himself.

A leadership structure was put in place where the stars had responsibility that went along with their prestige and accolades. The leaders subjugated their own interests to the interests of the team and allowed new leaders to enter the picture and take command when the time was right. One of their stars kept things light, even when the heat was on. The Reds did not allow disappointing finishes to finish them. They stayed positive. They kept trying. They tinkered with their success until they got it right.

Egos were not checked at the door, but they were managed. Everyone was held accountable for his actions and for his results. All players and coaches had the right, and indeed the responsibility, to bring issues out into the open and to resolve them openly and professionally. The team's stars came to understand and know that their best selves were found not in doing what was in their own individual self-interests but in doing what was best for the team.

And they ultimately found that it was balance across the team, not necessarily just pure power, that was the secret ingredient to becoming a champion and qualifying as a bona fide dynasty.

CHAPTER 8

Too Many Wrong Mistakes

The problem with Mantle, is Mantle.

—Casey Stengel

In the five years from 1960 to 1964, the New York Yankees won 97, 109, 96, 104, and 99 games, respectively, an average of 101 per year. They won the American League pennant in each of those five years and the World Series in two of them—1961 and 1962. There were several notable Yankee stars during this era, including Mickey Mantle, Roger Maris, Elston Howard, Bobby Richardson, Tony Kubek, and Whitey Ford. The high point was the 1961 season when Mantle and Maris gave chase to Babe Ruth's single-season home run record of 60, and Maris bested it on the last day of the season when he hit number 61. Many historians believe the 1961 Yankees were one of the best teams ever.

But the story of this dynasty is not so much that they won, how much, or why, but how quickly they began to lose, how far they fell, and how and why the dynasty ended. Two years after the last year of the dynasty, the Yankees finished tenth—dead last—in the American League and did not make the postseason until 1976, another 10 years. The title of this chapter is derived from one of Yogi Berra's famous "Yogisms"—"We made too many wrong mistakes." It is particularly appropriate for a chapter about the reasons for the end of this Yankee dynasty. To understand why the dynasty ended, it is important to start with a historical perspective.

Between 1921 and 1964, a period of 44 years, the New York Yankees won 29 pennants and 20 World Series. The great Yankees' teams over the 44-year period were built largely by two men. The first was Ed Barrow who was general manager from 1921 to 1939 and team president from 1939 to 1945. The second was George Weiss who was the head of the team's player-development system from 1932 to 1947 and general manager from 1947 to 1960.

The Yankees' majority owner was Jacob Ruppert Jr. Ruppert was a careful and successful businessman who paid attention to his baseball team and was very selective about those he chose to run it. During the 1920 season, he pursued Barrow and brought him to the team as "business manager"—which was at the time a job with the same duties that would come to be known as general manager.

Barrow would have a number of accomplishments with the Yankees, but it started with the fact that he aligned himself with the owner Ruppert. Barrow knew Ruppert's philosophies and how much could be spent on players. Barrow also continued his support of, and alignment with, Huggins, the manager. And Barrow had learned how to confront, and handle, Babe Ruth during the time the two were together with the Red Sox. The alignment of the three leaders—Ruppert, Barrow, and Huggins—was a main contributing factor in how well the Yankees managed (and disciplined) Ruth. This alignment was also one of the primary factors that contributed not only to the first Yankees' dynasty but also to the ones that would follow.

Barrow and Weiss met in 1920 when Weiss owned an Eastern league team. Weiss had contracted with Barrow and the Yankees to play an exhibition game against his team. When Babe Ruth did not accompany the Yankees to the game, Weiss refused to pay Barrow. A dispute arose and wound up on the desk of Commissioner Kenesaw Mountain Landis. Landis sided with Weiss. Barrow never forgot it and brought Weiss to the Yankees 12 years later.

Weiss learned from Barrow and adopted many of his qualities—working seven days a week, staying abreast of the progress of every player in the Yankees' farm system, and managing every detail down to approving every dollar that was spent by the Yankees.

By 1953, after Weiss had been the general manager for six years, the Yankees had at least 16 farm clubs and over 500 players in their farm system. Weiss was one of the best evaluators of talent in the history of the major leagues. But it would later be revealed that he had one major flaw.

In 1960, Weiss was still the general manager of the Yankees and Casey Stengel was the manager. In the 1950s, Weiss had made several multiplayer "blockbuster" trades; the last of which brought Roger Maris to the Yankees prior to the 1960 season. Weiss had also brought up outstanding players from the farm system, including three young infielders—second baseman Bobby Richardson, shortstop Tony Kubek, and third baseman Clete Boyer. The team had strong pitching, and Mickey Mantle was in the prime of his career. The Yankees were behind the curve on adding Black players but had become the 13th of 16 major league teams to integrate by adding Elston Howard to the team in 1956. By 1960, Howard had replaced Yogi Berra as the regular catcher. Maris hit 39 home runs and Mantle hit 40 that year. Maris won the American League's Most Valuable Player Award by three votes over Mantle. The 1960 New York Yankees went 97-57 and won the American League pennant by eight games.

In the 1960 World Series, the Yankees played the Pittsburgh Pirates and displayed extraordinary offensive firepower. The Yankees won Game Two 16-3, Game Three 10-0, and Game Six 12-0. But the Pirates also won three of the first six games and then won the seventh game 10-9 after a walk-off home run in one of the most exciting games in World Series history.

Despite many great performances by the team in the Series, owners Del Webb and Dan Topping removed both Stengel and Weiss from their jobs following the loss. The stated reason for the terminations was a new "mandatory retirement policy" which kicked in at age 65. Weiss just happened to be 65 that year and Stengel was 70. Stengel told the press, "I'll never make the mistake of being 70 again." Both Weiss and Stengel were quickly gobbled up by the new team in town—the New York Mets.

To replace Stengel, Topping and Webb chose 41-year-old Ralph Houk as the Yankees' new manager. Houk had shown great leadership on the battlefield in the Battle of the Bulge during World War II and was awarded the Silver Star, Bronze Star, and a Purple Heart. He had also played for the Yankees, served as a manager for the organization in the minor leagues, and had been a coach under Stengel. To replace Weiss, the Yankees chose Roy Hamey, a long-time baseball front office manager who had bounced around multiple teams and had mixed results.

The team received some negative publicity before the 1961 season. The Yankees' spring training hotel for 36 years in St. Petersburg, Florida, reiterated its refusal to allow the Yankees' Black players to stay there with their white teammates and the Yankees did not push back. Instead, they announced that they would move locations in three years, unless the hotel let them out of their contract sooner. The hotel quickly, and publicly, stated that they would not let the Yankees out of the contract. So, the Yankees stayed. The Yankees had only three Black players at spring training in 1961—Howard, Hector Lopez (an outfielder who was acquired in 1959), and catching prospect Jesse Gonder (who did not make the regular season roster) and mishandled the situation by not standing behind their Black players and forcing the issue.

Houk led the team that had been built by Weiss and Stengel into the 1961 season, but he had to reign in his famous temper. In the minor leagues, Houk had been chastised by the commissioner to cease and desist from his cursing at umpires. After his reprimand, and while on probation, Houk felt an umpire had wronged him in a close game. Houk ran up to the umpire and said "I'm not allowed to cuss you out, but I thought you might like to know I passed a kennel on my way to the ballpark and your mother is all right." Houk was reprimanded again.

The Yankees responded well to Houk in 1961 and won 109 games. Maris won another American League MVP Award and broke Babe Ruth's single-season home run record. Mantle hit .317 with 54 home runs and 128 RBIs. Whitey Ford led the pitching, winning 25 games and losing only 4. Richardson, Kubek, and Boyer, none of whom were yet over 25, continued to shine.

The Yankees easily handled the Cincinnati Reds in the 1961 World Series four games to one. They won the final game 13-5, with four doubles, a triple, and three home runs. Ford extended his World Series' scoreless inning pitching streak to 32, breaking the record set by Babe Ruth during his pitching days with the Red Sox. But Mantle was beginning to show his age. Due to a late season injury, he played in only two games in the Series and hit .167.

In 1962, the Yankees won their second straight American League pennant, but won 13 fewer games than they won in 1961. Maris' home run total dropped from 61 to 33 and Mantle's from 54 to 30. Mantle also played in 30 fewer games due to injuries. The Yankees played the San Francisco Giants in the 1962 World Series. The Giants, led by Black players Willie Mays, Willie McCovey, Orlando Cepeda, Felipe Alou, and Juan Marichal, were down 1-0 to the Yankees in the bottom of the ninth inning of Game 7. The Giants had two runners in scoring position when McCovey hit a rocket that started out like a World Series winning hit. But the ball dove instead of rose and traveled directly into the glove of Yankee second baseman Bobby Richardson. The Yankees were champions again. A week later, Houk and Hamey met with the media to discuss the next season. Both stated that the team had the talent to dominate for years to come.

In 1963, the Yankees won 104 games and the American League pennant by 10½ games. But Maris and Mantle were plagued with injuries. Maris played in only 90 games and hit 23 home runs. Mantle, then 31 years old, played in 65 games and hit 15 home runs. Attendance that year was down to the lowest it had been since World War II.

The Yankees played the Los Angeles Dodgers in the 1963 World Series. The Dodgers were led by pitchers Sandy Koufax and Don Drysdale and possessed speed and great defense. The team was also bolstered by strong seasons from Tommy Davis, Willie Davis, Jim Gilliam, John Roseboro, and Maury Wills, all of whom were Black. Koufax was almost unhittable in the Series and may have been at his all-time best. The Dodgers demolished the Yankees—sweeping them four games to none and limiting the Yankees to a grand total of four runs in the four games. Mantle hit .133 and struck out five times.

Yogi Berra was hired as manager in 1964 and got off to a slow start. He assumed the players would hold one another accountable as they had done in the past dynasty of 1947 to 1953. They didn't. They (particularly Mantle) poked fun at Berra in front of the team. When Berra finally did try and crack down on discipline, Mantle and others blatantly violated curfew by drinking in local bars until the wee hours of the morning.

A quarter of the way into the season, the Yankees found themselves in fifth place. They then roller-coastered their way through the year with a mixture of slumps and streaks. To make matters worse, the new general manager Ralph Houk was in over his head. He not only allowed but encouraged back chats between himself and the players about Berra doing a bad job. Players were critical of Berra's inability to communicate, not providing enough discipline and failing to effectively manage the pitching. Instead of addressing these issues directly with Berra, Houk reported them to owners Topping and Webb and added on that Berra couldn't control the players. As early as July 1964, Houk began to talk to Topping and Webb about replacing Berra, and in August, all three were in agreement that Berra would be dismissed from the manager position once the season was over. Houk made sure that Berra, and not himself, would take the fall for what appeared to be a lost year.

Against a backdrop of player disloyalty and an unqualified and dysfunctional general manager, Yogi Berra—then unknowingly a lame duck manager—guided the team down the home stretch. The Yankees made a great pennant run that included an 11-game winning streak and clinched their fifth straight American League pennant on October 3, the last day of the season.

In the 1964 World Series, the Yankees faced the St. Louis Cardinals, led by Bob Gibson, Lou Brock, Curt Flood, and Bill White—all young Black players on the rise. They beat the Yankees four games to three in the Series. Mantle hit well but was a liability on defense—failing to reach balls he once was able to get to easily. Roger Maris hit .200 and Whitey Ford pitched to an 8.44 ERA. As planned, Berra was removed as the team's manager after the season. Houk took his blame of Berra to the press, "I don't think Yogi was cut out to be a manager. It was my mistake. I miscalculated his ability to manage." He was wrong about Berra, who would later join Weiss and Stengel with the New York Mets and manage them to a National League pennant in 1973.

In August 1964, the Yankees were sold to the Columbia Broadcasting Company, more commonly known as CBS. Owners Topping and Webb made a profit of at least $6 million on the sale.

The CBS-owned New York Yankees went 77-85 in 1965 and finished sixth in the American League. The Yankees' 77 wins that year were the fewest for the franchise since 1925. The Yankees hit .235 as a team, eighth in the American League. Their team pitching ERA, which had been first or second in the American League from 1960 through 1963, dropped to fifth. The 1965 American League championship was won by the Minnesota Twins. The Twins had a number of Black stars including Tony Oliva, Earl Battey, Zolio Versalles, and Mudcat Grant. In the following year, 1966, the Yankees won only 70 games and finished 10th (among 10 teams) in the American League—26½ games behind the American League champions Baltimore Orioles. For the next seven years, the team would languish in mediocrity. They would not make the postseason again until 1976.

While there is some evidence that Webb and Topping stopped spending significant money on players once they decided to sell the team, the reasons for the dynasty coming to an end had little to do with whatever fiscal austerity that may have taken place. Instead, the demise of the Yankees was set in motion many years before and was caused by three separate things: (1) the failure to recognize and adapt to changes in the game, and in particular the failure to embrace integration; (2) poor leadership and decision making due to excessive turnover, on and off the field; and (3) the failure to properly manage their primary star.

Failure to Recognize and Adapt to Changes in the Game

The Yankees were way behind the curve on recruiting and signing Black players—a very available and inexpensive pool of talent. After adding catcher Elston Howard in 1956, the Yankees failed to add another Black potential starting player until they added Hector Lopez in 1959. It then took nearly four years until the Yankees had a third Black player who played significant innings—pitcher Al Downing.

Not only were the Yankees behind the curve in 1955 when they first integrated the team with Howard, they continued to lag behind well into the 1960s. By then, many teams were loaded with Black talent and many had become decidedly better than the Yankees because of it. This was evident during the last three World Series they played against the Giants, Dodgers, and Cardinals and was becoming evident throughout the American League.

The question of whether there is direct evidence that the Yankees' strategy was based on race discrimination is a complicated one. In George Weiss' Eastern League days, Black players played for and against his team. Topping had owned a pro football team and had at least one Black player. The two active decision makers on talent had each employed Black athletes in the past. Also, the Yankees received revenue from the Negro League games that were played in Yankee Stadium, so keeping the Negro Leagues in existence may have been in the Yankees best interests, and provided some (albeit weak and disingenuous) justification for their fail-ure to integrate their team more quickly and fully. And the Yankees did bring a Black player (Howard) up to the Yankees' major league team, but well after most (but not all) of the other franchises had integrated. They followed up with two more Black players—Lopez and Downing. But like their prior teams, Black players were few and far between.

The first Black players to sign with the minor league Yankees were signed in 1949, but none of the early signees were brought up to the major league team. And when given opportunities to acquire high end talent that was clearly suitable for the major leagues, the Yankees passed. An example is the case of Willie Mays. As noted in the *New York Times* by author John Klima, George Weiss kept an inner circle of scouts, includ-ing head of scouting Paul Krichell whom he had known since the 1920s. Klima believed those relationships coupled with the Yankees passing on opportunities for Black players constituted institutionalized discrimina-tion. It is hard to argue with this. As noted in Klima's article, an 18-year-old Willie Mays came to New York in 1949 to play in a Negro League game for the Birmingham Black Barons against the New York Cubans. While there, Joe Press, a junior Yankee scout, pleaded with Krichell to see Mays. In his letter to Krichell, Press described the Yankees opportunities with Black stars, "You could have practically all of them, just for the ask-ing." Krichell refused.

In 1950, the Yankees finally sent a scout to watch Mays play when Mays was in New York, but the Yankees again passed on pursuing him. The stated reason was "… although he could run and field a little, he couldn't hit curve balls." Both explanations were unjustifiable, even then. Mays was by all other accounts a phenomenal talent—especially in the field. Other teams—including the Braves, Dodgers, and Indians—were actively recruiting Mays. Red Sox scout George Digby said Mays was the greatest prospect he ever saw. Mays proceeded to sign with the Giants and played with them for 20 years. He is now generally regarded by virtually all historians in the top five of players all-time. Bill James ranks him sec-ond, behind Ruth.

The first Black player whom the team signed to one of their minor league teams and clearly had major league talent was Vic Power. Power hit .331 at AAA in 1952 but was not invited to the Yankees spring training the following year. And while the team did buy his contract from their minor league team after the 1953 season, Weiss almost immediately traded him to Philadelphia. Power would play in the major leagues for 12 years, made the All-Star team six times, and won seven Gold Gloves. There is no question that Power *did* have what it took to be a major league star, but the Yankees traded him instead of bringing him up to their major league team.

As noted in Burton and Benita Boxerman's book *George Weiss: Architect of the Golden Age Yankees*, Weiss' explanation in the early 1950s was "the cynical excuse that the Yankees were a winning ball club *without* the contribution of Black men." As the Boxermans point out, "That was a lame excuse for such inaction, especially when so many Black stars had begun to dominate every department of major league play." Weiss may have been pandering to what he perceived Yankees' fans wanted, and reportedly said, "I will never allow a Black man to wear a Yankee uniform. Box holders from Westchester don't want that sort of crowd. They would be offended to have to sit with n----s." Weiss denied making the statement. The Boxermans also noted that writers such as Roger Kahn and David Halberstam believed Weiss to be a vicious man and unable to empathize with any player, especially Black players. Jackie Robinson publicly stated in 1952 on a television show called "Youth Wants to Know" that the Yankees were "prejudiced due to their failure to sign a Black player within five years of integration." Weiss responded by stating, "With the exception of Jackie Robinson, we have been interested in just about every Negro player who has come up to the majors." Dodger pitcher Don Newcombe also believed that there was "innate prejudice … on the ball club and in that organization." Dick Young of the *New York Daily News* believed that baseball teams, like professional football teams, had an informal "quota" of Black players which limited their numbers.

What is also clear is that the Yankees' stalling in hiring Black players ultimately harmed the team. Many teams in both leagues were realizing not only the impact of Black talent but that the new diversity in the clubhouse was *good* for the team and for the fans. The advantages of diversity on teams have been shown to include increased creativity and less "group think"—where too many like-minded people devalue different ideas or sabotage or influence different opinions. Diversity among teammates has also been shown to require deeper concentration in order to understand others' ideas and arguments—thus, leading to more efficiency and productivity. In baseball, the Negro Leagues played a faster, more aggressive style of the game and the Black players brought that style with them to the major leagues. They also came as better conditioned athletes due in large part to being accustomed to playing two or three games in different cities in the same day. As a result of being in better shape, they were likely to perform better than less conditioned athletes late in the season, including in the World Series. Teams such as the Giants, Dodgers, Cardinals, Twins, and others were already realizing these advantages in the early 1960s.

On a wider level, diversity had a positive impact on fans. In the 1960s and 1970s, a whole generation of baseball fans, many of whom like this author grew up in small towns with no diversity in their populations, learned the value of diversity from watching sports on television. We grew up seeing the benefits of diversity and the value of people with different skin colors working together. We developed admiration for people of color rather than bigotry. Had the Yankees embraced the many opportunities they had to acquire Black players for the nearly 20 years between integration and the draft in 1965, they could have stockpiled an overwhelming amount of talent—so much so that the impact of the sale by Topping and Webb might have been just a blip on the screen. If this had occurred, the 1960 to 1964 Yankee dynasty may have continued well into the 1970s.

The Yankees also failed to notice and/or act on other trends in baseball in the 1960s. Major League Baseball was becoming a more pitcher-oriented game. Due in part to the number of home runs in 1961, rules changed to favor the pitcher. The strike zone became more pitcher friendly and teams began to raise the height of their pitching mounds. Suddenly, great pitchers such as Sandy Koufax, Juan Marichal, and Bob Gibson became more dominant than ever—and continued as such until the 1969 season when the rules were changed back to favor the hitters. During this pitching era, hitting statistics dropped. In the four seasons between 1965 and 1968, only 10 players hit over .300 for the year in the American League. The ten included three players who each did it twice—so it was only seven different players who accomplished this feat. In 1965, only two players hit 30 or more home runs. Pitching was king, and while other teams began to sign great starting pitchers, the Yankees again fell behind. For each year from 1960 to 1963, the Yankees finished first or second in the American League's ERA. By 1965, they had fallen to fifth.

The Yankees also failed to replace a significant number of their players who were breaking down with injuries. The best years of Maris and Mantle were behind them, and both seemed to be constantly injured. In the period from 1964 to 1966, Maris played an average of 102 games per year. Games played by Mantle over those three years dropped from 143 to 122 to 108. Tony Kubek would retire after the 1965 season at age 29 and Richardson left after the 1966 season at age 30. Tom Tresh sustained multiple injuries and stopped being productive at age 27 in 1966.

Poor Leadership and Decision Making on and off the Field

In Dan Heath's book *Upstream*, he focuses on the tendency for business leaders to continue to react to problems instead of spending the time to think through a way to prevent them before they occur. This happens because of a kind of inertia, when managers get into a mindset Heath calls "tunneling," where they simply move from problem to problem and react to crisis after crisis. "When you spend years responding to problems, you can sometimes overlook the fact that you could be preventing them," Heath said. "More often, managers don't recognize the problem at all. And they come up against something called inattentional blindness, a phenomenon in which the careful attention to one task causes missing altogether important information that is unrelated to that task. Something like lack of peripheral vision."

As far back as the 1950s, the Yankees failed to plan for Weiss' departure as they had done when Barrow retired and turned the reigns over to Weiss. This led to over a decade of poor leadership and decision making after Weiss' departure in 1960. On the surface, Topping and Webb seemed to do a fine job as owners during the 1960 to 1964 dynasty. But in reality, the success belonged to Weiss who had built the team in the 1950s. When Weiss was removed from the general manager position after the 1960 season, there was no solid succession plan in place to replace him. Neither of Weiss' replacements—Roy Hamey in advance of the 1961 season nor Ralph Houk in 1964—had Weiss' skills in running the farm system and scouting and signing players. While Hamey did bring up Tresh, Jim Bouton, Downing, and Joe Pepitone from the minor leagues, he made no blockbuster trades and acquired no new young stars for the franchise. In Hamey's only trade of significance, he sent Bill Skowron to the Dodgers for pitcher Stan Williams which allowed him to install Pepitone at first base. Like Hamey, Houk did not identify and sign any new players that turned into major league stars.

Houk was likely even worse than Hamey as a general manager. Houk was simply not an executive—he was a field manager, and in over his head when it came to negotiating with players.

Another leadership problem was there simply was not the unity between and among owners and other leaders as there had been with Ruppert, Barrow, and Huggins. In 1964, the players communicated with Houk about Berra's shortcomings as a manager, and Houk communicated with Webb and Topping, but no one communicated with Berra himself. Berra was left on an island to flounder. Due to the dysfunctional ways the communications were occurring, Berra didn't have a chance to succeed. And when Webb and Topping decided they were going to sell the team, they checked out as owners. Between 1962 and the end of the 1964 season, Webb was out running other businesses, Hamey and Topping became ill, Houk was in over his head, and Berra was struggling as a first-year manager. The musical chairs that went on with ownership and management directly impacted the team on the field. The owners did not disclose their plans to sell for two years, the general manager went behind the managers' backs to the owner, and none of the managers had a chance to establish any consistency or continuity on the field. There was no Ruppert, Barrow, or Weiss to reign things in and right the ship. And for a key period in the 1960s, no one was minding the store.

CBS also bears some responsibility for the downfall. They failed to take remedial action when attendance declined in 1963 and 1964. They failed to recognize the looming gaps in talent compared to other teams and their own lack of keeping up with the changes in the game.

On September 22, 1966, the team drew a total of 413 fans for a game against the White Sox. When the then Yankees' announcer Red Barber tried to get the TV cameras to pan the crowd to show the empty stadium,

CBS (who was covering the games for the team it owned) refused to do so. Then, CBS fired Barber.

CBS proceeded to mismanage the team making a series of bad trades which resulted in Maris going to the Cardinals, Clete Boyer to the Braves, and John Blanchard to the A's. The team got virtually nothing in return. During the eight years CBS owned the Yankees, the team made a profit in only one and reportedly lost a total of $11 million. Over the 1972 season, attendance dropped below one million for the first time since World War II. In 1973, they sold the team to ship builder George Steinbrenner for $11 million, a loss of over three million dollars. The Yankees would not become great again until the mid-1970s when the new ownership had added everyday players Reggie Jackson, Chris Chambliss, Willie Randolph, Roy White, Mickey Rivers, and Oscar Gamble, all of whom were Black.

Failure to Properly Manage Mickey Mantle

Another key reason for the downfall of the Yankees was the way they managed—or failed to manage—their premier superstar Mickey Mantle. When Casey Stengel first saw Mantle play in the Yankees' rookie camp in 1950, he said, "There's never been anything like this kid … He has more speed than any slugger and more slug than any speedster—and nobody has ever had more of both of 'em together." Stengel was right. As a young player, Mantle had a package of skills that made him one of the greatest talents to ever play the game.

Mantle was popular with his teammates. He would seek out and connect with rookies. In Bobby Richardson's autobiography, he talks of Mantle approaching him during his first day at Yankee Stadium, putting his arm around him, and helping Richardson negotiate the ins and outs of when to step into the batting cage. When Mantle saw that the team had given Kubek the number 34 (the lower the number, the higher the esteem), Mantle went to the trainer and said, "You better give him a lower number. He's going to be with the team a long time." Kubek promptly received number 10. Tom Tresh said, "As a young player, I worshipped Mickey. I was an outfielder and a switch hitter (like Mantle), but I would try and run like him and stand at the plate like he did."

Some teammates (including Tresh) admired him so much they named their sons after him.

Mantle was also known for being generous and always insisted he pick up the check at dinner. He allowed Joe Pepitone to stay with him for a month when Pepitone went through a divorce. Mantle and Ford would pool their endorsement income (e.g., from Gillette commercials), stash it in the clubhouse, and then take the team out for a night on the town. Like the pied piper, Mantle would lead groups of young players out to bars at night, often until the wee hours. He was also known for consistently giving money to panhandlers on street corners and others whom he knew were in trouble. His son Mickey Jr. recalled an incident where he was at a gas station with his dad. A Black man was inside the station and was beside himself because he needed new tires to get his family's Christmas presents to them. But the man did not have enough money for the tires, and he was being ignored by the attendant at the station. Mantle slapped down 300 dollars on the counter and ordered the attendant to put the tires on the man's car.

Mantle had a sense of humor, too, which resonated with his teammates. When Berra took over as manager in 1964, he met with the media. While answering questions, Berra was handed a telegram, smiled, and then read it to the press, "Our congratulations on your new job. We would appreciate it if you would give us our unconditional release so we can become pro golfers. It's signed White and Mickey." A genuinely funny action which likely helped Berra by lightening the tension which he always felt any time he had to speak to a crowd. One of Mantle's favorite tricks was to pick on one teammate during an important game. Before going out onto the field, Mantle would give a little pep talk and end it with "Go get 'em." The team would jump out of the dugout, and all but the unsuspecting victim would jump back in the dugout, allowing that player to go out on the field all by himself. This was essentially a sign of affection that signaled to the player he was accepted by the team. During one of the multiple times Mantle was not playing due to an injury, the press constantly hounded him for an update. Finally, Mantle got a piece of paper on which he printed, "Slight improvement. Be back in two weeks. So, don't ask." and taped the paper to his chest.

But Mantle's impact on his team was far more complex than being a great player, fighting through pain, being the guy who would give you the shirt off his back, and serving as the life of the party. His behavior required some very tough love from veteran players. When he struggled at the plate, he would smash bat racks and water coolers with his bat. His problems at the plate led to defensive lapses in the field. On one occasion when he let an easy pop fly land at his feet and then threw a tantrum, a Yankee veteran pitcher yelled at him, "You want to play? If not, don't screw around with our money. Just get the hell out of here because we want to win." The tantrums continued.

Manager Casey Stengel was strict with Mantle by getting on him when he missed signs or otherwise failed to follow instructions, which became part and parcel of Mantle's temper tantrums. Many of his mental errors came right after his strikeouts. When Mantle failed to run out grounders, Stengel called him out in front of his teammates in the dugout and then took his frustration to the *New York Press*, "Casey Raps Loafing Mantle," and "Casey Stengel Incensed at Mickey Mantle's Lack of Hustle." Mantle's typical response was to avoid the criticism, deflect (or ignore) it, and not own the offending behavior.

Mantle's childish behavior so predominated his 10 years with Stengel that when Stengel put together his all-time best team, Mantle was not on it. When Mantle was later confronted with Stengel leaving him off the team, Mantle deflected again, "Casey wanted me to be Babe Ruth, Ty Cobb and Joe DiMaggio all rolled into one ... it just never happened, you know." In the late 1950s, Stengel began to refer to Mantle as his "greatest disappointment." "The trouble with Mantle," Stengel said, "is Mantle." When Ralph Houk took over as manager in the 1961 season, his military style discipline seemed to work for a while with Mantle, and Mantle had particularly good years in 1961 and 1962. But by 1963 when it was clear Houk would be moved to the front office, Mantle played the rest of his career unchecked and largely undisciplined by the Yankees.

As for the humor, it was sometimes funny in an honest and genuine way—like the joke with Berra at the press conference. But on other occasions, it was far more troubling than funny. In Berra's first meeting with the team in spring training 1964, he decided to loosen up the team by starting off with telling them about his seemingly draconian ways about managing and then immediately take it back. This would have worked had Mantle not jumped in before Berra's punch line, slamming his bat on the floor of the clubhouse and saying, "I'm quittin'." Mantle's action—while slightly funny—was really weighted heavier toward disrespect. By taking the action he took and saying what he did, he showed up Berra in front of the team. Dick Young, one of the top baseball writers of the time noted of Mantle (and Ford), "Instead of using their immense influence with their teammates to ease their friend [Berra's] transition to manager, they undermined his authority with their overactive nightlife and scornful jokes." The "worship" that came from the rookies was carefully cultivated by Mantle.

Lurking under the many different sides and shades of Mickey Mantle was one big problem—alcoholism. Mickey Mantle was chronically addicted to alcohol. This condition impacted not only Mantle himself but virtually everything in his wake for at least 40 years. It was the dysfunctional foundation of his life and became part of the Yankees. This was apparent in 1964, the year Berra managed the team, but it had always existed and was still there during the period when the Yankee dynasty crashed beginning in 1965 and through the end of Mantle's career following the 1968 season.

"Time in a Bottle," a *Sports Illustrated* article, was written by Mantle in the first person and published April 18, 1994, about 16 months before his death in August 1995. Mantle wrote that he did not drink much at all when he came up with the Yankees in 1951 at the age of 19. But he began to drink with teammates, especially on the road, and his drinking escalated after the 1953 season when Billy Martin came to live with Mantle and his wife in the off-season. "With Billy and me, drinking was a competitive thing. We'd see who could drink the other under the table." As Mantle's drinking worsened, the Yankees addressed Mantle's alcohol-related behavior with tough love on the field from Stengel and other veterans and by assigning veteran Jerry Coleman to watch over him and be Mantle's roommate in the 1954 and 1955 seasons. Mantle acknowledged, "My drinking problems grew gradually as each year passed. My last four or five years with the Yankees (1964 or 1965 through 1968) I didn't realize I was ruining myself with all the drinking." Mantle added, "Today I can admit that my drinking shortened my career."

When on the road during the 1955 season, Coleman woke up in the middle of the night and saw Mantle with his "head in the toilet." The next day Mantle went six for eight in a doubleheader. In the later 1950s into the 1960s, Mantle's drinking escalated. Stengel was fired, the veterans retired, but Mantle's star continued to rise. Yankee players became accustomed to Mantle arriving at the stadium hungover, and then going out and hitting home runs. Younger players like Joe Pepitone, Tom Tresh, and Phil Lenz watched the great Mantle do this and were mesmerized. In one game in September 1962, Mantle had been drinking hard the night before. He woke up still drunk and a friend had to pump coffee in him for him to even have a chance to play that day. The friend drove him to the stadium, dropped him at the door, and handed him over to a Yankees' trainer. Mantle got up to bat in the bottom of the first inning barely able to stand up. But he connected on a pitch and hit it 460 ft. into the center field bleachers. When Mantle got to first base, he kept running down the right field line. The umpire had to reorient him by pointing to second, and Mantle made it around the bases. His teammates were doubled over in the dugout laughing. Mantle was taken out of the game after the first inning.

Part and parcel of the drinking was carousing and infidelity. Mantle did this regularly and as time went on, brazenly. Mantle's wife, Merlyn, noted that [Mickey Mantle] "… was married in a very small geographical region of his brain." The other Yankees' wives were aware of Mantle's behavior and felt bad for Merlyn. Unlike Sparky Anderson, the Cincinnati Reds' manager who ordered Pete Rose to stop engaging in infidelity in large part due to how it would be perceived by the wives of the other players on the team, the Yankees left this part of Mantle's behavior unchecked.

Mantle also cultivated others to enable his alcoholism. Mantle's father, two of his uncles, and ultimately one of his sons died of Hodgkin's disease, and Mantle would regularly rationalize his drinking because he thought he would die before he was 40 years old like they did. He said this again and again and would often cry when doing so. Others felt sorry for him and said they "understood" his drinking because of it. In *A Hero All His Life*, Mantle said, "It has been this way most of my life: If I said or did something wrong, the people who might have suffered for it would worry about my feelings being hurt. Even eight-year-olds made excuses for me." When Mantle hit the home run the day the umpire had to help him around the bases, his teammates laughed from the dugout. Enabling, always enabling.

Some gave him a pass on the drinking because of the pain he was in due to his many injuries. But it may have been the other way around. In his later years, Mantle confirmed what some writers had been saying for years—that Mantle's drinking and lifestyle actually contributed to his injuries. "Everybody tries to make the excuse that injuries shortened my career. Truth is, after I'd had a knee operation, the doctors would give me rehab work to do, but I wouldn't do it. I'd be out drinking." Whitey Herzog is quoted in Tony Kubek's book *Sixty-One—The Team the Record the Men*, "The press always tried to protect Mickey. If Mickey came in too hungover to play, the Yankees would say Mickey's leg was hurting, and that's what the press would write." Said Mantle, "God gave me a great body to play with, and I didn't take care of it. And I blame a lot of it on alcohol."

Unlike the unified discipline given Ruth by Ruppert, Barrow, and Huggins, there was no effective discipline given to Mickey Mantle during the period of the 1960 to 1964 dynasty. His bad behavior continued for the rest of his career, and then for most of the rest of his life. Berra didn't know how to handle it. Executives with new owner CBS just hoped that Mantle would keep showing up and bringing fans into the stadium. Mantle's behavior continued to go largely unchecked as the Yankee franchise floundered beginning in 1965.

Some organizations find themselves in a place where they have a person like Mantle—often a high performer such as a great salesperson, a rainmaker, or someone who provides great value in certain ways to the organization or team. The individual is sometimes one who obviously misbehaves. But more likely, it is more complicated. The person does favors for others—often a favor creating a "debt" which the misbehaving person can and will use to his advantage. Or the person is highly charismatic and is able to draw people in by the force of his personality. In either event, the individual is equal parts superstar and cancer. On one hand, this person does a bunch of seemingly great stuff (and believes others "owe" him). On the other hand, the person is a known superstar, and there would be all kinds of consequences if he were to leave the organization. What do you do?

Back to Ed Barrow and Babe Ruth. Seven years after Barrow put Ruth in his place when Ruth threatened to punch Barrow in front of the team in Boston, Ruth and the Yankees were struggling in 1925. It was a bad year for the team. The Yankees were 13½ games out of first place 42 games into the season. Babe Ruth was misbehaving, drinking, carousing, and coming to the stadium late for games. Manager Miller Huggins had to contend not only with Ruth but also with rabid New York fans who blamed Huggins and wanted him fired. By late August, things were unbearable as the Yankees plummeted to seventh place in the American League. But at the very moment it was necessary, Huggins was publicly supported by owner Jacob Ruppert, "Miller Huggins will be manager as long as he cares to be."

On August 29, Huggins finally suspended Ruth indefinitely for "misconduct off the playing field" and fined him $5,000. Ruth responded by stating that owner Ruppert would suspend the suspension and the fine, and he would never play for Huggins again. Ruppert stepped up again and stated, "Ruth would be suspended for as long as Huggins desired." Ruth then apologized to Huggins, but Huggins did not respond until September 7 when he told Ruth that he could come back on the team if he apologized to the team. Ruth did and never challenged Huggins again. Huggins, supported by a strong core leadership team, was able to stand up to the bully and the bully backed down.

Ruth responded well to the discipline, thus ushering in the first Yankee dynasty—the "Murderers' Row" team from 1926 to 1928. From 1926-1931, Ruth had the most productive six consecutive years of hitting of any player in baseball history. He averaged 50 home runs and 155 RBIs each year, and hit .347 over the six year period. However, when his game deteriorated after the six year stretch, he was shown the door.

After Ruth was discharged by the Yankees, he begged to be named the team manager, but he was never seriously considered. Ruth's wife later noted that Ruth spent the last years of his life waiting by the phone for a call to manage that never came. Ruth had behaved badly and ultimately had to face the music. The Yankees said no to the bully.

Back to the question posed—What do you do with the dysfunctional top performer? Yankee leadership handled Ruth as he should have been handled. But Yankee leadership mishandled Mantle, essentially by doing nothing. Mantle was coddled, enabled, and allowed to make mess after mess with the Yankees all the way through the 1968 season when he finally retired. What really matters in how an individual is handled is that it be addressed in a way that is best for the *team*. If it is *not* handled, the others on the team will get to a point where they no longer want to be part of things and will go elsewhere. The takeaways from the handling of Ruth and Mantle provide guidance to organizations. The best way to handle the Ruths and Mantles of the world:

1. Align the entire leadership team before dealing with the problem and get everyone on the same page.
2. Address the issue with the offending person immediately.
3. Provide clear and decisive correction to the offending person.
4. Follow through on the corrective action and do not tolerate any effort by the offender to create dissension in the leadership team (because the offender will try).
5. Tolerate the bad behavior only as long as absolutely necessary and be prepared to remove the individual from organization if it doesn't stop.

The Yankees in the era of Ruth handled things in these ways and thrived, the Yankees in the era of Mantle, not so much. While Mantle provided value for 12 or 13 years, he stopped making meaningful contributions in 1965. At precisely that point in time, Mickey Mantle should have been exited.

The end of this Yankees' dynasty teaches a number of lessons about leadership and organizational function. The Yankees failed to embrace the new availability of diverse talent, and they paid the price for at least 10 years, probably closer to 20. They became focused on what they thought their "fans wanted" and made wrong decisions because they did it for the wrong reasons. They also failed to keep focused on other changes in the game and other looming challenges such as the new focus on pitching and changes to the rules. Still further, they failed to recognize and address declining productivity of key players due primarily to injuries.

The Yankees also failed to properly navigate a season where their leadership changed multiple times on and off the field. There was no stability, and the team paid the price. For a while, they allowed dysfunction to

occur rather than make sure the entire leadership was aligned before taking action. Along with it, they let a talented star, dysfunctional in his own
way, run roughshod over everyone else.

Had the Yankees provided the right kind of discipline with Mickey
Mantle, pursued more great Black players like Willie Mays, and recognized the changes that were happening to the game, the 1960s version of
the team may have been the best and longest running dynasty in baseball
history.

CHAPTER 9

Chaos

Humility is not thinking less of yourself, it is thinking of yourself less.
—C.S. Lewis

In winning three World Series in the four years from 1915 to 1918, the Boston Red Sox served as a great example of a team overcoming obstacles to succeed. During the period of this dynasty, the Red Sox had to contend with the effects of World War I, a worldwide flu pandemic, a rival professional baseball league, the failure of that league, labor unrest among players, the departure of the Red Sox's best player, significant turnover in the leadership of the team, declining revenue across the league, the unsavory influences of gambling, and one of the most difficult personnel decisions in baseball history. In doing so, the team was led by two players who were complete opposites off the field, but who would work together on it to bring World Series championships to Boston for the last time until the 21st century.

One of the players who led the team was Babe Ruth. While Ruth would ultimately become better known for his ability to hit dramatic home runs, he came into the league as a pitcher. He was 20 years old in 1915 and had just one year before been released from reform school (St. Mary's Industrial School for Orphans, Delinquent, Incorrigible, and Wayward Boys) in Baltimore. He was loud, rude, crude, and seemed to want to fill his days (and nights) making up for lost time while at St. Mary's. He married a 16-year-old waitress—one of the first women he met in Boston. He ate, drank, and did pretty much everything else in excess. In spite of his flaws, he quickly transformed himself into the best left-handed pitcher in the American League in the Red Sox dynasty era.

The other leader was a six-year veteran named Harry Hooper. Hooper was college educated as an engineer, a leader among not only his teammates but other players across the league, and an outstanding outfielder.

Ruth himself called Hooper the best fielding outfielder in baseball. Newspapers of the day commended Hooper for his fine play and great character. Hooper made key hits, clutch catches, and run saving throws from his position in right field. He was hard working and dependable. Players of the time credited Hooper as being the best of his time in the clutch. He was simple, humble, and modest—the antithesis of Ruth. He led his team through unprecedented change and challenges which would have been anticipated by no one. Without both Ruth and Hooper, the Red Sox would likely not have won any championships, let alone three in four years.

In 1915, the Red Sox went 101-50 and won the American pennant by 2½ games over the Detroit Tigers. They had great pitching, including Ruth. In his first full year as a starting pitcher, he went 18-8 with an ERA of 2.44. With Tris Speaker in center field, Hooper in right, and Duffy Lewis in left, the Red Sox outfield was widely regarded as the best defensive outfield of the era.

The Red Sox won the 1915 World Series four games to one over the Philadelphia Phillies. In Game 5 of that Series, Harry Hooper hit two home runs that landed in the stands on one bounce—which under the rules of the time were counted as home runs. Hooper's batting average in the regular season was .235 but shot up to .350 in the World Series. The Red Sox player shares for winning the World Series in 1915 were $3,780.25 per player.

The 1915 also marked the second year of a rival baseball league called the Federal League. The league was initially well funded, and each of its eight teams built its own park. One of those parks was Weeghman Park built for the Chicago Federals a/k/a Whales. That park would later be named Wrigley Field. The Federal League patterned itself after the American and National Leagues and was initially successful in recruiting away players from the major leagues. Prior to the Federal League, the players in the major leagues had virtually no leverage in negotiating their salaries. But the Federal League provided for that leverage. The initial popularity of the new league among players and the salaries offered by its teams put pressure on the major league teams to pay higher salaries to keep their talent.

Some major league stars did not make the jump to the Federal League but certainly used the new league to their advantage in negotiating their salaries with major league teams. These players included Honus Wagner, Tris Speaker, and even the great pitcher Walter Johnson. But ultimately, the Federal League simply could not compete with the established major leagues and following an antitrust lawsuit which had been filed by the Federal League, the parties settled their disputes. The terms included a buyout of the Federal League's owners who were heavily in debt, the acquisition of many of the Federal League's parks by the major league's franchises, and amnesty for the players who had jumped ship from the American and National Leagues to play for Federal League teams. At the end of the 1915 season, the Federal League officially folded.

The Boston Red Sox, led by the business acumen of its owner Joseph Lannin and the leadership of Harry Hooper, sidestepped the drama associated with the Federal League altogether. Lannin, who had made his fortune in real estate development and hotels, saw the Federal League coming. He had proactively increased his payroll by 25 percent from 1914 to 1915 and had Ruth locked into a three-year contract which extended through the 1916 season. There is no evidence of Hooper seriously entertaining offers from the new league or even discussing such opportunities in the press. He kept his mouth shut. Rather, writings about Hooper during the era of player defections to the Federal League focused on his selfless team play and quiet leadership. By avoiding even testing the waters with the new league, Hooper demonstrated that he was all in with his team and was not going to abandon his teammates.

The end of the Federal League meant that there would be a horde of players looking for jobs on major league teams. Major league owners took advantage of the situation by cutting player salaries. Red Sox owner Joe Lannin did not go that far, but he did keep salaries relatively even from the year before.

With Hooper's steady leadership, another dominant pitching year from Ruth, and without Tris Speaker, the Red Sox has another great year in 1916. Ruth went 23-12 with a 1.75 ERA. He also pitched nine shutouts and led the league in innings pitched. Ruth had five famous mano-a-mano battles with Walter Johnson in 1916, winning four of them (5-1, 1-0, 1-0, and 2-1). In the fifth game, the Red Sox won but Ruth did not get the decision. Ruth was also starting to get attention for his batting skills, hitting ball after ball into the stands in batting practice before games. Due primarily to their pitching and defense, the Red Sox again won the American League pennant. The Red Sox then won their second World Series title in a row, besting Brooklyn four games to one. The amount of the shares paid to the winning Red Sox players increased to $3,910.36.

Hooper's most dramatic contribution to the Red Sox winning the series in 1916 was a catch he made in the outfield. With a Brooklyn runner on third base in Game 1, a ball was hit to shallow right field. Hooper had to immediately sprint forward to have a chance to make the catch. As the ball descended toward the ground, Hooper slid under it, made the catch, immediately bounced up, and threw a dart to home plate. The runner had tagged at third, and it seemed as if he would score easily. But the ball arrived slightly before the runner and the runner was out. While many writers covering the game thought that he stumbled, Hopper's slide was intentional and gave birth to the outfield slide that is performed by players today.

Following the 1916 season, Joe Lannin sold the Red Sox. He had reportedly earned $400,000 from the team but foresaw trouble in baseball due to the looming war. And the stress of ownership had worsened his health. The buyer was Harry Frazee, a 36-year-old wealthy theatrical owner with connections to gamblers.

In addition to the changes in ownership, the team changed managers. Boston manager Bill Carrigan resigned and was replaced by Jack Barry. Barry had learned the art of defensive alignments based on the hitter and the circumstances of the game from Connie Mack. He had also learned Mack's way of teaching players to communicate with one another on the field. Barry, who had never managed before, wisely deferred to Hooper on many of the duties traditionally performed by the manager including setting starting lineups, scheduling the pitching rotation, formulating game strategy, and even calling individual pitches—which Hooper would signal to the catcher from his position in right field. Hooper had already been performing many of these duties for the team but was now being formally recognized for assuming them. With changes in leadership on and off the field, Hooper assumed the role of the team's true leader going forward.

The "Preparedness Movement" in America had begun and as events in the world brought the United States closer to war throughout 1916 and into 1917. The United States made it official by declaring war against Germany on April 2, 1917—just a few days before the Major League Baseball season was to begin. Heading into the 1917 season, major league teams were very concerned about the impact of the war on its teams and their players. And efforts were made to try to exempt the players from being drafted. One such effort was American League president Ban Johnson's requirement that the teams in his league do close-order military drills in spring training. Army drill masters led the players in marching across their spring training fields carrying their bats as if they were rifles. By ordering the drills, Johnson was attempting to engage the teams in "military instruction" which would technically exempt the players from early conscription calls. The teams continued to do the drills in front of the fans when the regular season began, but by midseason, these efforts had lost their credibility. The leagues were forced to do things that actually aided the war effort such as playing benefit games, offering free admission to military personnel, and conducting patriotic parades.

While the most famous gambling scandal in Major League Baseball's history occurred in the 1919 World Series, gambling had been in the game for decades. It was perhaps at its worst level in the 1910s. A contributing factor was that the players were paid extraordinarily little at the time relative to the average wage paid to others. The highest paid player was Ty Cobb who made $20,000 a year, roughly $300,000 in today's dollars. On top of the low salaries, revenues were decreasing in the wartime economy. Attendance had decreased by 1.3 million from 1916 to 1917. As a result, owners had even less to spend on salaries. Given the depressed revenues due to the war and the manner in which the owners held salaries even (or lowered them) after the failure of the Federal League, the underpaid players became easy marks for gamblers.

New Red Sox owner Frazee had been known to consort with gamblers such as Sport Sullivan (who would become a prominent figure in the 1919 Black Sox scandal) and Jim Costello. Frazee entertained them at Red Sox games and not surprisingly, Fenway Park was a known hot spot for gambling. A group of gamblers came regularly to Red Sox games where they situated themselves in the right field bleachers just behind where Harry Hooper played. They could be heard offering and accepting bets over virtually everything that went on in the game. When Sullivan told them to be less brazen about their activities, they passed notes and developed a system of hand signals to communicate with one another.

The Red Sox had started strong in 1917 and the gamblers (who generally bet on the team to win) had fared well. But the Red Sox began slumping in June, and by June 16, 1917, the Red Sox had lost 8 of their last 11 games. The team had fallen 2½ games behind the Chicago White Sox who were in town for a game. Babe Ruth was pitching that day and a large number of gamblers showed up intent on recouping their recent losses. The attendance was less than 10,000 so many seats were available in the box areas around the infield. But a strangely large number of fans sat in the right field bleachers close to the gamblers.

June 16, 1917 was a rainy day in Boston and the field at Fenway Park was wet. The White Sox were ahead 2-0 in the top of the fourth inning as rain continued to fall. The rule on rainouts was that if a game was called due to rain before 4½ innings were completed, the game would be canceled, and it would be replayed at a later date. With two outs and a runner on in the top of the fourth, a group of fans from the gamblers' section jumped onto the field, ran across it, and sat in another section of the stadium that was covered. As intended by the culprits, the game was delayed for several minutes.

The Boston batters went down one, two, three in the bottom of the fourth. In the top of the fifth, Ruth got two outs against the White Sox. As the rain worsened, a group of roughly 300 from the right field bleachers then jumped the fence and ran out onto the field. If the game was called before the last out in the top of the fifth, it would be canceled and would have to be replayed. The gamblers who had bet on Boston would be off the hook for their bets. When the fans came onto the field, they did not attack the players or umpires, they just stood around on the field delaying play. Frazee had only a handful of police at the ballpark that day and the officers were nowhere to be found. So, there was not even a threat that the fans would face harm for coming onto the field. Boston manager Barry was able to persuade the fans to get off the field, but just as they did a second wave came out of the gamblers' section. This group was violent and went after the players. The teams were forced to get off the field and go into the clubhouse. The second group delayed the game for an additional 35 minutes. By that time, it was clear what was going on and the umpires refused to call the game. After 45 minutes the game was restarted, and the White Sox ultimately won 7-2.

American League president Ban Johnson ordered Frazee to take action against the gamblers, proclaiming "Either the gamblers go or Frazee goes," but Frazee did nothing. It was not in Frazee's or any of the other teams' best interests to ban gamblers as they too bought tickets and attended games. But Johnson persisted by doing his own investigation. It ultimately resulted in the conviction of 33 gamblers who operated at Fenway Park in Boston.

The Red Sox played well in 1917, winning 90 games. Hooper had another solid year at bat and in the field and Ruth had another extraordinary year pitching winning 24 games, finishing 35 of 38 games he started and pitching six shutouts. His ERA over 326.1 innings was 2.01. But the team finished second in the American League that year to the Chicago White Sox. It was the one year of four in which the Red Sox did not win the World Series.

In March 1918, more than 100 soldiers at Camp Funston in Fort Riley, Kansas, became ill with the flu. Within one week, the number grew to 500. Flu activity spread through the United States and Europe throughout the year. By May 1918, hundreds of thousands of soldiers traveled across the Atlantic each month as they deployed for the war. They carried the flu—which would later be recognized as a pandemic known as the "Spanish Flu"—with them. The flu came in waves, one of which emerged at Camp Devens, a U.S. Army training camp just outside Boston. By the end of September, 14,000 flu cases were reported there. The symptoms and speed at which people were inflicted was horrific. Dr. Victor Vaughn, Surgeon General of the U.S. Army, described the soldiers in the hospital, "The faces wore a bluish cast, a cough brought up the blood-stained sputum. In the morning, the dead bodies are stacked up like cordwood." The most horrific symptoms were bleeding not only from the nose and mouth but from the eyes and ears. The basic treatments that were offered were enemas, whiskey, and bloodletting.

At the time the flu began to spread, Congress passed the Sedition Act, making it a crime to say or publish anything that cast the government or the war effort in a negative light. So as the virus began to spread, the nation wasn't told. Simultaneously, Wilson made the decision to send troops on barges to Europe, knowing full well the health risks they were taking. Those barges became known as floating coffins. In the span of 12 months, the average U.S. life expectancy dropped almost 12 years. Babe Ruth caught the flu at least twice and several other Red Sox players fell ill. On one of the occasions Ruth got sick, he was wrongly given the caustic compound silver nitrate for a sore throat. The treatment caused Ruth to begin choking and passed out. He was rushed to the hospital and there were rumors that he was on his deathbed. He survived but remained hospitalized for multiple days. Before the end of 1918, the flu would kill over 675,000 people in the United States at a time when the nation's population was only 110 million. The virus hit Boston and Massachusetts particularly hard. The flu for U.S. troops would be more deadly than the war itself. When Woodrow Wilson was stricken in 1919 with the illness that led to his death, it may very well have been that the illness was the Spanish Flu itself.

The baseball season nonetheless began on April 16, 1918. By that time, many major leaguers had either been drafted or volunteered to fight in the war. Jack Barry joined the over 200 major league players (including at least 13 Red Sox players) to not be in major league camps due to military service. Many more followed later in 1918. In July, the "work or fight" rule was established. It required all men with "nonessential" jobs to enlist, make themselves draft-eligible, or apply for work directly related to the war. Some major leaguers actually took jobs with wartime suppliers and manufacturers, but in reality, just played for the company's baseball teams. The Red Sox and other major league teams struggled to put full teams on the field.

The Red Sox manager Jack Barry was replaced by Ed Barrow for the 1918 season. Barrow was the third manager during the Red Sox's four-year dynasty. Barrow was known for being a tough disciplinarian, including keeping Ruth in check, but he had very limited experience managing the game on the field at the major league level. Once again, enter Harry Hooper. Hooper would advise Barrow on every aspect of the game on the field from line-up selection to game strategy. Hooper was even more involved than he had been before with Barry, and he became the de facto manager on the field. Barrow and Hooper each realized that the team needed them in these unique roles, and they aligned their interests in a way that best served the team.

The new leadership arrangement also gave Hooper the platform he needed to advance his idea on an important personnel decision—how and where to play Babe Ruth. Ruth had continued to pitch through the 1917 season, but Ruth had also demonstrated the ability to hit—particularly home runs. Ruth had actually led the team in slugging percentage, a statistic that did not exist at the time, in each of his first three full years with the team. This included 1915 when Tris Speaker was still with the club. Ruth also struck out a lot during those years, but he batted ninth as the pitcher always did. As such, he typically swung freely for the fences without any real downside of striking out. Hooper noticed Ruth's hitting power and believed that Ruth would add additional value to the team if he developed more discipline and played in the field on days he didn't pitch. Hooper began an effort to convince Barrow to use Ruth in this way.

Barrow initially disagreed believing he would be second guessed if he moved the left-handed pitcher into the outfield. The general sentiment among the writers (still in the dead-ball era) was to agree with Barrow. Ruth, as planned, started the year as a full-time pitcher. But Hooper didn't give up. He tried many arguments with Barrow, all to no avail. Finally, Hooper settled on the argument that since attendance went up whenever Ruth pitched, it would likely go up every game if Ruth played in the field. Knowing the value of a dollar, and having $50,000 invested in the team, Barrow finally agreed. But he assigned Hooper two additional jobs: helping Ruth develop his batting skills and playing next to him to aid Ruth in the outfield. He also held Hooper accountable—noting that if Ruth failed as a full-time hitter, Hooper would be responsible.

On May 6, 1918, Babe Ruth started his first game at a position other than pitcher. He played left field and Hooper played center, the first of some 60 games that year where the two would play those two positions next to one another. In the first game starting in the field, Ruth hit a home run, his second in two days (he had hit one pitching in the prior game). He hit another, and another, and one month into his new role he was hitting almost .500. Half of his hits went for extra bases. It took a while, but Ruth also turned into a good fielder. Along the way, he lost interest in pitching.

Boston went on to win the American League pennant in 1918, led in hitting by Ruth and Hooper. Barrow also continued to ask Ruth to pitch, particularly as the team's pitching ranks thinned due to players leaving for military service or "essential service" jobs. Ruth sometimes objected, but mostly obeyed Barrow, and won 13 games with an ERA of 2.22 as a starting pitcher. Hooper, in addition to his new role as "comanager" and Babe Ruth's personal coach, had the best year at the plate in his 10-year career to that point hitting .289.

One of the interesting statistical metrics for the Red Sox was that Hooper's personal performance improved during the stage of his career when he assumed increased leadership responsibility.

In the following year of 1919, Ruth's final year with the Red Sox, he hit a single-season record 29 home runs and batted in 113 runs. He was on his way to becoming a major power hitter. Later, Hooper witnessed first-hand Ruth's transformation and the remarkable adulation he would receive from the public, who could not get enough from Ruth. During the 1918 season as the war raged and Ruth started to hit home runs, newspapers focused more on Ruth's performance than on the team's. Wireless news cable messages sent nightly overseas to the air forces in Europe would include two sports metrics: (1) the scores of the games and (2) how Ruth did that day. As Joe DiMaggio would do during the next World War, Babe Ruth provided Americans with a hero during a time of crisis. And he would become the poster child for the new era of power hitting in baseball.

But in 1918, Ruth was still young and very immature and would go through slumps during which he did not exhibit the plate discipline that Barrow wanted. During one at bat during a game in Washington, DC, in early July 1918, Ruth struck out on three straight pitches. Barrow confronted Ruth—calling his last swing and miss a bum play. Ruth talked back to Barrow and (as he had done with Barrow earlier in the year before he backed down) threatened to punch Barrow in the nose. Barrow fined Ruth $500. Ruth left the dugout mid-game and then left the stadium. Ruth threatened to join a shipyard industrial team but returned two days later. When Barrow reprimanded him in front of the team, Ruth ripped off his uniform and threatened to quit again. Hooper intervened and mediated the dispute. He persuaded both men to talk through their dispute, resulting in Ruth apologizing. By defusing a situation which could have resulted in Ruth being kicked off the team for good, Hooper may have saved the pennant for the Red Sox. And Ruth's performance and Hooper's recommendation on how to use Ruth were equally remarkable. In what may have been the apex of the dead ball era, the 1918 Boston Red Sox *as a team* hit only four home runs in addition to Ruth's 11. Ruth's offensive contributions powered the Red Sox to the American League pennant by the slim margin of 2½ games over Cleveland. Similar to stepping in to help address Ruth's disagreements with Barrow, Hooper's thoughtfulness, diligence, and follow through in managing Ruth as a hitter was essential to the Red Sox winning the pennant.

After much debate among the teams and their owners, the decision was made to end the 1918 regular season early (on September 2) due to the war. Seven double headers were played that day as teams hurried to get games (and ticket revenue) in by the deadline. While the teams played an odd number of games, ranging from 123 to 131, the two best teams, the Red Sox and the Chicago Cubs, made it to the World Series that year. Due to wartime travel restrictions, the Series would be played in a 3-4 format. The first three games would be played in Chicago and the last four would be played at Fenway Park. The teams would travel together on the same train. "The Star-Spangled Banner" was played at the games for the first time as part of the effort to unify the nation. Carrier pigeons brought score updates to the troops at Camp Devens. The challenges and distractions of the times were everywhere. Another Spanish Flu outbreak took place in the first week of September due in part to a "Win the War for Freedom" parade of over 4,000 returning sailors on September 3 on the streets of Boston. Some historians blame the playing of the World Series itself as a contributing factor to the second wave of the flu virus. Boston became the epicenter of the outbreak in 1918. And on top of it all, a terrorist bombed the Federal Building in Chicago on the eve of the first game of the Series.

Hooper's most important contribution in the 1918 World Series was off the field. In yet another twist on the events during the dynasty period, it became evident during the Series that attendance was way down, and that the players' World Series shares would be impacted. Overall attendance during the regular season went down even more from 1917 to 1918 than it had from 1916 to 1917—this time by over three million fans. Less than half of the 16 teams made a profit in 1918. Only 20,000 fans showed up for the first game of the 1918 World Series despite the fact that it had been moved from the Cubs' park to the White Sox's home, Comiskey Park, which could hold 32,000 fans. This was over twice what the Cubs' park could hold at the time. The attendance in Games 2 and 3 was not much better. Due to the lower demand, the three game box seat packages that sold for $15 in 1917 cost only $9 in 1918.

As the teams took the train from Chicago to Boston after the first three games, the players on both teams discussed the rumors that their World Series' shares would be shorted or even eliminated. They knew their shares would not be what they had been in the past but the players depended on the money. The players as a group were angry and ready to strike. Thankfully, they turned to Hooper to seek his advice. Hooper's first suggestion was to meet face-to-face with the owners prior to Game 5 in Boston. The players from both teams agreed and unanimously appointed Hooper their leader. The players had no union and no real negotiating leverage.

When the players' committee attempted to confer with the owners, the owners refused to meet. The players then made a series of demands including one which would require a guaranteed amount for the shares, and that at least part of that amount be paid to the Red Cross instead of the players. This latter point was suggested by Hooper knowing that the public would likely view the players as greedy for asking for *any* guaranteed shares in the war-time economy. Ultimately, the players voted to not play until the issue was resolved, and a hastily scheduled meeting took place in the umpires' room at the time Game 5 was scheduled to begin.

The owners' group appeared late and were drunk. Their presentation included a tearful plea from American League president Johnson in which he threw his arms around Hooper's neck and begged him to play. Hooper rejected the plea and realized that the owners were in no condition to negotiate. But he was also aware that in the stands waiting for the players to come on the field were dozens of wounded soldiers dressed in blue and khaki uniforms, some of them missing limbs. It was doubtful that the waiting crowd would have any sympathy for the players delaying the game because of concerns over their World Series shares.

Hooper led a meeting of both teams in which he wisely counseled them about where fans would stand on the players' action in the war-time economy and how lucky the players were to be serving on the ballfield and not a battlefield in Europe. The players unanimously agreed with Hooper and after securing an agreement from the owners to not take action against any of the players, they agreed to play the game. Hooper scripted a prepared statement that was read to the crowd. It said in essence that the players would play the game out of respect to the fans, including those among them who were wounded in battle. Hooper, acting in some ways as Marvin Miller would some 50 years later, had the insight and wisdom under pressure to avoid what could have been a public relations disaster for not only the players, but for professional baseball as a whole.

The teams went on the field to play. The Red Sox won the Series four games to two, and each Boston player received a winning share of $1,102.51, less than a third of what the Red Sox had received in 1915 and 1916. But it was better than nothing. As Hooper had expected, the press lambasted the players—but the Series was played, something that was not assured during the negotiations. Hooper had the acumen to keep the players organized and aligned. The press accurately reported Hooper's role as a leader rather than one of the insurgent players. Hooper's steady and even-handed leadership carried the day.

There are many lessons to be learned from Harry Hooper's leadership. During a time when the Red Sox went through significant changes in leadership from the top, Hooper ran the team from his position in right field. While his title was not that of manager, management came to him for answers and for action. Hooper partnered with perhaps the greatest player the game has ever seen to guide his team to three championships in four years. He also joined with other team leaders to manage that great player when he misbehaved and was instrumental in transforming that player into an all-time great.

There are dozens of books written about Babe Ruth, but this author could find only one written about Harry Hooper, *Harry Hooper: An American Baseball Life* written by Paul Zingg. Zingg's book is based in part on the letters Hooper wrote to his wife during his playing days. The book paints an extraordinary portrait of Hooper, the man, as well as Hooper the player. The letters, some of which Hooper wrote while his team was out on the town during road trips, were preserved by the Hooper family and are a foundational resource for baseball historians. Zingg's book reveals very little drama in Hooper's life, but instead chronicles a life of humble consistency, stability, and focus on others—the fundamentals of extraordinary leadership.

There was no job description for Hooper—he did not have a defined leadership role. Instead, he assumed those roles in real time, and on an as-needed basis. He navigated his team through the forces of an economy in deep recession, greedy owners, greedy players, labor unrest, team conflict, selfish misbehavior by teammates, gambling, war, and a major pandemic. During the almost annual change of managers, Hooper's steady leadership kept things intact. His teammates naturally turned to him when the chips were down, and Hooper responded matter-of-factly and without fanfare. The outside world knew little of Hooper's contributions. And indeed, most of Hooper's efforts were not mentioned by any of the many newspapers in Boston in those times. But his efforts were well known not only by the men who played with him, but those who played against him.

Harry Hooper was selfless at a time when it was very tempting, and understandable, to be selfish. He did not create problems. He solved them. He was always a net positive. Hooper was steady, didn't bring attention to himself, and on many occasions saved the day for the Red Sox. And while doing so (and maybe because of it), Hooper's own *personal* performance metrics improved. This is another telltale sign of a natural leader—an uptick in personal productivity during a stretch of challenging leadership responsibility. Instead of bemoaning his leadership duties, he embraced them, and the proof showed in the box scores. Hooper was a jewel—quiet, unassuming, a highly successful influencer of those around him, and model of humility. While he didn't serve on the battlefield in Europe, he demonstrated a sense of command that would have allowed him to thrive there. Instead, he commanded battles on the home front, and he won.

This book identifies those select players on the dynasty teams who made contributions that were not as recognizable as those of the high profile stars on their teams. But without these players and their contributions, their teams would not have been as successful, and some may not have even been dynasties. They were men about whom negative words were virtually never spoken—and include Bobby Brown, Jack Barry, Red Rolfe, Buck O'Neil, and others. But Harry Hooper may have been the greatest of them all.

CHAPTER 10

Moments of Impact

If you haven't found it yet, keep looking.

—Steve Jobs

The 1996 to 2000 New York Yankee dynasty was the team's fifth dynasty, and perhaps the best. They were led by a manager who at age 55 transformed himself into a great leader—in part because he came to terms with a dark family secret that had haunted him since his childhood. After transforming himself, he did the same for his players by courageously stepping up and communicating key lessons in key moments. This manager arrived just in time for the rookie years of two players who would become all-time great players and first ballot Hall of Famers. The manager, Joe Torre, and the two players, Derek Jeter and Mariano Rivera, were extraordinarily humble and selfless—qualities that would become foundational pieces of the team's culture. By their efforts, these men built trust in the clubhouse and success on the field.

This Yankee team fought for baseball supremacy with the Atlanta Braves. During the period of 1991 to 2005, the Braves were extraordinary. They won 14 divisional titles. The only year they didn't win was the strike shortened 1994 season when there was no postseason. They had a starting pitching rotation that was historically second to none, and had four players—pitchers Gregg Maddux, Dave Smoltz, and Tom Glavine and third baseman Chipper Jones, who were elected to the Hall of Fame. Over the 14-year period, the Braves *averaged* 97.3 wins, and the 1995 World Series champion team is considered by some historians as one of the best single-season teams ever. But while being regarded by many historians as a "dynasty," the fact of the matter is that they were not. There are at least three reasons for this:

1. The Braves were not the best team of their era.

   The Braves played in five World Series and won one from 1991 to 2005. The Yankees of that same period of time played in six World Series and won four. In two years—1996 and 1999—the two teams met head to head in the World Series and the Yankees won each time. The Yankees beat the Braves four games to two in 1996 and won by a 4-0 sweep in 1999. In the strike shortened 1994 season, the Braves were 68-46 but second in their Division by six games to the Montreal Expos when play stopped. The Yankees were 70-43, first in their Division, and 6½ games ahead of the Baltimore Orioles. The Yankees of the era from 1991 to 2005 were simply better than the Braves, and it is very difficult to argue that a team was a dynasty during an era when they weren't the best team of their time.

2. The Yankees played in a better league.

   In the 14-year period between 1991 and 2005 when a World Series was played, the American League won 10 World Series and the National League won four. Four of the American League wins were by a sweep. The only National League winners other than the Braves in 1995 were the then Florida Marlins who won in 1997 and 2003 and the Arizona Diamondbacks who won in 2001. Interleague play began in 1997, and the American League had a better overall record in interleague games than the National league in 6 of the 10 years between 1997 and 2006, and for each of the next 11 years. The American League was a competitively better league than the National League during the era.

3. The Yankees played in a far better division.

   The Braves began this era in the National League's Western Division, which included the Dodgers and Giants who were both very good teams. But the Braves played in that Division for only three years. After the teams were realigned before the 1994 season, the Braves were placed in the National League's Eastern Division which included the Philadelphia Phillies, New York Mets, Washington Nationals, and Florida Marlins. The Braves won this Division 11 years in a row (1995–2005) by an *average* of 9.7 games each year. During that era, teams played 18 games against each team in their own Division. So, the Braves played a total of 72 games annually against those four teams. They did have to contend with the World Series winning Marlins, but the Marlins tore down the team after their 1997 championship season to do a rebuild, went 54-108 the next year, and had a losing record each successive year through 2002. The Yankees played in the American League's Eastern Division which included the Boston Red Sox, Toronto Blue Jays, Baltimore Orioles, and Detroit Tigers. This Division was the best in baseball over the dynasty period and produced the World Series' champion in 7 of the 14 years when a champion was crowned. The National League's Eastern Division produced only three champions in the era. The differences in competition may have also been a factor in the Yankees being a better team. They faced stronger competition throughout the year and often had to survive a pennant race to make the postseason.

During the Yankees' five-year dynasty run, their postseason record was 46-16, a winning percentage of .742. In 1998, the Yankees won a whopping 114 games, the third most wins all time. The Yankees of this era were historically great. They are one of only three teams to win at least four titles in five years in the history of Major League Baseball.

Interestingly, the Yankees were not statistically dominant during the regular seasons of their dynasty period. They did not lead the American League in batting or home runs in any of the five dynasty years. No Yankee player won either the MVP or Cy Young Award during the dynasty period.

At least part of the explanation for the Yankees' lack of statistical dominance in the American League was that the competition in the league was fierce. The Blue Jays won the World Series in 1992 and 1993. The Orioles, led by Cal Ripken, Roberto Alomar, and Rafael Palmeiro, were very strong in the era. The Orioles finished second to the Yankees by only four games in 1996 and beat the Yankees to win the American League Eastern Division Series in 1997 while winning 98 games. In 1999, the Red Sox, led by pitchers Pedro Martinez and Nomar Garciaparra, won 94 games and finished just four games behind the first place Yankees. In 2000, the Red Sox got even closer—finishing 2.5 games behind.

Perhaps the best competition in the American League during the Yankee dynasty was the Cleveland Indians. The Indians, led by Manny Ramirez, Jim Thome, and David Justice, averaged 92.2 wins over the five-year period. The Indians were the only team in baseball to beat the Yankees in the postseason during the dynasty period—beating them in the Division Series in 1997. In addition to these strong American League teams, the Seattle Mariners, Texas Rangers, and the Billy Beane Oakland A's also showed flashes of great play in the American League during the Yankee dynasty period.

This may explain why the Yankees became so dominant in the *postseason*. Unlike the Braves, the Yankees had consistent tough competition during the regular season. Save the 1998 season where they won by 22 games, the Yankees never had a cakewalk through their Division and had to stay focused and competitive the entire 162 games to win. They simply had to play at a very high level to win during the regular season. Perhaps, this "iron sharpening iron" made them stronger for their postseason runs.

The Yankees were led by manager Joe Torre. Torre was a very good catcher and third baseman in his playing days, made nine All-Star teams, and had one extraordinary season in 1971 when he won the National League's MVP Award. His older brother, Frank, had also played, and while a 16-year-old watching Frank play for the then Milwaukee Braves in the 1957 World Series, Joe Torre began to dream about playing in the World Series himself. But he never made it as a player.

At the end of his playing days, Torre managed three teams: the New York Mets, the Atlanta Braves, and the St. Louis Cardinals. Torre did not make the postseason (and thus, not the World Series) with any of the teams he managed and had an overall record as a manager of 894-1,003. He was fired by each team, and at the time of his third firing, he held the record for the most games played and managed combined without making the World Series. Upon his mid-season firing in 1995 by the Cardinals, Torre thought he would never have the opportunity to manage again let alone make it to the World Series, "I felt as though the window had slammed shut." Torre was 55 years old.

In Bob Buford's book *Halftime*, he explores the challenges that people face at the stage of life where Torre was in 1995. Whether getting ready to retire after a successful career, coming to a time where there is no more passion for one's chosen career, or like Torre, being terminated in that career, there is challenge and uncertainty. Buford explains how to "take stock" with your circumstances as you contemplate the next stage (the "second half") of life. He advises to make peace with your first half—take time, be deliberate, share the journey, be honest, be patient, and have faith.

Buford notes that a major part of making peace at halftime is to get over any regrets left over from the first half. "Since you cannot go back and undo past mistakes, you really have only two options," said Buford, "You can dwell on them and become consumed with the effects they may have had on your family and career. Or you can come to terms with them through grace, accepting them as poignant markers from which you can learn something valuable for the second half." At his initial press conference with the New York press after being hired before the 1996 season, Torre was repeatedly asked about his losing record and whether he felt he was over the hill. One writer referred to him as "Clueless Joe" in the next day's paper. In response to the questions about his managerial record and whether he was qualified to do the job for the Yankees, Torre responded with humor and optimism, and calmly asked the writers to wait and see.

Buford also cautions against moving too quickly at halftime, because it increases the chances that you might repeat mistakes made in the past. After his firing by the Cardinals in the summer of 1995, Torre and his wife moved from St. Louis to Cincinnati to get closer to his wife's family. He traveled with friends. He had been living and breathing Major League Baseball since his rookie season as a player in 1960, and he benefited from the time away. Torre did not actively pursue managerial jobs because he thought that he might go back into broadcasting. But he didn't actively seek a job there either. He simply took his time, remained deliberate, and continued to remain open to all possibilities. When the Yankees extended an offer as the team's general manager, Torre declined due to the year around demands of the job. He trusted his instincts on what was best for him. And by waiting, Torre kept the door open for that one perfect opportunity to come his way—the Yankees' managerial job. As Buford notes and Torre demonstrated, patience is a key component of navigating halftime.

Buford also advises to "share the journey" during halftime, to be honest by asking the hard questions, to not fudge on the answers, and to have faith. Torre had gone through two divorces before he met his third wife, Ali. He and Ali had been married since 1987, and Ali had noticed that when she asked Torre to talk about their marriage and relationship, he would become aloof, guarded, and tense. As a result of Torre's reactions, Ali was proactive about seeking change. In doing so, she convinced Torre to attend a Life Success seminar. At the seminar, couples were asked to open up about their personal lives—not only to each other but to other couples. It was there that Ali learned for the first time that Torre's upbringing was dominated by a highly abusive father. Joe's father, Joe Sr., physically and emotionally abused his mother in front of him and his brothers and sisters. The fact that his father was a police detective made it all the more intimidating. The entire family felt afraid and trapped with no way out. It became so bad that Torre avoided his father altogether and learned the wrong approach to handle confrontation.

Until the seminar, which occurred in December 1995 while Torre was in "halftime," Torre had kept this trauma bottled up. As a result of his father's abuse, Torre did not deal well with conflict, but simply avoided it. By opening up at the seminar about the abuse, Torre developed a deeper understanding of himself and found an inner peace he did not have before.

Torre's learning to handle confrontation was also very timely as he prepared to interact with his new boss, Yankees' owner George Steinbrenner, and deal with the fallout from the prior Yankee manager Buck Showalter. Steinbrenner was famous for his private and public outbursts directed at players and managers. In the 23 years since he bought the Yankees, Steinbrenner had changed managers 21 times and regularly berated those managers in the press. Showalter, like Steinbrenner, had a style of management that favored keeping subordinates uncomfortable. As a result, the Yankee team that Torre inherited included very little trust of management (and of each other) among the players. Torre would have to navigate confrontations and conflict in multiple directions. And he would have to change the culture in the clubhouse to build trust. By opening up about a dark childhood secret, Torre became better equipped to do the job that had to be done with the Yankees. Had his wife, Ali, not introduced him to the seminar in the first place, his personal transformation would likely have not occurred. As Buford says, "Your second-half self is your genuine self, so be honest enough to discover it." Torre confronted this head-on, just weeks before he would go to spring training with his new team.

Torre's development as a person and a leader would continue throughout the Yankee dynasty. He would learn to trust his key players and enlist them to help convey key messages to the team. Torre would learn to not always "follow the book" in his managerial decision making, but instead to trust his gut. The Yankees would face a number of situations where their success was in the balance, and Torre's faith in himself and his team would be tested.

The year 1996 marked the first full major league season for shortstop Derek Jeter and pitcher Mariano Rivera. These two players would serve as the foundational players for the Yankees during the dynasty period and for years thereafter. Jeter was obviously a special player from the very beginning. He was humble, aware, and always in the moment. He seemed to understand better than anyone what it took to succeed as a team. Before spring training, when asked by the press who would be the team's shortstop, Torre announced that it would be Jeter. At the time Torre made the statement, there were two returning veterans who were candidates for the position and each was likely to be taken aback by Torre's statement. When asked by reporters about the statement, Jeter recognized the potential impact of Torre's statement on his teammates and said—tactfully correcting Torre—"I'm going to get an *opportunity* to play shortstop."

In April 1996, the team started to stage winning comebacks after being down early in games—usually after the sixth inning. Many were started or extended with hits from Jeter. Torre observed that the veteran players began to look for something special from Jeter when it was needed in a game. Jeter usually delivered. He hit .314 his rookie year and was unanimously voted for the American League's Rookie of the Year Award. He was even better in the playoffs during the run for the World Series championship—batting .388 over the 15 post season games. In the first regular season game, Jeter made an outstanding catch on a pop fly and hit a home run. When he hit the home run, there was no celebration, trying to get the ball, and so on as is common for rookies on all of their "firsts" in the majors. Jeter was too humble to attract attention in that way. Instead, he stayed focused and stuck to business. Jeter always seemed calm, poised, and kept it about the team.

It wasn't until deep in the season when Jeter made an obvious rookie mistake. He was thrown out trying to steal third base with two outs when he was already in scoring position and the Yankees lost the game by one run. Oftentimes when players make mistakes, they will come in off the field and avoid the manager—typically by looking for a seat on the other end of the dugout. When Jeter first came off the field after his base running mistake, he went directly toward where Torre was sitting and sat down *between* Torre and bench coach Don Zimmer. Jeter knew he had made a mistake, and that is how he chose to communicate that acknowledgment to his manager.

In the first playoff game in 1996, Jeter was hitless in his first three at bats and left a total of five men on base because of it. The Yankees lost the game, and the media tried to make something of it with Torre in the postgame press conference by questioning what he would do with Jeter. Before Torre could decide what to do, Jeter walked by Torre's office before he left the stadium, stuck his head in the door, and said, "Mr. T, tomorrow's the biggest game of your life. Make sure you get your rest." By addressing the tension proactively and with humor, Jeter again showed his awareness of the situation. He knew Torre would be concerned about how to handle it, and by taking the initiative, Jeter took the pressure off Torre. In Game 2, Jeter went three for five including a leadoff single in the 12th inning that led to him scoring the winning run. He then proceeded to hit .412 in the Series.

Jeter went on to be a 14-time All-Star. He finished his career with 3,465 hits, the sixth most in the history of baseball, and his career batting average was .310. Jeter led the Yankees to five World Series championships (one in 2009 in addition to the four in the dynasty period) and was elected to the Hall of Fame in his first year of eligibility with 99.7 percent of the vote. He played in at least 145 games in all but three of his full years with the Yankees. He is recognized as an all-time great on an all-time great franchise—just as much for his intangible winning qualities as his statistics.

Mariano Rivera was born, raised, and basically never left the small fishing village in Panama called Puerto Caimito until he signed his first contract with the Yankees. Rivera's family home was a two-room cement structure with a tin roof, no running water, and no electricity. Rivera had an eighth-grade education, worked on his father's fishing boat, and dreamed of being a mechanic. When he tried out for the Yankees in 1990, he was six-foot-one and weighed 150 pounds. He had to travel by bus for an hour and a half to get to Panama City and then had a 20-minute walk through a barrio to get to the stadium. He was dressed in an old, frayed shirt and had a hole in one of his shoes. He did not have a glove. He threw nine pitches for the Yankee scouts. His pitching was not as fast as some of the others trying out, but he showed excellent control. He was asked back for more tryouts, and the Yankees made the decision to sign him.

Rivera's first contract with the Yankees provided for a payment of $2,000, a new baseball glove and a pair of cleats. When he signed with the Yankees, Rivera did not speak English and knew little of the major leagues except that there was two of them—American and National—and that Rod Carew, who was also born in Panama, had played there. He did not know of either Babe Ruth or Hank Aaron.

Rivera pitched well in the minors and pitched even better after recovering from an elbow operation in 1992. When he was called up by the Yankees' big-league team in 1995, he had never seen a big-league stadium.

Before the 1996 season started, the Yankees had talks with the Seattle Mariners to trade Rivera. Rivera handled the situation much like the strong-minded Jeter, he viewed distractions as the enemy and did not allow any doubt to come into his mind. And as it turned out, Torre made the decision to keep Rivera. The team was immediately rewarded. In the first six weeks of 1996, Rivera's ERA was 0.83 with one stretch of 15 innings without allowing a hit. At the end of the regular season, he finished third in the Cy Young voting. In games where the Yankees led after six innings, due in large part to relief innings from Mariano Rivera, the team was 70-3.

Rivera had three main breakthrough points in his career. The first was in 1997 when he started the year struggling after having an extraordinary year in 1996. Torre addressed the issue directly with Rivera and told him to just be himself and not try and be perfect. By trying to do too much, Rivera had lost his confidence and his pitching had been affected.

Rivera took the constructive criticism to heart. From that point forward, Rivera decided to no longer think about what inning it was when he pitched. It was his form of controlling himself and not falling into the trap of doing too much. Rivera turned things around and completed 12 saves in a row. Rivera later credited Torre for establishing an environment where players believed in themselves but were totally devoid of arrogance.

The second breakthrough point also happened in 1997. When warming up before a game with teammate Ramiro Mendoza, Rivera's throws started breaking significantly to the right when they got to the target. The break was so sharp that Mendoza refused to continue to try and catch Rivera's pitches. Rivera had no idea why the ball was moving. He was trying to throw the same pitch each time. After two or three weeks of training, Rivera began to harness the new pitch. He learned that all it took was to put a little bit more pressure on the ball with his middle finger. The famous Rivera cutter had been born.

The third breakthrough took place in 1999. In a July game against the Braves, Rivera came in the game in the ninth inning in a classic save situation. Before the first Braves batter came up, Rivera had an overwhelming feeling of his own greatness and let himself feel the adulation from the crowd. But then he bounced a pitch to the Braves' Chipper Jones and walked him. Rivera then gave up three more hits including a game ending home run from Andruw Jones. He had not only lost the save but the game. He learned the lesson of resisting the temptation of getting too full of himself. Rivera gave up a grand total of one earned run over the remainder of the 1999 season, including streaks of 30 and two-thirds scoreless innings and 22 consecutive saves.

Over the course of his career, Rivera would be a 13-time All-Star and finished in the top three in the Cy Young voting four times, a remarkable feat for a relief pitcher. Rivera was later elected into the Hall of Fame by a unanimous vote of the eligible baseball writers, the only player in baseball history to be so selected. Rivera's greatness was not just due to his strong right arm, but his strong mind and his humility.

Joe Torre's transformation as a leader between his prior experience with the Mets, Braves, and Cardinals and his time with the Yankees was tangibly evident from the beginning. Torre had grown up with a great deal of tension in his life, and he had learned to better address it in the seminar he attended with his wife in December 1995. Like Jeter and Rivera, and maybe in a way that resonated with the entire team, Torre developed the strength of mind to not allow tension to creep in.

Over the course of his managerial career, Torre had also learned the importance of remaining calm with his team. He didn't yell at players, call them out in the press, or micromanage. Torre had personally felt the sting of being on the wrong side of such behavior. After a loss in a game in 1983, Braves owner Ted Turner screamed at Torre about some moves Torre had made during the game. Others with the Braves team were in the area and heard it. The next day, when Turner greeted him warmly and with a smile, Torre invited Turner into his office. In their private meeting, Torre very directly told Turner to never yell at him in front of others again. Turner never did, but the incident demonstrated such little professional respect that the relationship was never the same. Turner had lost the most essential element of a leadership relationship—trust. And Torre never forgot it. Over his Yankee years, there would be many interactions with players where Torre continually built trust with his players. Establishing trust also allowed him to more easily communicate with his players about needed areas of improvement. He spoke to them plainly, honestly, and in real time. Players learned this about Torre, and it brought the additional benefit of the players feeling comfortable coming forward to Torre when they had a problem.

The Yankees finished 92-70 in 1996 and won the American League's Eastern Division. After winning the League Division Series 3-1 over the Texas Rangers, the Yankees faced the Baltimore Orioles in the American League's championship series. During the 1996 season, Torre's oldest brother Rocco died. Torre was particularly close to Rocco, who had been instrumental in standing up to their abusive father and getting him out of the house, and was devastated by the loss. During the American League's Championship Series against the Orioles, Torre had a dream that he heard a knock on his hotel door, and when he opened it, Rocco was there with a peaceful contented look on his face. Torre interpreted the dream to mean that his team would beat Baltimore, and it left him with an even deeper peace and confidence that he could lead his team to victory. The Yankees did beat the Orioles four games to two. During an on-camera interview after the final win against Baltimore, Torre was asked about how Rocco's death affected him. He broke down in tears on national television.

The Yankees would play the Atlanta Braves in the 1996 World Series. The Braves had won the year before and came back as an even stronger team in 1996. The Braves won Game 1 in New York behind the pitching of John Smoltz. Greg Maddux would pitch Game 2. It was at this point, after a time of personal growth in the off-season and the further calming influence of his dream about Rocco, when Torre would show his new mettle with his owner. Steinbrenner stormed into Torre's office after the Game 1 loss and asked what Torre was going to do about it. Torre was seated at his desk and without looking up calmly told Steinbrenner not to expect to win Game 2 either, but that he [Torre] had confidence that the Yankees would prevail in the Series. Steinbrenner was disarmed, and Torre's confidence in his team would prove to be well founded.

The Yankees did lose Game 2 to the Braves and Greg Maddux, 4-0, and faced a must win in Game 3 which would be played in Atlanta. The Yankees went ahead 2-0, but Torre was about to have another opportunity to test his newfound ability to confront a challenging situation. The Braves had loaded the bases, and power hitter Fred McGriff was up. One big hit by McGriff, and with the Yankees down two games to none, the Series might be blown open. Torre faced the decision of whether to take out his starting pitcher David Cone, or leave him in to pitch to McGriff. Torre went out to the mound and got right in Cone's face and asked how he felt. Cone responded by stating he was okay and said, "I'll get this guy for you." Torre wanted to be sure he was properly reading his pitcher, "This game is very important. I've got to know the truth, so don't bullshit me." When Cone responded again in the affirmative, "I can get him," Torre not only heard the words but he saw the look in Cone's eyes. He knew that his pitcher was telling the truth. McGriff popped out and the Yankees would win the game 5-2.

Game 4 was one of the most dramatic games in World Series' history. The Yankees were behind 6-0 after five innings but as they had done so many times during the regular season, staged a comeback initiated by Derek Jeter. The Yankees chipped away at the lead, tied the game 6-6, and ultimately won 8-6 in 10 innings when the Braves dropped a pop fly. Torre recalled never once thinking negatively after the Yankees had lost the first two games to the Braves. Instead, he simply kept believing that good things would happen. His transformation as a calm leader who addressed confrontation positively and head on had translated into wins on the field—*especially* when it mattered most. The Yankees would go on to win the next two games, and the World Series, four games to two.

In 1997, the Yankees won 96 games but finished second to Baltimore in their Division. The Yankees made it to the playoffs as a wild card team but lost in the American League's Division Series three games to two to Cleveland. In 1998, the Yankees started slow—losing four of their first five games. Rumors began to circulate that Torre might be fired. Instead of avoiding the conflict as he might have done before, he faced it. He called a team meeting and prepared for it with carefully drafted notes. He was honest with the team about the fact that he did not sleep the night before but instead thought about the reasons why the team was not winning. He told the team that he had prepared detailed notes and then spoke from them—calmly, directly, and honestly. The team spoke about the reality that Torre could be fired. It worked. They won 64 of their next 80 games—a winning percentage of .800 over nearly half a season.

The Yankees won 114 games in the 1998 season, the third-highest season victory total in Major League Baseball's history. The statistics did not reflect great dominance by any one player, but instead demonstrated consistent success across the team. No one player hit over 30 home runs but 10 players hit at least 10. Six pitchers won 10 or more games. The balance and success carried on into the 1998 postseason where the Yankees won 9 of 11 games and swept the San Diego Padres in the World Series four games to none. In the past, Torre may not have addressed problems directly and in real time, instead hoping that things would work out. But during the 1998 Yankee season, the new Joe Torre stepped in and took action. His efforts led to a championship.

In March 1999 when Torre was diagnosed with prostate cancer, he immediately left the team to have surgery and asked his key leaders to deliver the news to the team. The surgery was successful and as soon as he could, Torre opened up to the team about his condition. Torre believed it deepened the trust the players had in him. On May 18, almost two months to the day after his surgery, Torre was back managing the team. The Yankees were not as dominant as the 1998 team but led the

American League's Eastern Division for most of the year and won the Division championship. In the 1999 postseason, the Yankees were again dominant, winning 9 of 11 postseason games, including a 4-0 sweep of the Atlanta Braves in the World Series.

In 2000, the Yankees won only 87, the fewest of any team that qualified for the postseason that year. It took five games to beat the Oakland Athletics in the American League's Division Series. The Yankees proceeded to win the American League's championship over the Seattle Mariners, and the World Series over their cross-town rival, the New York Mets.

The Yankees continued to win after the 2000 season, making the playoffs for the next seven years. They played in the World Series twice during that period but did not win either. It is difficult to pinpoint the exact reasons the team did not win again until years later (2009). As noted, it is simply very difficult to do so in this era. Jeter later said that he thought the teams after 2000 were not quite the same in terms of a team first attitude, that too many players became too selfish. He felt this one thing could have made the difference.

This Yankee dynasty teaches us much about leaders developing and continuing to evolve—even late in their careers. Leaders, like Torre, must sometimes first allow themselves to be personally transformed in ways that make them better equipped to address the challenges ahead. This transformation can be difficult, and even painful, but it can lead to a new level of success. Joe Torre teaches us that it is never too late to embrace positive change.

The Yankee dynasty also recognized the value of a young natural leader and allowed him to flourish early on in his career. Derek Jeter modeled the selfless and humble culture that Torre sought to promote, and the rest of the players—young and old—followed. Instead of selfishly standing in the way, the Yankee veteran players accepted Jeter as their leader. With constant humility and selflessness, and never arrogance, Jeter embraced the opportunity. He aided Torre in building trust and helped message that Torre had the players' backs, and that they had his.

The success of the Yankees also reveals the importance of a leader recognizing and properly handling potential teaching moments. For Torre, these usually took two minutes or less, and many were during a game when a big pitch or hit was necessary. The words he chose and the way he spoke mattered. His calmness resonated. He spoke honestly, even when the news was tough. He was authentic. Many of Torre's teaching moments allowed the recipient to make it through his own personal barriers. The bottom line is Torre helped his players find the best versions of themselves. And by doing so, he built the trust in the clubhouse and a dynasty on the field.

CHAPTER 11

Smartest Guy in the Room

Someone is sitting in the shade today because someone planted a tree a long time ago.

—Warren Buffett

The New York Yankees won the American League pennant each year from 1926 to 1928 and the World Series in 1927 and 1928. Each of the two World Series wins was by a 4-0 sweep. The 1927 team went 110-44 and is regarded by many historians as the best single-season team of all-time. The best known Yankees of this era were Babe Ruth, then in the prime of his great career, and Lou Gehrig, whose career was just starting to take off. But the story of this dynasty is much deeper than just the talents of Ruth, Gehrig, and the other individual players on this Yankees' team—it is really about the man who created this version of the Yankees and the foundation for the future he put in place. The components of this foundation could apply to any company, group, or team which is being built to last. The New York Yankees would become the most successful and most valuable franchise in the history of American professional sports.

Jacob Ruppert was the third-generation owner of a family beer brewing business which sold the "Knickerbocker" brand, and he had a passion for baseball. He played baseball when he was young and found that he was better as a leader of the team rather than a player. He was fastidious, well-dressed, and precise. Ruppert was careful with his words, and in spite of being born and raised in the United States, he would frequently speak with a thick German accent much like his grandfather who had immigrated to the United States from Bavaria. Ruppert got just close enough to Tammany Hall to advance his business interests and stayed far enough away to avoid scandal. Due in part to his Tammany connections, Ruppert served in the U.S. House of Representatives from 1898 to 1907 representing the "Silk Stocking District" in Manhattan.

By virtue of careful planning and a more robust sales model for his beer enterprise, Ruppert became wildly successful in business. He gave his full attention to his business interests and would do the same with his baseball team. Ruppert had been in the market for a team, but as of the beginning of 1914, he had thus far failed in his efforts. He had first sought to buy the Chicago Cubs and then the New York Giants. But unlike many others who had sought to purchase a major league team, and some who already owned one, Ruppert was free of legal problems and was the type of owner the league was looking for. As a result, he was given an opportunity to buy the Yankees. But he had competition from Tillinghast L'Hommedieu Huston, an engineer by trade who was a hero in the Spanish American War and then stayed in Cuba to make a fortune building harbors. Once Ruppert and Huston became aware of their mutual interest in the team, they got together and decided to go in as equal partners. In 1915, Ruppert and Huston purchased the Yankees for $460,000 and assumed $20,000 in existing debt obligations. It would prove to be a good investment.

The new owners took over the team in advance of the 1915 season. The Yankees they had purchased came with very little star power and had finished sixth in the American League in 1914. They fared little better on the field in the first few years under new ownership but did manage to improve by the end of the decade—finishing third in both 1919 and 1920. Due to better players and an increasingly better product on the field, fan interest increased, and attendance had tripled by 1920. Much to the chagrin of the New York Giants and their ownership, the Yankees began to outdraw them in their own stadium—the Polo Grounds where the Yankees were the Giants' tenant.

The new big attraction in baseball in 1919 was Babe Ruth the hitter, who was being transitioned by the Boston Red Sox from pitcher to an everyday player. Ruppert admired Ruth and saw what he could do for fan attendance. As a result, Ruppert made it his business to get to know Red Sox owner Harry Frazee who lived in New York, and Ruppert learned about Frazee's financial circumstances. Frazee was in the business of producing Broadway shows and was prone to wide swings in cash flow. Ruppert did not hide his interest in Ruth and made multiple offers for him to Frazee. Finally, in December 1919, Ruppert caught Frazee in a particularly difficult financial state due to low attendance at Red Sox games and poor box office revenues from his Broadway shows. Ruppert had also learned that Frazee's lenders were calling in loans. In dire straits for cash, Frazee agreed to sell Ruth to the Yankees for $100,000 plus a $300,000 personal loan from Ruppert which was secured by a mortgage on Boston's Fenway Park.

Prohibition had just started in 1920, and while Ruppert was able to refit his breweries to produce soda, glass bottles, and other products to offset some of the loss, the business still took a big hit. But by acquiring Ruth and building up the Yankees, Ruppert was able to effectively redirect his capital into a business that would become wildly profitable during the Prohibition era. The beauty of the Ruth acquisition was not just the fact that they were getting Ruth, but that part of the transaction involved Frazee owing a big debt to Ruppert. This gave Ruppert leverage over Frazee which Ruppert would use to the Yankees' advantage in acquiring Red Sox players in a series of future transactions. These players included Waite Hoyt, Joe Dugan, and Herb Pennock who would all become key components of the Yankees' dynasty of 1926 to 1928. Of the 24 players on the Yankees' 1923 roster, 11 were acquired from Boston.

Ruppert also did a superb job in selecting lieutenants to run the team. His first such choice was Miller Huggins, who was hired to be the Yankees' manager in 1918. When Ruppert met Huggins, he was taken by Huggins' knowledge of the nuances of baseball and his ability to organize and lead a team. Huggins was also cerebral and something of a loner, but he inspired the feeling in others that he knew the game backward and forward. He was known as a leader who did not criticize his players publicly, as did many of the managers of that era. Instead, Huggins did so privately away from the rest of the team. While Huggins was small in stature, he was tough, too, and did not get pushed around. This quality would serve him well in his many battles with Babe Ruth (whom—perhaps ironically given the battles that were to come—Huggins had urged Ruppert to acquire).

When Ruppert acquired Ruth, he sent Huggins to California to meet Ruth on a golf course to negotiate his salary. Huggins had a direct talk with Ruth—telling him it would be "all business." In spite of some back-talk from Ruth about wanting more money, Huggins got the job done and Ruth signed with the Yankees. From the very beginning, Huggins was firm with Ruth about his behavior and would have multiple battles with him over everything from his on-the-field behavior with umpires to his off-the-field behavior with alcohol and women. Huggins fined and suspended Ruth on multiple occasions. When Ruth complained about the discipline to Ruppert, Ruppert would support Huggins, not just privately, but in the newspapers.

After the completion of Ruth's first season with the Yankees in 1920, Ruppert approached Red Sox manager Ed Barrow and made him the Yankees' "business manager," a job now known as the general manager. Barrow was a large man who had been a boxer when he was young. He once went four rounds with the first heavyweight champion of gloved boxing, John L. Sullivan. Barrow's size and forcefulness made him uniquely qualified to handle Babe Ruth. Barrow had managed Ruth in Boston and stood up to him on numerous occasions, including once when Ruth challenged him to a fight in front of the team. Barrow had stood up to Ruth, and Ruth had backed down. At the urging of right fielder Harry Hooper, Burrow was the manager who made the decision to change Ruth from a starting pitcher to an everyday player.

Ruppert was one of the first owners to formally divide team leadership between on-the-field manager and off-the-field general manager. Barrow adjusted easily to his role off-the-field and was rarely seen on it. Most importantly, Ruppert made it clear that he, Barrow, and Huggins must always be aligned and on the same page. Barrow made as much clear directly to Huggins when Barrow was hired by clarifying their roles. Barrow was to provide the players and Huggins was to manage the team on the field.

But Ruppert did not stop with just signing great players and putting together a solid management team. In 1920, largely because they had been outdrawing the Giants, the Yankees were informed that the Giants were evicting them from the Polo Grounds following the 1922 season. Once again, Ruppert thought big—this time deciding to build a brand-new ballpark for the Yankees. But he first had to find the land on which to build it. He first set out to vet locations in Manhattan—but finally settled on a 10-acre plot in the Bronx, within sight of the Polo Grounds, which was owned by the William Waldorf Astor estate. Ruppert ponied up another $500,000 to $700,000 (depending on which report is to be believed) to acquire the land. Ruppert then set about to build the greatest sports facility in America at the time—Yankee Stadium.

Team owners Ruppert and Huston initially planned to use the stadium as part of New York City's bid to be selected as host for the 1928 Olympic Games. As a result, the initial construction included a quarter mile running track around the outside of the stadium. While the City did not get the bid for Olympics, the track remained, and thus became the first "warning track" around the outfield wall of a baseball stadium.

The largeness and beauty of the Stadium in the time it was built cannot be overstated. The building was the tallest in the area except for the Bronx County Courthouse. It was the first sports structure in North America with three tiers, and it could seat at least 60,000 fans. It was also one of the first "multipurpose" facilities. It would serve not only as the Yankees' home stadium but also as the home of the football New York Giants. It was the site of the 1958 NFL Championship game ("The Greatest Game Ever Played"), boxing championship matches, numerous concerts, and multiple Papal Masses. The press named it "The House that Ruth built." When the stadium was completed Ruppert said, "Yankee Stadium is a mistake—not mine, but the Giants'."

More importantly for the New York Yankees' team, the new stadium was a great place to work. It had large, comfortable "clubhouses" for players instead of cramped locker rooms. The dugouts included cushioned seats and wooden floors. The new electronic scoreboard was large enough to show the scoring in each inning of every game being played that day in both the American and National Leagues. There was a new office for the manager with room to meet with the players. A pay phone was installed in the Yankees' clubhouse—largely for use by Ruth. The new stadium had an elevator allowing easier access to the new team offices which were moved from downtown into the stadium itself. The stadium's signature design feature was an arched copper frieze that would line the top of the highest points of the stadium. The right field wall was a mere 290 ft. away—perfect for Babe Ruth's left-handed batting stroke to hit home runs. But the center field wall was 500 ft. away, which would favor teams (like the then current Yankees) who had pitchers with great control. Instead of naming the facility for himself, Ruppert insisted on the name "Yankee Stadium." Above all, the new facility reflected the values and sensibilities of Jacob Ruppert and was part of the new brand and a new image for the Yankees.

Ruppert's sensitivity to the conditions of his players also manifested itself in the team's travel accommodations. The Yankees stayed in only the finest hotels on the road. The trains were equipped with separate drawing rooms for executive leadership, Huggins and the coaches, and Ruth. No player slept in the "lower berths" which were loud and uncomfortable. All would have a more comfortable upper berth. Ruppert also enhanced the team's visual brand—the pinstripe uniform and the interlocking "NY" insignia on the jerseys. He reportedly chose the pinstripes because he thought they would make Ruth look slimmer. He furnished the team with three sets of uniforms instead of one—an effort to introduce a clean and neat look to his team. Major league uniforms of the day appeared rumpled and were often dirty. Each of the Yankees' players would have three sets of uniforms— and the team kept them clean and pressed—providing a neater and cleaner look. Ruppert also made it clear that there would be no facial hair allowed other than trimmed moustaches, a standard that remained until the 1970s. For decades to come, players understood what it meant to be a New York Yankee.

Co-owner Huston was out of the country when Ruppert hired Huggins. Huston was not supportive of the new manager and went public with his concerns. He was rumored to be a drinking partner of Ruth's and undercut Ruppert's, Barrow's, and Huggins' efforts to reign in their top star by telling Ruth he would take care of Ruth's fines. Following the second straight Yankees' World Series loss to the Giants in 1922, Huston addressed the press in a bar at the Commodore Hotel. While dramatically wiping several drinking glasses off a table, Huston loudly proclaimed that Huggins was done as the Yankees' manager. Upon learning of this, Ruppert had had enough. He waited until Huston finished his work supervising the construction of the stadium and simply bought out Huston's interest in the team. The reports of the amount paid by Ruppert varied between $1.25 and $1.5 million. Any figure in this range represented an excellent return on Huston's 1915 investment of $230,000. The moment the deal with Huston was signed, Ruppert sent out a telegram to the team stating, "I am now the sole owner of the Yankees. Miller Huggins is my manager. Jacob Ruppert." Said Ed Barrow, "Peace came to the Yankees after that." The three leaders—Ruppert, Barrow, and Huggins—were now perfectly (and comfortably) aligned.

The Yankees would win the World Series in 1923, but they did not get back into the World Series until 1926, the first year of the dynasty. In 1924, the Yankees finished second to the Washington Senators who won their only World Series that year. Ruth was spectacular, hitting .378 with 46 home runs and 124 runs batted in. But as he aged and failed to take care of himself, his weight and overall poor health became increasingly problematic. This played out in dramatic fashion over the 1925 season.

When Ruth went on his annual trip to Hot Springs, Arkansas in advance of the Yankees' 1925 spring training, he weighed in at 256 pounds—at least 30 pounds over his optimal playing weight. Instead of getting into shape, he mostly drank and chased women. He also got sick with an upper respiratory infection, something that seemed to happen annually to Ruth. When he arrived at spring training in Florida, Ruth said he had a temperature of "one hundred and five and eight-fifths." Following spring training, the team took its regular trip north to New York City, stopping along the way to play exhibition games. Somewhere around Ashville, North Carolina, Ruth became feverish and started to experience body aches. As he exited the train, he collapsed. He recovered temporarily but missed the train to New York and a rumor was started that he was dead.

By the time he did arrive in New York, he was sick again—vomiting continually and then passing out in the men's room, hitting his head. There has been much debate over the years on the root cause of his illness. Some said it was venereal disease. Others have said he ate too many hot dogs. When finally diagnosed, it was determined that Ruth was suffering from an intestinal abscess which was directly caused by the carelessness in what, and how much, he ate and drank. It was referred to in the newspapers as "The bellyache heard around the world." On April 17, 1925, Ruth had surgery and would remain hospitalized through May 26. When released, he still looked sickly and weak; Ruppert and Barrow suggested he take more time off. Ruth refused and demanded to play but hit only .250 over June and July with few home runs. He began to eat and drink again in excess and gained back the weight he lost during his hospitalization. By August, Ruth was hitting so poorly that Huggins sent in a pinch hitter for him. At least one writer who covered the team thought Ruth would never again be the superstar he was between 1919 and 1924.

Ruth's relationship with Huggins had never been good and it worsened in 1925. In August, it came to a head. After disobeying curfew and twice disobeying Huggins' orders (on whether to sacrifice a runner or hit away) during a game, action was clearly necessary. Huggins suspended Ruth and fined him $5,000. Ruth responded with attitude and back talk; Huggins ordered him to leave the premises. Ruth tried without success to appeal to Ruppert and then to Commissioner Landis. He publicly berated Huggins and said he wouldn't play for the Yankees if Huggins remained as the manager. Ruppert responded in the press, "I'm behind Huggins to the limit. There will be no remission of the fine, and the suspension will last as long as Huggins wants it to last." When asked about Ruth's statement that he wouldn't play for the Yankees if Huggins remained the manager, Ruppert was clear: "Huggins will be the manager as long as he wants to be the manager."

Ruth was skewered by the press—for his conduct, his drinking, and his chronic infidelity. He was carrying on a public relationship with an artist's model named Claire Hodgson, and became separated from his wife Helen, who had a nervous breakdown. When Ruth visited her in the hospital, he invited the press in with him. Then, Ruth broke down, sobbing. Photos of the scene appeared in the papers. Ruth tried to apologize to Huggins, but Huggins wouldn't meet with him. When Ruth was finally able to see Huggins, he asked if he could play. Huggins responded, "No, sir." When Ruth asked if he could practice, Huggins gave him the same response. Ruth continued to come back to the stadium over the coming days and each time Huggins gave him the same answers. Finally, when Huggins agreed to hear out the then contrite Ruth, Huggins made him apologize in front of the entire team. After nine days of very tough love from a unified Yankees' leadership team, Ruth was finally allowed back on the team. Ruth would finally step in line.

Ruth's new attitude became evident during the off-season. He hired a personal trainer, Artie McGovern, who famously worked Ruth into shape. He turned down an exhibition tour that would have paid him $25,000. When he reported to spring training in 1926, he weighed 212 pounds—44 pounds lighter than he had been the prior season. But for the coordinated discipline meted out by the Yankees in the 1925 season, it is very possible that Ruth's physical transformation would not have occurred. And absent a healthy Ruth, the Yankees' seasons to follow would have likely been more like 1925 than as they did in the 1926 to 1928 dynasty.

As the 1925 season ended, Ruppert had his leadership team in place, had built the team's new facility, and had finally gotten Ruth's attention. But like many of the great dynasties, the Finley A's of the 1970s, Big Red Machine of the 1970s, and the Connie Mack A's, the Yankees had to continue to tinker with their team to get to the top. Part of the team was already in place. Ruth and left-fielder Bob Meusel had been in place since 1921. In 1923, Ruppert continued to cash in on his continuing influence over Boston owner Harry Frazee by acquiring third baseman Joe Dugan and the team's headline starting pitchers Waite Hoyt and Herb Pennock. The rest of the dynasty team would be built piece by piece over the next few years—mainly due to Paul Krichell and the Yankees' scouting group. These players included pitcher George Pipgrass, center fielder Earle Combs, shortstop Mark Koenig, and second baseman Tony Lazzeri. Koenig and Lazzeri were acquired for the 1926 season when the dynasty began. Pitcher Urban Shocker, originally with the Yankees' farm system, would be acquired back from the St. Louis Browns. And Krichell found the great Lou Gehrig, who was at the time playing at Columbia University, and convinced him to sign with the Yankees.

After the disastrous 1925 season and the organization's discipline of Ruth, the Yankees came back with a vengeance in 1926 to launch their dynasty. Ruth hit for an average of .378 and led the league in home runs (47) and runs batted in (146). Ruth also showed a new discipline at the plate—leading the league with 144 walks. Gehrig began to show his offensive prowess by hitting 47 doubles and a remarkable 20 triples. After having finished seventh the season before, the Yankees won the American League pennant in 1926. In the World Series, Ruth broke a World Series record by hitting three home runs in one game and a record four overall. And while the team would lose the Series in seven games to the St. Louis Cardinals (the last out coming on Ruth's unsuccessful attempt to steal second base), the Yankees were becoming the dominant team that Ruppert envisioned.

Lost in all the drama over Ruth was the launch of the career of Lou Gehrig. By the 1927 season, Gehrig was on his way to his record consecutive game streak of 2,130. He lived at home with his parents, rarely drank, and followed the team rules. He was as shy as Ruth was loud, as manageable as Ruth had been incorrigible, as steady as Ruth was unpredictable, and as clean living as Ruth was hedonistic. Gehrig played an excellent first base. While his hitting statistics would rival Ruth's, the way he swung the bat—hitting down on the ball resulting line drives— was the opposite of Ruth's uppercut swing which led to towering fly balls. But in spite of their differences, they were together the greatest back-to-back power hitters in MLB history. On any credible all-time best starting nine players list, Ruth is in the outfield and Gehrig is at first base.

The 1927 version of the Yankees was the best team of that dynasty. Like many of the other dynasty teams, the Yankees came from behind to win many of their games. Their home games typically started at 3:30 in the afternoon and the game was typically in the seventh or eighth inning by 5:00—the time the team often caught fire —earning them the nickname "Five O'clock Lightning." Five o'clock coincided with the end of the workday and was marked by loud horns from local factories. The horns inspired the Yankees and caused dread in the hearts of opposing pitchers. The Yankees were in first place in the American League from opening day until the end of the season, finishing 110-44, 19 games ahead of Connie Mack's Philadelphia A's. Ruth and Gehrig competed for the home run title over the course of the year. Ruth famously won with 60 to Gehrig's 47. Together, they hit almost 25 percent of the home runs hit in the entire American League. Yankees' second baseman Tony Lazzeri finished third in the AL with 18. Center fielder Earle Combs led the American League with 231 hits and 23 triples. The team as a whole scored 975 runs, averaged 10.6 hits per game and a team batting average of .307. Individual batting averages were off the charts: Gehrig .373, Combs .356, Meusel .337, Lazzeri .309, and Ruth .356. After wins, the team would sing "Roll out the Barrel" and "The Sidewalks of New York" as they made their way to the clubhouse. The Yankees demolished the Pittsburgh Pirates in the World Series by sweeping them in four games.

The 1928 team was also dominant, winning 101 games and again winning the World Series by sweep, this time over the St. Louis Cardinals (avenging their loss in 1926). Ruth hit 54 home runs and tied with Gehrig for first in the American League in runs batted in, each hitting

142. In the World Series sweep, Gehrig hit .545 and Ruth .625. Between them, they hit seven home runs and knocked in 13 runs. Ruppert doubled down on the Yankees' dominance by investing another $400,000 in Yankee Stadium—increasing capacity from 60,000 to 72,000.

One of the ingredients of the success of this Yankees' dynasty is that each player had a clearly defined role that did not change. Earl Combs batted first and was expected to get on base which he did as well as anyone. Shortstop Mark Koenig batted second and was charged with moving Combs over and putting him in scoring position for Ruth and Gehrig who batted third and fourth in the lineup. Gehrig and Ruth were nearly always allowed to "hit away," as was the fifth batter Bob Meusel. Meusel would also trade outfield positions with Ruth depending on the amount of ground to cover in different ballparks—Meusel taking the larger area to give Ruth's legs a rest. Second baseman Tony Lazzeri batted sixth, played a great second base, and hit for average and power. Together, the six became known as "Murderers' Row."

There were other roles, some based more on superstition than talent. Huggins would only deliver messages to the dugout via reserve third baseman Mike Gazella. Ruth put a notch in his bat after each home run. Shocker would not allow anyone to touch his glove on days he pitched. Joe Dugan never threw the ball back to the pitcher during infield practice. Even bat boy Eddie Bennett got in on the act. Bennett was disabled and very short of stature because of a childhood spinal injury and lost both his parents in the 1918 Flu Pandemic. He was handpicked by Jacob Ruppert. Pitcher Wilcy Moore required that Bennett catch his first warm-up pitch. And before games, Bennet would play catch with Ruth. The two would throw the ball back and forth along the third base line, and Ruth would start throwing the ball progressively higher over Bennett's head causing him to run to get it each time. The crowd would howl.

The culture was very businesslike. Players had to check in at the stadium at 10:00 in the morning for the 3:30 games. Huggins would school players individually in his office about the finer points of the game. The team lineup would stay the same each game except for substitutions at a given position. The order was not changed. The team was expected to run out on the field right after the third out of an inning and typically would be standing on the dugout steps ready to go at that very moment. There does not appear to have been any fights on the field in 1927, and only one player (Dugan) was thrown out of a game. Waite Hoyt believed that the Yankees' togetherness and professionalism in this era was carried forward to later Yankees' teams. And it was no coincidence that these were they very qualities exhibited by their owner Jacob Ruppert.

This Yankees' dynasty should have run longer but ran directly into Connie Mack's second Philadelphia A's dynasty. In the years from 1929 to 1931, the Yankees finished 18, 16, and 13.5 games behind the A's. Ruth continued to put up big offensive numbers through the 1932 season when the Yankees again won the World Series. But then Ruth began to fade, and the Yankees quickly dispatched him. Ruth begged Ruppert to manage the Yankees after the untimely death of Miller Huggins in 1929 and thereafter. But Ruppert would not have it, uttering his famous inquiry: "How can Ruth manage a team when he can't even manage himself?" Huggins died late in the 1929 season due to chronic illness which was probably tied to his stress level. Gehrig would play until 1939 and would die of ALS in 1941. Ruppert died in 1939 and in a trust designated Barrow as the team's president. Seven players from the Yankees' dynasty team plus Huggins, Barrow, and Ruppert are now in the Hall of Fame.

While the Yankees of this era typically harken back black and white images of Ruth and Gehrig, it is Jacob Ruppert who was primarily responsible for the team's success, and there is much to learn from the manner in which he purchased and ran the franchise. First, Ruppert made extraordinarily wise decisions in hiring the team's leaders and key players. In Jim Collins' book *Good to Great*, he notes that in studying the great companies, they first "got the right people on the bus." This, of course, emphasizes the importance of hiring—especially early on—in an organization or management tenure. Ruppert made good decisions with his two key leaders, Barrow and Huggins, and his best player Ruth—though he went through some rough patches. His partnership with Huston also served the organization well during the first eight years of their ownership (and especially during the construction of Yankee Stadium), but when a change was required, Ruppert made it by buying out Huston. Ruppert's judgment in hiring and guiding other leaders was one of his many outstanding traits as a leader.

Ruppert then coordinated his management team—himself, General Manager Ed Barrow, and Manager Miller Huggins such that they would always be on the same page. Following Huston's exit, the players knew that they could not go around any one of the three to get more favorable treatment from another. Ruppert not only supported the other two internally but also proclaimed his support publicly. When Huggins was struggling with Ruth or was beginning to hear it from the fans, Ruppert often would proactively support him in a clear and unqualified way. When Barrow was hired, he immediately threw his support behind Huggins and never wavered.

Ruppert could mete out firm discipline when necessary. Ruth was one of the most difficult discipline problems in the history of baseball. Ruppert, Barrow, and Huggins tried everything, but Ruth would not amend his ways. It finally took a lengthy suspension, a big fine, and very direct talk. After a dismal season, Ruth finally saw the light and took it upon himself to get in shape and turn things around. The Yankees' leadership was finally able to get the most important member of the team to change his total approach to the game. Quite clearly, the Yankees would not have reached the heights they reached but for their leaders digging in and not relenting in their discipline of Ruth.

Ruppert delegated authority and then allowed his lieutenants to delegate. When Ruppert hired Huggins, he repeatedly stated his support. When Ruppert hired Barrow, he gave like support and then Barrow stated his support for Huggins, too. Barrow was free to make decisions related to the running of the team and players that the Yankees acquired. And Huggins was given the authority to make decisions on the field. When Barrow saw a problem with Ruppert being too involved in the clubhouse, he felt comfortable enough to say as much to Ruppert, and Ruppert backed off. Each man had the right to speak up if he felt something needed to change, and the others listened.

Ruppert also created a great place to work. Ruppert understood the importance of the team's place of work and spent the dollars it took to build Yankee Stadium with the finest of fields, clubhouses, and dugouts. The expenditure at the time was difficult for him because his main revenue stream—the brewing of beer—had been leveled by Prohibition. But

Ruppert saw the opportunity, found the funding, and built the stadium. The team responded by winning the World Series in the year it was built and by reaching the World Series in five of the first six years of the stadium's existence.

Ruppert further created a team brand with not only the uniforms and logo but also with a way of conducting business that was unique to the Yankees. The professionalism Ruppert displayed ultimately became the culture of his team. He created a certain look and feel of what it was to be a Yankee. The players had pride in themselves individually, and as a group. Even Ruth, for the most part, behaved like a professional when he was on the field. Ultimately, there became a mystique, or even magic, that accompanied the Yankees for decades. This all began with Ruppert.

Ruppert, Barrow, and Huggins also showed innovation and established workable systems that the team repeated every day. The same lineup, in the same order, was put out on the field in most games. Players were expected to be at the stadium at the same time each day. The team was expected to be ready to run out on the field from the dugout at the same time. Everyone on the team, all the way down to the team's batboy, knew their roles. And they repeated them over and over and over. Systems and continuity are important to any team or group, and the Yankees reflected this.

Even after becoming successful, Ruppert continued to work to find the right mix of players. It took the completion of Murderers' Row by adding Gehrig, Combs, Koenig, and Lazzeri to Ruth and Meusel to do it. Ruppert used (some would say exploited) Red Sox owner Harry Frazee after becoming his major creditor because of the loan Ruppert gave Frazee in order to acquire Ruth. Ruppert clearly used that influence in future trades. Ruth, Dugan, Hoyt, and Pennock—all key members of the dynasty team—were former Red Sox. Ruppert could have remained very good and continued to sell tickets and make a profit after acquiring Ruth. Instead, he continued to relentlessly target excellence; the team improved and reached the pinnacle of baseball success.

And like all the dynasty teams, the Yankees' players got to the point where they felt a kind of confidence—a high level of certainty that they would win. It was not braggadocio or even cockiness; they simply knew when they stepped on the field that things would go their way. This feeling does not come by accident. It is a culmination of the many fundamentals established by the leaders of the team. The personal qualities that made the New York Yankees phenomenal include sound judgment, great insight into people, smart hiring decisions (and correcting those that turned out to be not so smart), an aligned leadership team, firm discipline when necessary to correct bad behavior, a brand, an image, a great place to work, and sound business systems consistently applied. The New York Yankees were designed, planned, and carefully cultivated by the greatest executive leader of his time—and perhaps in the history of baseball—the smartest guy in the room, Jacob Ruppert.

Afterword

A Life Well Lived

On March 25, 2021, as the manuscript for this book was being finalized, Bobby Brown died. He was 96 years old. It had been over 26 years since he had been President of the American League, 36 years since he left his cardiology practice, and 68 years after he had retired as a Major League Baseball player.

Five days later, Brown's memorial service was held at Christ Chapel Bible Church in Fort Worth, Texas. I made the trip up to Fort Worth from my home in Houston. I chose to drive rather than fly to have more time to ponder the life of this great man and the impact he had on my life. After over 30 years of studying professional baseball history, I had concluded that Bobby Brown was one of my favorite players. But why? He was not a Hall of Famer, played in parts of only seven years in the big leagues, was never an all-star, and I was never a big Yankee fan.

But as I learned more about the game and its history, I ran across more and more information about Brown's career and life. Much of this is in Chapter 1 of this book, but some of it bears repeating. While his regular-season statistics were unremarkable, his star shined in the World Series. He played in four separate Fall Classics, each of which Yankees won. His batting average across the 17 games spanning those four World Series was .439, second all-time among players in World Series games with over 40 plate appearances. He trails only David "Big Papi" Ortiz of the Boston Red Sox.

Brown did not just hit for average in these games, but he hit with power—including five doubles and three triples—and to this day, he has the fifth highest slugging percentage in World Series history, behind only Ortiz, Reggie Jackson, Lou Gehrig, and Babe Ruth. When it mattered most, Bobby Brown brought his very best.

Perhaps, even more impressive than his World Series statistics was what he accomplished before, during, and after his professional baseball career. Brown served in both the Navy and the Army, and due to his service obligations, attended two colleges—UCLA and Stanford—and then Tulane Medical School. He played baseball at all three and had season batting averages of .463 at Stanford in 1943, .444 at UCLA in 1944, and with eligibility remaining when he entered medical school, .500 at Tulane in 1945. He is now in the sports hall of fame at each university.

Brown retired from baseball mid-season in 1954 at age 29 to serve his medical residency. After completing it, he established a cardiology practice in Fort Worth, where he served heart patients for 25 years. Brown left his cardiology practice in 1984 upon being asked to serve as the President of the American League for 10 years until his retirement in 1994.

Despite his other-worldly life accomplishments, I always felt there was even more to this man. In December 2019, I learned part of the rest of the story. I was able to contact the Brown family through Dallas journalist Leslie Minora, who herself has written on Brown. She introduced me to Brown's daughters Beverley Dale and Kaydee Bailey. I contacted them, and they could not have been more helpful and gracious. They arranged for me to meet with Dr. Brown at his home in Fort Worth. In doing so, they carefully protected his privacy and noted that one of the conditions for interviewing Brown was that my book "not be about him." I gladly (but now somewhat regrettably) agreed.

On December 18, 2019, I was led into the living room of the great Bobby Brown and was invited to sit down on his couch a few feet from where he sat in his recliner. He was dressed sharply in a purple sweater over a bright white t-shirt and corduroy slacks. He stood to greet me with a firm handshake and looked me solidly in the eye. He did not look anywhere close to his age, which was 95 at the time.

I immediately felt a unique presence I had not experienced before, even when meeting other great athletes, business executives, and heads of state. There was a steadiness about him, a kind of certainty, and confidence. But he was also very kind to me, soft-spoken, and very gracious like his daughters. He had a quick wit. And he quickly confirmed what I had read many times before: he had unflinching integrity.

I was immediately struck that he did not want to talk about himself but was happy to speak of others. Brown was a "top prospect" coming out of high school in today's parlance and may have been the top high school player in the nation for at least his senior year. When I asked him about his extraordinary play in high school, he gave credit to his team, noting that they were so good that they even beat the University of California in an exhibition game. He went out of his way to mention a high school teammate named Sheehan, a star pitcher "who almost never lost" and later served and died in World War II. Arthur Edmunt Sheehan, Jr. served as a Staff Sergeant Waist Gunner in the U.S. Army Air Corps, 360th Bomber Squadron, 303rd Bomber Group; and was killed in action on September 28, 1944, over Suppingen, Germany.

When I asked Brown about his many workouts (at least five) with major league teams while still in high school, he wanted to talk about his experience with the Cincinnati Reds and, in particular, two Reds' veterans, Jimmy Gleason and Bobby Mattick. They helped a 16-year-old Brown feel comfortable on a trip to Chicago with a major league team to play at Wrigley Field.

I believe Brown wanted Staff Sergeant Sheehan, shortstop Mattick, and outfielder Gleason recognized in print, and I am honored to oblige.

Brown emphasized the culture of the great Yankee teams on which he played. "The Yankees looked for players who could meld with the team as a whole," he said, "and they scouted players who knew how to play in big games." There were no cliques. Bad guys were not kept. I do not doubt that the presence of Bobby Brown enhanced this kind of culture with the Yankees and modeled the same in each other organization he served throughout his long life.

He spoke of the professionalism in the Yankee culture, which did not have to be enforced by ownership or even manager Casey Stengel. Veteran players Joe DiMaggio, Yogi Berra, Phil Rizzuto, and Tommy Henrich took care of that themselves—directly and in real time. The veterans taught young players how to act and dress. There was no bat flipping, trash-talking, or even taunting opposing players or umpires from the bench. "If you practiced that," said Brown, "we can get you back to Newark." The Yankees were not there to put on a show, but to win ballgames.

In response to questions about his first contract that at the time equaled the highest bonus ever paid a young ballplayer, Brown credited his father's negotiating skills and described that process. And when "bonus baby" Brown arrived to play with the Yankees, he created such instant respect that he didn't receive the hazing and mistreatment that other "bonus babies" received in those times.

He told me stories about Joe DiMaggio, Mickey Mantle, and Yogi Berra. His paths crossed many times with Jackie Robinson, including when they attended UCLA at the same time. He spoke about his long-time friend and Yankee teammate Jerry Coleman who flew multiple missions as a fighter pilot in the Korean conflict and served as a dive bomber at Guadalcanal. He noted that infielder Gil McDougald was named an all-star at every position in the infield and then adopted multiple foster children throughout his life. I gave Brown a copy of David Halberstam's book, *1949*, which provides excellent historical detail on Brown's Yankee teams. In response, Brown went out of his way to express his sorrow that Halberstam was killed in a car accident in California in 2007.

He attributed his extraordinary hitting in World Series games to "waiting for a good ball to hit and swinging as hard as he could," He said he never felt pressure during those games. He went out of his way to compliment Don Newcombe and Roy Campanella, who played for the Dodger teams who the Yankees consistently beat in each World Series played during Brown's career. He showed me a photo of a triple he hit in the World Series to point out all the *others* in the photo who later made the Hall of Fame. When I asked him to describe his major league career, he quickly replied, "Pretty damn good for a medical student."

He showed me what the Brown family refers to as "Dad's wall"—a collection of photos of Brown with presidents, generals, star athletes, star entertainers, and others. He was particularly fond of Bill White, President of the National League at the same time Brown was President of the American League. He noted that they still exchange Christmas cards. Many of the photos showed Brown with his late wife, Sara. While tearing up, Brown described her as "perfect" and noted that they only had two arguments in 61 years. One was on a golf course, after which Brown quit playing golf.

As I departed from Brown's home, I felt blessed by the experience and, in general, much better than when I arrived. I think Bobby Brown had that effect on many people.

At Brown's memorial service, four men eulogized him, long-time friend and baseball historian Talmage Boston, church pastor Dr. Ted

Kitchens, Brown's son-in-law Bill Bailey, and Brown's son Pete Brown. "Amazing Grace" was played. Brown's survivors included his three children and their spouses, 10 grandchildren and their spouses, and 14 great grandchildren, all of whom were at the service. Brown had clearly succeeded as the patriarch of a great and close-knit family.

Brown's daughters had previously introduced me to Talmage Boston, who, much like myself, is a lawyer who's passionate about baseball. Like everyone else I met associated with Bobby Brown, Boston was kind to me and helpful with this project. Boston knew Brown 40 years and kicked off his eulogy by noting that his relationship with Bobby Brown was the seed that inspired him to write about baseball history. I understand exactly how he feels.

Boston is probably the foremost authority among historians on the history of Brown's remarkable life, and he shared much of that during his remarks. He noted that Brown was the first person to play a full major league schedule of games in a season while attending medical school in the off-season. This kept Brown from attending spring training for any of the seasons in which he played. Boston noted that when Brown was asked if he ever thought about how much better he could have been had he attended spring training, Brown consistently answered, "I think about it daily."

Boston also summarized Brown's remarkable military service in Korea, which interrupted his baseball career for 19 months—right in the middle of his prime. He began as a battalion surgeon near the front lines, and his service then made Brown the only big-league ballplayer to serve in America's ground forces in that war. Boston captivated those at the service with a story of Brown's life on October 1, 1952:

> Put yourself in Bobby's shoes ... His Yankee teammates were playing in the first game of the 1952 World Series, which of course they went on to win ... . That day Bobby said he was "trudging up a harbor platform for a quarter of a mile with everything he owned on his back going into Korea" and he had just learned that Sara had delivered their first child Pete in Dallas, while Bobby was flying over the Pacific. The war then caused him to miss the entire 1953 season and the World Series that year, which the Yankees won again.

Boston also spoke of Brown's career as a cardiologist for over 25 years and noted the crucial similarity between being a great big-league hitter and a great cardiologist: "Both require the practitioner to deal with and conquer fear." He then described the terror that must have gripped batters, who, without a batting helmet, stepped up to the plate against Bob Feller and other great fastball pitchers of the day, and the fact that the hitter couldn't think about the danger associated with getting hit in the head. In comparing baseball to cardiology, Boston provided a quote from Brown to the *New York Times*: "Cardiology cases all involve a certain amount of fear. There's lots of trauma and almost every heart case has significant problems. The patient depends on you, and often there's an emergency, and you've got to be really on." "Bobby *overcame all fear*" noted Boston, "and was *really on* for his Yankee teammates in ballgames *and* his heart patients in Fort Worth."

Boston then gave many examples of Brown's contributions as President of the American League, which included providing guidance on defining the strike zone and driving the ban on smokeless tobacco from the minor leagues. While President, Brown served under four commissioners: Peter Ueberroth, Bart Giamatti, Fay Vincent, and Bud Selig. Brown also had a friendly tennis rivalry with President George H.W. Bush. As Boston noted, Brown was born to hit fast-moving balls.

The eulogy from Dr. Kitchens included the story of how Brown came to his religious faith through his relationship with his wife and later in life, he participated in many "Q & A" sessions with Dr. Kitchens sitting on a stool near the pulpit during Sunday church services. Before Brown began attending the church, he heard Dr. Kitchens do a series on the Book of Revelation and felt the need to call Kitchens to ask his approval to attend church on those days. Kitchens noted this was the first time, and the last, anyone "asked permission" to come to see him preach.

Dr. Brown's son Pete and son-in-law Bill Bailey each gave moving presentations from the perspective of being members of the Brown family, including a story from Pete Brown regarding an exchange they had late in Bobby Brown's life. Son Pete had to tell his father that he was no longer fit to drive. Bobby agreed and handed over his keys. A few weeks later, father and son were talking on the phone, and Bobby mentioned he was going to the dentist. When Pete inquired how his father was going to get to the dentist without a car, Bobby responded by telling him that the dentist was going to pick *him* up and take him to the appointment. So went the life of Bobby Brown.

Much like the most extraordinary and unique leaders in organizations today, Bobby Brown wasn't just loved; he was revered. Very few ever attain this status. We don't often experience leaders like this, but we're certain of their greatness when we do. Brown's life teaches us about what we should look for in our best leaders: unflinching integrity, humility, and consistent kindness. His life history also shows one can serve as this type of leader from any level within an organization, including as a platooning third baseman or a low-ranking officer in the military. Being the President or CEO is not required.

Other key characteristics of Brown empowered him to succeed in many different areas of life: the ability to face and navigate fear and danger, to stay calm under pressure, and to connect and inspire all who come in contact with him—even rookie authors. Talmage Boston noted that Brown lived his life in a way that "he always did the right thing, even when no one was looking." To me, Brown was one of the greatest of the Greatest Generation. Dr. Kitchens summed it up best when he called Brown's time on earth "a life well lived."

Everyone needs a Bobby Brown in their lives and their careers. I was with him for less than one day, very late in his life, yet I somehow felt his continued encouragement as I powered through this project. I felt a small sense of what it must have felt like to be his teammate facing a tough at-bat, a soldier on the front lines in need of life-saving surgery, a heart patient facing a life or death operation, or one of Brown's family or friends going through a tough time. Though I was only with him in person for a regrettably brief time, I could not have written this book without him. His extraordinary ability to lift up others—even when they didn't know he was doing it—is, I believe, his most impressive quality. And *that* particular quality did not disappear with his death. It survives in the hearts and minds of the people who knew him. I was one of the lucky ones who did.

About the Author

Ted Meyer is a lawyer based in Houston, Texas, who represents companies of all sizes nationwide as well as individual executives in matters relating to employment and organizational excellence. He has been rated by Chambers, Best Lawyers, and Super Lawyers for nearly 20 years and has been Board Certified in Labor and Employment Law by the Texas Board of Legal Specialization since 1997. He has counseled and advised some of the largest employers in the world on how to improve their organizations and has done similar work representing smaller teams and groups including churches and nonprofit organizations. Ted is also a self-taught baseball historian with a deep passion and respect for the history of the game and the racial integration of it. Ted has pursued both passions side by side for over 30 years.

References

2020. "How Does Diversity Affect the Performance of Sports Teams?" at OnlineMasters.ohio.edu/blog/

2020 Websites: Alamac.com; History.com; Taxbrackets.org; ThePeopleHistory.com; TreasuryDirect.gov; Weather.gov; BleacherReport.com; thebaseballscholar.com; sbnation.com.

Alexander, C. 1991. *Our Game: An American Baseball History.* New York, NY: MJF Books.

Amore, D. 2018. *A Franchise On the Rise: The First Twenty Years of the New York Yankees.* New York, NY. Sports Publishing.

Anderson, S., and S. Burick. 1978. *The Main Spark.* New York, NY: Doubleday & Company, Inc.

Anicetti, D. May 05, 2020. "Top 20 Major League Baseball Teams of All-Time." Available at www.fueledbysports.com

Aranoff, J. 2009. *Going Going . . . Caught!: Baseball's Great Outfield Catches as Described by Those Who Saw Them, 1887–1964.* Jefferson, NC: McFarland & Company, Inc.

Armour, M. 2014. *The Great Eight.* Lincoln, NE: University of Nebraska Press, Lincoln Press and Society for American Baseball Research.

Armour, M. (n.d.). *Baseball Integration 1947–1986.* Society for American Baseball Research. Retrieved 2020, from https://sabr.org.

Armour, M., and Daniel, L. 2003. *Paths to Glory.* Dulles, VA: Brassey's.

Baker, K., and J. Tracy. (n.d.). "Special Report: War, Fever and Baseball in 1918." Retrieved 2020, from Axios.com.

Bankes, J. 1991. *The Pittsburgh Crawfords: The Lives and Times of Baseball's Most Exciting Team.* Dubuque, IA: William C. Brown.

Banks, P., and R. Waddell. December 21, 2018. "Story of the Most Heroic, Egregious Idiot in Cubs History." Retrieved 2020, from TheSportsBank.net.

Barra, A. 2009. *Yogi Berra: Eternal Yankee.* New York, NY: W.W. Norton and Company.

Beer, J., and O. Charleston. 2019. *The Life and Legend of Baseball's Greatest Forgotten Player.* Lincoln, NE: University of Nebraska Press.

Bench, J. and W. Brashler. 1979. *Catch You Later.* New York, NY: Harper & Row Publishers.

Bingham, W. July 09, 1962. The Yankees Desperate Gamble. *Sports Illustrated.*

Bingham, W. July 31, 1961. Assault on the Record. *Sports Illustrated.*

Boston, T. 2005. *1939: Baseball's Tipping Point.* Albany, NY: Bright Sky Press.

Boston, T. 2009. *Baseball and the Baby Boomer: A History, Commentary and Memoir*. Houston, TX: Bright Sky Press.

Boxerman, B.A., and B.W. Boxerman. 2016. *George Weiss: Architect of the Golden Age Yankees*. Jefferson, NC: McFarland and Company, Inc.

Bregman, R. January 01, 1977. A's Fans Mourn Charlie O., the Mule. *The Sporting News*.

Brown, B. December 18, 2019. Personal communication [in-person interview].

Buford, B. 1994. *Halftime: Moving from Success to Significance*. Grand Rapids, MI: Zondervan.

Burns, K. 1994. *Baseball* [Television Documentary Miniseries]. U.S.A.: Public Broadcasting System.

Carlo, D. 2010. *The Bibliography of Phil Rizzuto*. Chicago, IL: Triumph Books.

Clark, T. 1976. *Champagne and Baloney: The Rise and Fall of the Finley A's*. New York, NY: Harper and Row.

Cohen, J. 2013. "Heat Waves Throughout History." Retrieved 2020, from History.com.

Cohen, M. July 16, 1919. *Baseball as a National Religion*. Framingham, MA: The Dial.

Cohen, S. 2018. *Yankees 1936–1939, Baseball's Greatest Dynasty: Lou Gehrig, Joe DiMaggio and the Birth of a New Era*. New York, NY: Skyhorse Publishing.

Coleman, J., with Goldstein, R. 2008. *An American Journey: My Life On the Field, In the Air, and On the Air*. Chicago, IL: Triumph Books.

Collins, J. 2001. *Good to Great*. New York, NY: HarperCollins Publishing.

Collins, J. 2001. *Good to Great: Why Some Companies Make the Leap . . . and Others Don't*. New York, NY: HarperCollins Publishers, Inc.

Conrads, D. (n.d.). *Johnny Kling*. Retrieved 2020, from Pendergastkc.org.

Cramer, R.W. 2000. *Joe DiMaggio: The Hero's Life*. New York, NY: Simon and Schuster.

Creamer, R.W. 1974. *Babe: The Legend Comes to Life*. New York, NY: Simon and Schuster.

Creamer, R.W. 1984. *Stengel: His Life and Times*. London: Sterling Lord Literistic.

Creamer, R.W. 1992. *Babe: The Legend Comes to Life*. New York, NY: Simon and Schuster.

Creamer, R.W. 1984. *Stengel: His Life and Times*. New York, NY: Simon and Schuster.

Creamer, R.W. 1995. *Mantle Remembered*. New York, NY: Warner Books Inc.

Crossman, M. January 31, 2020. "Carlton Fisk's Iconic 1975 Home Run and the Rat That Changed Television." Retrieved 2020, from MassLive.com.

Dailey, A. April 12, 1949. "The Strange Case of Bobby Brown." *The New York Times*.

Daneshavar, D., C. Nowinski, A. McKee, and R. Cantu. 2011. "The Epidemiology of Sports-Related Concussion." Retrieved 2020, from www.sportsmed.theclinics.com.

Davis, E.G. 2007. *Get 'Em Laughing: Public Speaking Humor, Quotes, and Illustrations*. Bloomington, IN. Trafford Publishing.

Dreier, P. 2013. "The Real Story of Baseball's Integration That You Won't See in 42." *The Atlantic*.

Eig, J. 2005. *The Luckiest Man. The Life and Death of Lou Gehrig*. New York, NY: Simon and Schuster.

Enders, E. 2003. *100 Years of the World Series: 1903-2004*. New York, NY: Sterling Publishing Co., Inc.

Enders, E. 2005. *1903-2004 100 Years of the World Series*. New York, NY: Sterling Publishing Company.

Featherson, A. (n.d.) The Demise of the New York Yankees, 1964-1966. Retrieved 2020, from DiamondsintheDusk.com.

Freedman, L. 2017. *Connie Mack's First Dynasty: The Philadelphia Athletics, 1910–1914*. Jefferson, NC: McFarland and Company, Inc.

Frommer, H. 2008. *Five O'clock Lightening*. Lanham, MD: Taylor Trade Publishing.

Furling, W.B. August 30, 1970. "Johnny Bench: Supercatcher for the Big Red Machine." *The New York Times*.

Gaffney, D. 2000. "What Made DiMaggio a Great Player." Retrieved 2020, from www.pbs.org.

Goldberg-Strassler, J. January 17, 2014. "Fifth Third Fire Brings Back Memories of Past Ballpark Blazes." Retrieved 2020, from https://ballparkdigest.com

Golenbock, P. 1975. *Dynasty: The New York Yankees 1949–1964*. Englewood Cliffs, NJ: Prentice-Hall International, Inc.

Golenbock, P. 1975. *Dynasty: The New York Yankees 1949–1964*. New York, NY: Prentice-Hall.

Graham, R. June 16, 1928. Huggins an Ideal Leader. *The New York Sun*.

Greenberg, H., with I. Berkow. 1989. *Hank Greenberg: The Story of My Life*. Chicago, IL: Triumph Books.

Greene, C. 2015. "Mustaches and Mayhem: Charlie O's Three-Time Champions." Retrieved 2020, from https://sabr.org.

Guilbault, J. July 16, 2020. "Top 25 MLB Teams of All-Time." Retrieved 2020, from Lineups.com

Halbarstam, D. 1989. *Summer of '49*. New York, NY: HarperCollins.

Haupert, M., and K. Winter. 2003. *Pay Ball: Estimating the Profitability of the New York Yankees*. La Crosse, WI: University of Wisconsin—La Crosse.

Heath, D. 2020. *Upstream: The Quest to Solve Problems Before They Happen*. New York, NY: Avid River Press.

Heitz, J. 2011. "1970–1971: A Retrospective...or is it?" Retrieved 2020, from Fansided.com

Hogan, L. 2006. "Shades of Glory: The Negro Leagues and the Story of African-American Baseball." *National Geographic.*

Holway, J. 2011. *The Complete Book of Baseball's Negro Leagues: The Other Half of Baseball History.* Fern Park, FL: Hastings House.

Howard, A., and R. Wimbash. 2001. *Elston and Me: The Story of the First Black Yankee.* Columbia, MO: University of Missouri Press.

James, B. 2001. *The New Bill James Historical Baseball Abstract, Revised.* New York, NY: Free Press, a Division of Simon and Schuster.

James, B. May 05, 2011. *The Greatest Team in Baseball History Part II.* Retrieved 2020, from Billjamesonline.com.

Jenkinson, B. 2007. *The Year Babe Ruth Hit 104 Home Runs.* New York, NY: Carroll and Graf Publishers.

Kahn, R. 2014. *Rickey and Robinson: The True, Untold Story of the Integration of Baseball.* New York, NY: Rodale.

Kashatus, B. 1999. *Connie Mack's '29 Triumph.* Jefferson, NC: McFarland and Company, Inc.

Keene, K., R. Sinibaldi, and D. Hickey. 1997. *The Babe in Red Stockings: An In-depth Chronicle of Babe Ruth with the Boston Red Sox 1914-1919.* Champaign, IL: Sagamore Publishing.

Kelly, M. (n.d.). On Account of War. Retrieved 2020, from https://baseballhall.org/hall-of-fame.

Kennedy, K. 2011. *56: Joe DiMaggio and the Last Magic Number in Sports.* New York, NY: *Sports Illustrated Books.*

King, S. (n.d.). *The Strangest Month in the Strange Career of Rube Waddell.* Philadelphia, PA. Retrieved 2020, from https://sabr.org.

Klima, J. September 12, 2009. "When the Yankees Were Not Ready For Willie Mays." *The New York Times.*

Kubek, T., and T. Pluto. 1987. *Sixty-One: The Team, The Record, The Men.* New York, NY: Macmillan Publishing Company.

Leavy, J. 2010. *The Last Boy.* New York, NY: HarperCollins Publishers.

Leavy, J. 2018. *The Big Fella: Babe Ruth and the World he Created.* New York, NY: HarperCollins Publishers.

Leggett, W. September 28, 1964. Out in Front with a New Look. *Sports Illustrated.*

Leggett, W. October 05, 1970. That Big Red Machine has Developed a Few Sputters. *Sports Illustrated.*

Leggett, W. March 13, 1972. Reds Who Go Grunt in the Spring, Tra La. *Sports Illustrated.*

Lester, L., and S. Miller. 2001. *Black Baseball in Pittsburgh.* Charleston, SC: Arcadia Publishing.

Levitt, D. 2008. *Ed Barrow: The Bulldog Who Built the Yankee's First Dynasty*. Lincoln, NE: Nebraska Press.

Levy, A. 2000. *Rube Waddell: The Zany, Brilliant Life of a Strikeout Artist*. Jefferson, NC: McFarland and Company.

Libbey, B., and V. Blue. 1972. *Vida: His Own Story*. Englewood Cliffs, NJ: Prentice Hall.

Lieb, F. 1976. *Baseball as I Have Known It*. New York, NY: Coward, McGann & Geoghegan.

Locker, B. January 20, 2020. Personal communication [phone interview].

Macht, N. 2007. *Connie Mack And the Early Years of Baseball*. Lincoln, NE: University of Nebraska Press.

Macht, N. 2012. *Connie Mack: The Turbulent & Triumphant Years 1915–1931*. Lincoln, NE: University of Nebraska Press.

Macht, N. 2015. *The Grand Old Man of Baseball: Connie Mack in His Final Years, 1932–1956*. Lincoln, NE: University of Nebraska Press.

Macht, N. October 26, 2020. *Personal communication* [Phone Interview].

Macht, N. (n.d.). "Jack Barry." Retrieved 2020, from https://sabr.org.

Mack, C. 1950. *My 66 Years on the Big Leagues: The Great Story of America's National Game*. Philadelphia, PA: Universal House.

Mack, C. III. October 19, 2020. Personal communication [phone interview].

Mann, J. June 21, 1965. Decline and Fall of a Dynasty. *Sports Illustrated*.

Mantle, M. 1994. Time in a Bottle. *Sports Illustrated*.

Mantle, M., with H. Gluck. 1985. *The Mick: An American Hero: The Legend and the Glory*. New York, NY: a Jove Book published by arrangement with The Doubleday Publishing Group, a Division of Random House.

Mantle, M., M. Mantle, Jr. D. Mantle, and D. Mantle. 1996. *A Hero All His Life*. New York, NY: HarperCollins.

Markusen, B. 1998. *Baseball's Last Dynasty: Charlie Finley's Oakland A's*. Indianapolis, IN: Masters Press.

Markusen, B. 2002. *A Baseball Dynasty: Charlie Finley's Swingin A's*. Haworth, NJ: St. Johann Press.

Matthewson, C. 2015. *Pitching in a Pinch; or Baseball from the Inside*. Charles Town, WV: Jefferson Publication.

McGreal, C. August 17, 2010. "Lou Gehrig Killed by Baseball not Lou Gehrig's Disease, Study Findings Suggest." Retrieved 2020, from TheGuardian.com.

Monteville, L. 2004. *Ted Williams: The Biography of an American Hero*. New York, NY: Doubleday.

Montville, L. 2006. *The Big Bam: The Life and Times of Babe Ruth*. New York, NY: Doubleday.

Morgan, J. and D. Falkner. 1993. *A Life in Baseball*. New York, NY: W.W. Norton & Company.

Muder, W., and B. Howsam, B. (n.d). "Engineered Cincinnati Dynasty." Retrieved 2020, https://baseballhall.org/hall-of-fame.

Murphy, C. 2007. *Crazy 08: How a Cast of Cranks, Rogues, Boneheads and Magnates Created the Greatest Year in Baseball History.* New York, NY: Harper Collins Publishers, Inc.

Murray, J. July 07, 1994. *"His Dignity and Style Add to the Legend,"* Retrieved from https://latimes.com

Nack, W. August 19, 1996. "The Team that Time Forgot. *Sports Illustrated.*

Neil, B. 1996. *I was Right on Time: My Journey from the Negro Leagues to the Majors.* New York, NY: Simon & Schuster.

Nemec, D., S. Hanks., D. Johnson., and D. Raskin. 1999. *20th Century Baseball Chronicle Year-By-Year History of Major League Baseball.* New York, NY: Publications International Ltd.

Neyer, R. and E. Epstein. 2000. *Baseball Dynasties. The Greatest Teams of All Time.* New York, NY. WW Norton and Company

Neyer, R., and E. Epstein. (n.d.). *Baseball Dynasties.* Retrieved 2020, from www.baseball-almanac.com.

O'Brien, D. (n.d.). "Rube Waddell." Retrieved 2020, from https://sabr.org.

Perry, D. 2010. *Reggie Jackson.* New York, NY: HarperCollins Publishers, Inc.

Perry, D. January 31, 2014. "The Curiosities of Rube Waddell." Retrieved 2020, from CBSSports.com.

Pessah, J. 2020. *Yogi: A Life Behind the Mask.* New York, NY: Little Brown and Company, a Division of Hachette Book Group.

Pormrenke, J. 2012. Call the Game! The 1917 Fenway Park Gamblers Riot. Retrieved 2020, from Mcfarlandbooks.com.

Posada, J. with G. Brozek. 2015. *The Journey Home: My Life in Pinstripes.* New York, NY: HarperCollins Publishers.

Rader, B. 2008. *Baseball: A History of America's Game.* Champaign, IL: University of Illinois Press.

Rapp, D. 2018. *Tinker to Evers to Chance: The Chicago Cubs and the Dawn of Modern America.* Chicago, IL: The University of Chicago Press.

Reuter, J. March 19, 2014. *Bleacher Report's Official Rankings of the 50 Greatest Teams in MLB History.* Retrieved 2020, from Bleacherreport.com.

Ribowsky, M. 1996. *Josh Gibson: The Power and the Darkness.* New York, NY: Simon and Schuster.

Richardson, B., with D. Thomas. 2012. *Impact Player: Leaving a Lasting Legacy On and Off the Field.* Carol Stream, IL: Tyndale House Publishers.

Ritter, L. 1966. *Glory of Their Times: The Story of the Early Days of Baseball Told by the Men who Played it.* New York, NY. Macmillan and Company, Inc.

Rivera, M., with W. Coffey. 2014. *The Closer: My Story.* New York, NY: Back Bay Books/Little, Brown and Company.

Roberts, R. and J. Smith, J. 2020. *War Fever: Boston, Baseball, and America in the Shadow of The Great War*. New York, NY: Basic Books.

Rogers, P. September 03, 2014. *An Evening with Bobby Brown*. Allen, TX: Allen Public Library film: ACTV.

Rryal, G. (n.d.). *Frank Chance*. Retrieved 2020, from https://sabr.org.

Sandomir, R. March 16, 2013. "End of the World as the Yankees Knew It." *The New York Times*.

Schaal, E. December 12, 2017. *The Greatest Dynasties in Major League Baseball History*. Retrieved 2020, from Sportscasting.com.

Schall, E. June 16, 2017. *The 8 Greatest Teams of All Time*. Retrieved 2020, from Sportscasting.com.

Schechter, G. (n.d.). "Charlie Faust." Retrieved 2020, from https://sabr.org.

Schonenfield, D. January 27, 2015. Ranking Baseball's Dynasties. Retrieved 2020, from ESPN.com.

Schoor, Gene. 1958 *Mickey Mantle of the Yankees*. New York, NY: Putnam.

Simers, T. November 6, 2009. Joe Torre, witness to domestic abuse, helps others to manage. Retrieved 2020, from www.latimes.com.

Siwoff, S. 1991. *The 1991 Elias Baseball Analyst*. New York, NY: Touchstone.

Skipper, D. (n.d.). "Connie Mack." Retrieved 2020, from https://sabr.org.

Thomas, Henry. 1998. *Walter Johnson: Baseball's Big Train*. Lincoln, NE: University of Nebraska Press.

Thomson, C. (n.d.). "*Sparky Anderson*." Retrieved 2020, from https://sabr.org.

Torre, J., and T. Verducci. 2009. *Joe Torre: The Yankee Years*. New York, NY: Doubleday, a division of Random House.

Torre, J., with T. Verducci. 1997. *Chasing the Dream: My Lifelong Journey to the World Series*. New York, NY: Bantam Books.

Twombly, W. October 27, 1973. Charlie O. *The Sporting News*.

Tye, L. 2009. *Satchel: The Life and Times of an American Legend*. New York, NY: Random House.

Vaccaro, M. 2007. *1941—The Greatest Year on Sports*. New York, NY: Doubleday.

Vecsey, G. 2006. *Baseball: A History of America's Favorite Game*. New York, NY: Random House Publishing Group.

Vitty, C. (n.d.). "Red Rolfe." Retrieved 2020, from https://sabr.org.

Weintraub, R. 2011. *The House That Ruth Built*. New York, NY: Bay Back Books.

Wertheim, J. July 02, 2018. Johnny Bench is Seeking a new Challenge at age 70. *Sports Illustrated*.

Will, G. 1990. *Men at Work*. New York, NY: Macmillan Publishing Company.

Zingg, P. 1993. *Harry Hooper: An American Baseball Life*. Urbana and Chicago, IL: University of Illinois Press.

Acknowledgments

There are many people to thank for their contributions to this book. I first want to recognize the five extraordinary people who served as my editing team. Becky Diaz, Dick Ebling, Bob Ford, John Martinson, and Scott McLellan all reviewed and commented on each draft of each chapter of my Manuscript, and provided the encouragement, affirmation and correction that were all essential to the completion of the book. The final product is far more entertaining, concise and historically accurate than it ever would have been without them. Many others, including Danette Alfonso, Connie Anderson, John Burchfield, Melinda Dworaczyk, Tracy Foreman, Carl Garraffo, Brett Hurst, Nick Lanza, Tamara Le, Malcolm Mazow, Jenny Meyer, Chris Miner, David Parks, and Trey Thompson read and commented on specific chapters along the way and each provided timely encouragement and affirmation. Words alone cannot convey how much I appreciate the contributions from all who took their very valuable time to make this book better.

I thank prominent authors Talmage Boston, Norman Macht, and Connie Mack III for helping me navigate the writing and publishing process; and recognize Cassidy Lent, Reference Librarian with the Bart Giamatti Research Center at the National Baseball Hall of Fame and Museum, for tracking down the many source materials I requested. And I thank Faye Coulter who found many rare source materials scouring garage sales deep in the piney woods of east Texas.

Many talented professionals added value to the book. They included artist Isabelle Zimmerman from the University of Houston School of Art who painted the picture that appears on the cover. Filmmaker/photographer Charlie Giesler produced the videos that will appear on my social media pages and helped me with the live presentations I have done to promote the book. Chris Marlin, Darrin McMurray, and Leslie Minora made key introductions that allowed me to reach many of the individuals I interviewed. Darla Burney served as "the starter" of the manuscript and did the heavy lifting required to get it substantially complete. Then,

Connie Anderson came in as "the closer" to find the issues in the text that I missed, and earned the save.

I am of course grateful to Business Expert Press (BEP) for publishing this book, and to the many professionals at BEP who made specific contributions along the way, including Managing Executive Editor Scott Isenberg, Collections Editor Michael Provitera, Director of Production/Marketing Charlene Kronstedt, Gunabala Saladi and her team at Exeter Premedia Services, and no doubt others who will contribute during the publication process.

I also wish to thank many friends from Memorial Drive Presbyterian Church in Houston, Texas including Pastors Alf Halvorson and Brett Hurst, Mike Handel, the members of the Great Group, and those involved with Men's Life who each offered encouragement and affirmation at many points along the way. I also must recognize my law firm Blank Rome for allowing me the time during the COVID-19 Pandemic to do the main writing of this book, and three terrific lawyers, Nikki Kessling, Alix Udelson and Josh Huber who each took on significant shares of my workload while this book was being written, published, and promoted.

Finally, one does not get through the process of authoring a book without a great family, and I am proud to recognize mine: Doug, Carolyn, Tamara, Tracy, Sarah, Francie, Grant, Quang, Whitney, Riley, Chelon, Colette, and our latest arrival, Lily.

Index